Agustín Rubini
Fintech in a Flash

Agustín Rubini

Fintech in a Flash

—

Financial Technology Made Easy

Third Edition

ISBN 978-1-5474-1716-2
e-ISBN (PDF) 978-1-5474-0105-5
e-ISBN (EPUB) 978-1-5474-0107-9

Library of Congress Control Number: 2018963411

Bibliographic information published by the Deutsche Nationalbibliothek
The Deutsche Nationalbibliothek lists this publication in the Deutsche Nationalbibliografie; detailed bibliographic data are available on the Internet at http://dnb.dnb.de.

© 2019 Agustín Rubini
Published by Walter de Gruyter Inc., Boston/Berlin
Printing and binding: CPI books GmbH, Leck
Typesetting: MacPS, LLC, Carmel

www.degruyter.com

The dedication of this book
Is split two ways with my wife and child
To my son Luca,
And to my wife Elena,

without you this book would have
been completed two years earlier
but it would have been a lot darker.

About De|G PRESS

Five Stars as a Rule

De|G PRESS, the startup born out of one of the world's most venerable publishers, De Gruyter, promises to bring you an unbiased, valuable, and meticulously edited work on important topics in the fields of business, information technology, computing, engineering, and mathematics. By selecting the finest authors to present, without bias, information necessary for their chosen topic *for professionals*, in the depth you would hope for, we wish to satisfy your needs and earn our five-star ranking.

In keeping with these principles, the books you read from De|G PRESS will be practical, efficient and, if we have done our job right, yield many returns on their price.

We invite businesses to order our books in bulk in print or electronic form as a best solution to meeting the learning needs of your organization, or parts of your organization, in a most cost-effective manner.

There is no better way to learn about a subject in depth than from a book that is efficient, clear, well organized, and information rich. A great book can provide life-changing knowledge. We hope that with De|G PRESS books you will find that to be the case.

DOI 10.1515/9781547401055-203

Acknowledgments

Many thanks to the following people for their hard work and dedication:
Research
- Florence de Borja
- Ronalea Talaboc
- Christina Pomoni
- James Pepper
Editing
- Katie Uniacke
Proofreading
- Brian Cross
Cover design
- Ilian Georgiev
Interior design
- Shabbir Hussain
Illustrations
- Bloomingsun

DOI 10.1515/9781547401055-204

About the Author

Financial savant, author, and advocate, **Agustín Rubini** has many interests and is devoted to excelling in these fields. With many years of experience as a financial industry strategist, Agustín is passionate about the world of finance and the future of financial services. He spends much of his time speaking and writing about fintech and advising businesses on innovation and digital transformation.

He has a strong background in developing digital strategy, driving innovation in the financial services industry, and is well-versed in the disruptive effect of technology on the industry. As a means of helping others understand the complexities of the financial services industry, Agustín wrote and published *Fintech in a Flash*, a comprehensive guide to financial technology. A resident of London, Agustín's love of the UK led to the release of his first book, a novel about a young Latin American's first trip to London. An advocate of child welfare, arts and culture, and a proponent of education, Agustín combines his love of science and technology, knowledge, and compassion to effect positive change and offer a better understanding of our complex world.

DOI 10.1515/9781547401055-205

Contents

Prologue

When I started working in financial services, just starting out in management consulting, I would have never dreamed of writing a book on the topic. My first impression of the industry was that it was highly regulated, static, boring ...

Boy, how wrong I was! I was right when I said it was highly regulated. But static and boring? Not at all.

Financial services is one of the most important industries, as the expression used in *Cabaret* goes—"money makes the world go round."

Since I started in banking, I've seen a lot of changes. However, over the past few years, the change rate has been exponential. While going digital used to be a nice thing to do, it is now a necessity for any serious financial services institution.

The application of new technologies to financial services creates loads of opportunities for disruption, as well as many job opportunities for the people that have the right skill set. I believe it is the most exciting place to be for the next decade.

However, getting up to speed in this sector is not that easy. The amount of news and analysis that's generated on a daily basis is so huge that keeping up to date feels like climbing a mountain.

My motivation for creating this book, and the online blog that complements it, was to provide an entry point to this exciting industry. *Fintech in a Flash* aims to provide an overview of the whole sector, and readers that start off with no knowledge of the industry will come out the other side with an intermediate understanding. This can help seasoned financial services professionals as well as new entrants into the industry.

I hope that by reading this book, and following the blog, you develop knowledge of and love for this industry.

DOI 10.1515/9781547401055-207

Chapter 1
The Booming World of Fintech

What Is the Fintech Industry?

The financial technology—or fintech—industry refers to the group of companies that are introducing innovation into financial services through the use of modern technologies. Some fintech firms compete directly with banks, while others have partnered with them or supply them with good or services. What is clear is that fintech companies are improving the financial services world through introducing innovative ideas, allowing for speedy delivery and increasing competition.

Financial technology integrates various types of financial services into the day to day lives of customers. Millennials, as well as the generations coming up behind them, are used to technology and want to manage their money in an easy and quick manner, instead of walking to physical branches to perform transactions and other operations.

Fintech is redefining financial services in the 21st century. Originally, the term applied to technology used in the back-end of established trade and consumer financial institutions. It has expanded to include various innovations in technology, including cryptocurrencies, machine learning, robo advice and the internet of things.

Areas of Fintech

In this section, we provide a preview of what will be covered in the book. Feel free to skip to any chapter that interests you, or read the chapters in order.

In our "New Entrants to Banking" chapter, we look at the new business models that are being introduced to challenge traditional banking, such as aggregators and infrastructure providers. We also reflect on how open banking and APIs will change the industry.

In our "Rethinking Payments and Remittances" chapter, we will explore how fintech is paving the way for innovating the way people send and receive money. We look at peer-to-peer payments, mobile apps, cryptocurrency transfers, social payments, and nanopayments. Innovations in remittances are particularly beneficial to migrant workers, who need to send money to their families at home.

In our "Digital Lending Innovation" chapter, we look at peer-to-peer lending marketplaces, as well as other forms of lending and forms of credit scoring, which allow more people to access the market. We analyze different niches, including consumer lending, student lending, business lending, and mortgages.

In our "Commercial Banking Transformation" chapter, we examine how this sector is being revolutionized, which are the new banks to look out for, and how the

DOI 10.1515/9781547401055-001

value-added services space for small and medium enterprises is starting to merge with traditional banking services.

In our "Next Generation Commerce" chapter, we look at how fintech influences retail shopping. We analyze the different technologies, such as mobile point-of-sale terminals and tablet-based point of sales. Additionally, we examine online commerce and the companies that are disrupting the space, making commerce easier and cheaper for all parties. We also look at how mobile wallets are slowly replacing cash and plastic cards.

In our "Crowdfunding and Crowdinvesting" chapter, we appraise this new way of obtaining funds for all sorts of different purposes, including social purposes and investing in firms. We also consider crowdinvesting, which allows individuals and companies to invest their money in small businesses in exchange for stock.

In our "Innovative Wealth Management" chapter, we find out how fintech can be used to democratize investments by using technologies such as robo-advisors, which can offer low-cost investment advice, artificial intelligence, and advanced analytics.

In "The Power of Big Data and Artificial Intelligence" chapter, we examine how the increase in the power of analytics can help provide better insights into customers and their behaviors. We look at the use cases that are being developed specifically for the financial services industry.

In "The Internet of Things" chapter, we explore how connected devices in the cloud can communicate with each other and even perform payments smartly. We consider use cases using blockchain, in insurance, real estate, and in lending.

In our "Blockchain and Distributed Ledgers" chapter, we explain distributed ledgers in a way that is simple to understand. We cover the main cryptocurrencies that have emerged and the areas that are most likely to be disrupted by this new way of storing data.

In "The Rise of InsurTech" chapter, we look at how new business models could potentially change the fintech industry by introducing a peer-to-peer framework. We also find out how blockchain, smart contracts, and the internet of things impact this area.

In our "Identification, Cybersecurity, and RegTech" chapter, we look at how these key enablers have evolved and provide the foundations for future growth all across the different fintech themes.

 ## Short History of Fintech

It is difficult to pinpoint when financial technology began, but the 1950s are a good reference point. Technology is a key component of the financial services sector in various ways.

The 1950s saw the introduction of credit cards. Instead of carrying cash, people used these cards to pay for their purchases. ATMs were introduced in the 1960s, meaning that people no longer had to visit bank branches for certain transactions.

In the 1960s, banks started using mainframe computers for record keeping and data storage. In the 1970s, firms began to trade stocks electronically. In 1981 the first IBM PC was invented, ending the dominance of time-sharing terminal computing. In the 1990s, e-commerce business models and the internet thrived. Because of this, retail investors could experiment with online stock trading. In the 1990s, e-commerce business models and the internet thrived. Because of this, retail investors could experiment with online stock trading.

During the 50 years of fintech developments, innovators have created sophisticated treasury management, risk management, data analysis tools, and trade processing for financial services firms and institutional banks.

Currently, fintech is digitizing retail financial services through crowdfunding platforms, robo-advisors for retirement and wealth planning, payment apps, mobile wallets, and the like. Fintech provides access to alternative and private investment opportunities, as well as online lending platforms.

However, despite the fact that fintech is flourishing, banks have not been greatly affected. The main reason for this is that fintech and banks complement each other. Banks have realized that technology is a strategic asset and that it needs to be taken seriously.

Why Is Fintech Important?

Money makes the world go round—and financial services regulate how fast it spins. Disruption caused by fintech drives the financial industry to be smarter and more agile and allows it to deal with important problems in the world. For example, automated investing paves the way for all social classes to invest and see returns on their money. It also allows people in developing countries to transact, even if they don't have a bank account. Yet the fintech industry has a lot of room for growth and improvement, and financial infrastructures should be revised for the benefit of consumers.

Fintech disruptors can also help develop better methodologies for risk assessment. For instance, OnDeck and Kabbage use information to assess the performance of small businesses using more than 1500 data points. Avant underwrites consumers using machine learning. Kickstarter taps into people's wisdom to fund start-ups by allowing crowds to fund their preferred ideas. This means that more customers can get access to lending services.

Since the financial crisis in 2008, regulators have enforced strict compliance with bank regulations to make finance safer. Fintech can help regulators secure financial transactions and serve customers better by introducing technologies that automate regulation checks and sophisticated crime detection algorithms.

Why Has Fintech Become Popular Now?

The fintech sector received a huge influx of funds in 2014. The start-ups that received funding are hungry and ambitious and want to disrupt the banking sector. There are several factors that have contributed to the fact that fintech is flourishing now.

One of these is that fintech promises healthy returns on investments and growth opportunities, even though the business models are not yet fully understood. For example, nobody knows whether peer-to-peer financing is a model that can be sustained in the long term.

Additionally, new technologies have been emerging in several industries that can also be applied to financial services. These include blockchain technology, advanced machine learning software, micro-sized card readers and chips, and powerful servers capable of performing intelligent analytics. Social networks and micromarketing have also broken down the barriers to entering the industry, as some fintechs can achieve very low acquisition costs, as little as 1% of the costs of national and community banks.

Customer expectations also drive this increased interest in the industry. Previous generations failed to experience a respect-based, personalized, and one-to-one relationship with their banks; but millennials demand it. With advanced personalization and internet technologies, they can access the kind of banking relationships that they have come to expect. The use of data provides the potential for financial services companies to know and treat their customers better.

Finally, regulation changes have also helped fintech. Generally, regulations can hinder influx of capital and growth. They can slow things down because they are there to protect and control the public. However, many regulators have recognized the value of technology and have provided innovation sandboxes or bent the rules for small players. The lack of regulation for some segments, such as peer-to-peer lending, has helped new companies grow at a fast pace.

 Global Fintech Investment

Fintech has experienced substantial growth due to heavy investments and new trends in the financial industry. It has produced different financial services products that can disrupt the way in which customers transact with their banks. In the beginning, firms were experimenting with fintech. However, as companies mature, investments are now mostly value driven.

Global investments pour into fintech start-ups. From 2015 to 2017, the total investment in fintech exceeded $122 billion. In 2017, $31 billion were invested in fintech, an investment similar to 2016.

In H1 2018, global investment for financial technology companies was over $57.9 billion across 875 deals. This was higher than the total for 2017. The median size per deal rose from $14 million in 2017 to $25 million in 2018. RegTech in H1 2018 totalled $1.37 billion, also higher than the total for 2017. In the US, companies received $14.2 billion, with investment banking and RegTech becoming hot areas.

China saw big deals in 2017 with three mega deals, including Dianrong ($220 million), Feidee ($200 million), and Dashu Finance ($117 million). In 2018, other mega deals occurred including Dianrong ($290 million), WeCash ($160 million), Meili Jinrong ($130 million) and Ant Financial got a huge funding round of $14 billion. In addition, Alibaba, JD Finance, and Tencent made regional investments to expand their domestic reach.[1]

Venture capitalists used to dominate fintech funding, yet from 2016, private and corporate investors were also ramping up their investments. In Q3 2017, global investment in fintech companies reached $8.3 billion across 274 deals while venture capitalists put in $3.3 billion, raising their corporate role to 18.4% participation as opposed to 16.0% in 2016. US companies accounted for more than 50% of the biggest global deals, including Intacct ($850 million), CardConnect ($750 million), Xactly ($564 million), and more.[2]

According to CB Insights, 2017 was a record year for VC-backed fintech as it reached $16.6 billion, up 336.8% from 2013 and 20.3% from 2016, and 2018 is headed for another record.[3]

In the United Kingdom, in 2017, investors placed more than $1.1 billion in British fintech start-ups with London attracting more than 90% of investments. Some key deals include Prodigy Finance ($240 million), Neyber ($149.1 million), Monitise ($97.3 million), and Revolut ($76 million). In 2018 Revolut ($250 million), eToro ($100 million), Flender ($60 million) and MoneyFarm ($54 million) got funding too.[4]

Main Fintech Hubs

Some regions are more open to fintech innovation than others. The factors that contribute to fintech growth include government support, a developed culture of innovation, proximity to customers, specialized talent, and flexible regulations.

Considering these factors, the places that have the best environments for fintech are London, Singapore, New York, Silicon Valley, Hong Kong, and Shanghai. These centers have seen many years of either financial or technological (in the case of Silicon Valley) development. They also understand that it is important to collaborate with an ecosystem of firms to achieve greater results.

In Europe, London combines booming technology with the world's largest financial services sector. Some of the companies based in London are Atom Bank, Funding Circle, Monzo, Worldpay, and Zopa. The success stories of Worldpay and Transfer-Wise show that London can stand independently and scale up companies. London is strong in retail banking, neobanking, foreign exchange, and wealth management.

Moving on to the US, New York is home to Wall Street, the largest capital base in the world. It has considerable human talent and huge investors. OnDeck and Betterment are two big fintechs based here. Silicon Valley is linked with technology in general, and much of that has been directed toward finance. Venture capitals are huge in this area, and there is substantial expertise in scaling up companies. PayPal, Square, LendingClub, and Sofi are based here.

In Asia, Hong Kong is an important point of reference, as it is the largest Asian financial center. They are especially strong in B2B solutions since Hong Kong is involved in so much trade. The proximity to China is also a strategic asset. WeLend, a lending platform, is the biggest success story that has come out of this city. Singapore has also created a top financial center. The government is investing heavily to support the sector, and has even created a regulatory sandbox for innovating safely. Finally, Shanghai can't be ignored. China is the biggest fintech market based on the amount invested and the total usage. Shanghai is strong in asset management, liquidity management, and blockchain. "Unicorns" such as Ant Financial, Lufax, and ZhongAn are based here.

The Fintech Unicorns

Fintech is disrupting the way that people carry out financial transactions. Quite a number of fintech firms have reached a valuation of at least $1 billion in net worth, and the term "Unicorn" has been coined to describe these promising companies, which have reached a significant size but remain private. In this section, we examine this club. Investors see these companies as the ones that will have the biggest impact in the world of finance. In terms of categories, unicorns dominate the lending and payments space, taking up 75% of the aggregate valuation of these firms.

The American Unicorns

America is the continent with the highest number of unicorns, even though the total valuation of these companies is far behind Asia.

There are several unicorns in the lending space. Worth at least $4.4 billion, **SoFi** is a San Francisco-based peer-to-peer loans provider. It provides mortgages, student loan refinancing, and other personal loans. It recently acquired Zenbax, which will allow SoFi to perform the basic functions of a bank. Established in 2011, it has provided about $25 billion worth of loans since it started.

Another unicorn in lending is Chicago-based **Avant**. Valued at $2 billion, it uses machine-learning protocols, algorithms, standard consumer data, and analytical tools to determine the loan terms it offers to its borrowers. In October 2013, it commenced operations in the United Kingdom and Canada.

San Francisco-based **Affirm**, valued at $1.8 billion, is a hire purchase provider, that allows people and businesses to buy products and pay them off in instalments. It works with over 1200 retailers and the technology allows retailers to increase order size by up to 50%.

Atlanta-based **Kabbage** offers loans to consumers and small businesses through its automated lending platform. It has written over $4 billion worth of loans and has partnered with Santander bank. It is worth $1.3 billion.

San Francisco-based **Tradeshift** provides a flexible business platform that allows collaborative accounts payable and procurement automation. It connects buyers and suppliers. The company was founded in 2009 and counts HSBC and Goldman Sachs as investors. It is valued at $1.1 billion.

In the insurance sector, **Oscar** is worth about $3.2 billion. Founded in 2013 in New York, it offers digital health insurance, which includes unlimited telemedicine consultations and free generic medication for its members.

Clover Health is a digital health insurance company founded in San Francisco in 2013, worth $1.2 billion, and has attracted capital from Alphabet GV and Sequoia Capital.

Credit Karma is a company offering online credit reports free of charge by allowing targeted advertising of financial products. Established in San Francisco in 2007, it has at least 35 million users. Credit Karma is currently worth at least $4 billion. In 2016, Credit Karma acquired OnePrice Taxes, an online tax preparation and filing service, to directly compete with TurboTax and H&R Block.[5]

Gusto provides cloud-based software for employees' and contractors' payroll, benefits, and workers' compensation. It is worth $1 billion.

Symphony, founded in 2014 in Palo Alto, CA, is a cloud-based messaging and collaboration platform with bank grade security, and several investment banks are both investors and clients. The company has offices in New York, Hong Kong, Singapore, Stockholm, and London and its current valuation is $1 billion.[6]

In the payments sector, San Francisco-based **Stripe** provides online payment processing for companies. Established in 2010, it boasts of Fitbit, Twitter, Lyft, Kickstarter, Pinterest, Salesforce.com, The Guardian, and Reddit as some of its clients. Stripe's ease of implementation is what made the company so successful. It was valued in October 2018 at $20 billion in a round of funding.

AvidXchange offers accountancy automation software, which eliminates manual processes and allows companies to become more efficient. AvidXchange was founded in 2000 in Charlotte, NC, and has a current valuation of $1.4 billion.

Coinbase, founded in California in 2012, is a brokerage that established itself as the cryptocurrency market achieved a valuation of $1.6 billion in 2017, when they secured $100 million in funding.

In the same area, **Circle** is an internet finance company built on blockchain technology. It enables quick money transfers and cryptocurrency trading. Based in Boston, it is worth $3 billion.

In the investment sector, **RobinHood Markets Inc.**, headquartered in Palo Alto, became the first unicorn in the wealth management sector. It is positioned as the stock trading place for millennials, and it offers commission-free trading. Its current valuation is $5.6 billion in 2018, after securing a round of $363 million.

San Francisco-based **Zenefits**, founded in 2013, is a payroll, HR and health insurance provider which is valued at $2 billion, although it has faced several problems over the past years so its valuation might be a bit out of date since its last round of funding.

Also from San Francisco, founded in 2017, **Brex** is a B2B focused company building a corporate credit card product that has higher limits, automates expense management and integrates with accounting systems seamlessly. It is valued at $1.1 billion.

The only unicorn in the Americas coming from outside the US is Brazilian-born **Nubank**. Valued at around $2.1 billion, it offers more than 3 million customers next generation mobile banking. It counts Tencent Holdings as one of its lead investors.

The Asian Unicorns

Asia is the king of high-value fintechs, with China being the main hub. The main reason for the high valuations lies in the sheer number of people living there. In China alone there are over 500 million smartphone users.

The biggest fintech in the world, **Ant Financial** operates the Sesame credit rating system and the Alipay payment platform. It is said to be worth over $150 billion, making it the biggest fintech company globally. The company's IPO is expected during the first half of 2019.[7] In June 2018, it raised $14 billion.

In the lending arena, **Lufax** is a Shanghai-based peer-to-peer financing and loans platform with at least 20,000 loans approved since it began its operations in 2011. It is valued at $18.5 billion.

In the same space, **Jimubox** is an online peer-to-peer lending platform for individuals and small businesses. Worth about $1 billion, it is popular in China and currently experiencing significant growth. Founded in 2013, its headquarters are in Beijing.

Also in lending, **Tuandaiwang** is a peer-to-peer lending platform from Dongguan founded in 2012 and has written more than $11.4 billion in loans.

In the same space, **9f Group** is a fintech platform that includes peer-to-peer lending as well as other services, and has more than 38 million registered users. It is valued at $1 billion.

In the investments area, Beijing-based **Tiger Brokers** is a brokerage service for Chinese investors wanting to invest overseas. It is valued at $1 billion.

In the payments area, **Lakala Payment** provides online and offline third party payment services. Valued at $1.6 billion, it is based in Beijing and caters to convenience stores and supermarkets to acquire customers.

In the same space, born in India, **One97** is the company behind Paytm, an online platform for online shopping and bill payment. Founded in 2000 in New Delhi, India, Paytm transacts 800,000 orders daily with 50 million registered wallets.

Hangzhou-based **Cgtz**, founded in 2014, is a platform that provides investment and loan related products to Chinese consumers and small businesses. It has a valuation of $1.4 billion.

Producing risk control software, founded in 2013, Hangzou-based **Tongdun Technologies** works with over 7,000 institutions across China and is valued at around $1 billion.

In the insurance arena, headquartered in Gurgaon and founded in 2008, **Policybazaar.com** is a leading online life insurance and general insurance aggregator in India backed by Softbank. It is valued at $1 billion and is planning an IPO very soon.

Unicorns of the Rest of the World

In the banking arena, **Atom Bank** is a mobile banking application that offers personal and business banking products. Based in Durham, UK, it has a valuation of $1.25 billion.

In the same space, Manchester-based **ACORN OakNorth** is a specialist in structured lending solutions to businesses. They also sell white labelled software for lending to banks. It is valued at $2.3 billion.

In the payments space, valued at $1.6 billion, is **TransferWise**. It provides international money transfers online at reduced fees. Founded in 2010, with headquarters in London, it has transferred at least $4.7 billion since its launch. At present, it is transferring around $783 million monthly.

Klarna is yet another user-friendly payment system for web and mobile. Established in Stockholm in 2005, it is worth about $2.5 billion and has processed at least $9 billion worth of transactions in the space of a year.

In the value-added services space, New Zealand-based **Xero**, founded in 2006, provides cloud-based accounting software for small businesses. Listed on the Australian Securities Exchange, it is worth at least $1.3 billion.

Based in Zurich and founded in 1991, **Avaloq** provides BPO services and digital banking software. It is valued at $1 billion.

Based in Peterborough UK, **BGL Group** provides insurance and financial products as well as price comparison engines such as comparethemarket.com. Founded in 1991, it is valued at $3 billion.

Noteworthy Exits

Every entrepreneur's dream is to have a glorious exit to cash in all the hard work that was put into the business. The main exit strategies applicable are a company acquisition or an Initial Public Offering. In this section, we look at key deals.

Square is a fintech start-up offering sellers tools to start, run, and grow businesses. On November 18, 2015, Square announced $9 per share for its 27,000,000 Class A common stock in its initial public offering. This valued the company at $2.9 billion. In September 2017, Square was granted a crowdfunding patent, seeking to enable merchants to use the Square point-of-sale (POS) terminal and be evaluated based on its processed transactions history. The patent also provides information on return on investment and other indicators.

Worldpay is a pioneer in multi-currency processing, card payments, and contactless and online payments.

When it went public in October 2015, Worldpay priced its shares at £2.40 per share, thus generating a market valuation of £4.8 billion. Its IPO was the biggest in the United Kingdom for that year.

P PayPal

PayPal went public for the second time in July 2015, after its spinoff from eBay. Established in 1998, its first IPO was in February 2002. eBay bought PayPal for $1.5 billion in July 2002. In its second IPO, PayPal had a market value of $46.6 billion. Its shares jumped as high as $42.55 or 11% during the morning trading. However, eBay shares dipped to $26.50 or 2%.

 First Data.

First Data is a leader in commerce-enabling solutions and technology with at least 4,000 financial institutions. On October 1, 2015, First Data announced its IPO of Class A common stock consisting of 160,000,000 shares, at a price of between $18 and $20 per share.

▦ LendingClub

LendingClub is a peer-to-peer lending firm in San Francisco, California. By December 31, 2015, LendingClub originated $15.98 billion worth of loans. LendingClub announced the price of its IPO on December 10, 2014. As the world's largest peer-to-peer marketplace, it offered 58,000,000 common stock shares at $15 per share. The price plummeted after a scandal which made its CEO resign, and the price per share went down to $3.50. Since then the stock has been recovering, and current valuation for LendingClub is around $2 billion.

OnDeck›

OnDeck is an online lending platform for small businesses. On December 16, 2014, it announced its IPO price at $20 per share for 11,500,000 common stock shares. The shares traded on the NYSE on December 17, 2014. The value of the stock has gone down, and in November 2018, it was trading at around $9.

Y◉DLEE

Yodlee is a US-based software company providing an account aggregation service so users can view their bank, email, credit card, investment, travel rewards, and the like on just one screen. Yodlee announced on October 2, 2014, the $12 per share price of its 6,250,000 common stock shares in its IPO on the NASDAQ but was sold to Envestnet for a reported $660 million in August 2015.

✺coupa

California-based **Coupa** uses its cloud architecture to provide spend-optimization software focusing on expense management, accounts payable, and procurement. The company went public in 2016 for $18 per share and saw its shares double during the first day of trading. The company's market cap is $3.6 billion.[8]

China Rapid Finance

China Rapid Finance is another innovator offering online, offline, and multi-channel lending platforms in China, connecting investors and borrowers. Since commencing, it has provided at least $2 billion in loans and the market cap is $163 million. The company went public in April 2017, offering 10 million ADRs (American Depositary Receipts) at $6 per ADR and a total size of $60 million.[9]

JD Finance

JD Finance is a consumer finance spin-off of China's JD.com, an e-commerce company. It offers various online financial services to China's companies, start-ups, and consumers. Valuation is at $34 billion.

IHS Markit

Valued at $20.6 billion and established in 2003 in London, **Markit** provides financial data and information. It began as a platform for credit derivative pricing. The company raised $1.28 billion in its 2014 IPO, pricing its shares at $24 per share.[10]

ZhongAn Insurance

In the InsurTech space, **ZhongAn** is the first Chinese-licensed internet insurance company. It is reshaping the country's conventional insurance by using an online model to lower distribution and operating costs. Its IPO happened in 2017 and its current market cap is $43.21 billion.[11]

Qudian.com

Qudian, a Chinese online microloan provider, went public on October 2017, pricing as the fourth-largest US IPO. The main investors included Ant Financial Services Group, Beijing Phoenix Wealth Holding Group, Hangzhou Liaison Interactive, and Kunlun Worldwide. Qudian's growth is mainly driven by its online cash loans, which account for 83.3% of its total revenue. On the other hand, the Chinese government rolled out a series of regulations in December 2017 to leverage the potential risks in this industry.[12] The company's current valuation is $1.6 billion.

PPdai, a leading online consumer finance marketplace with strong brand recognition, went public in December 2017. The main investors included Sequoia Capital China, Alibaba Group, Lightspeed China Partners, Legend Capital, and SIG Asia Investments. The company was launched in 2007 and is the first online consumer finance marketplace in China connecting borrowers and investors. With more than 57 million cumulative registered users in Q3 2017, PPdai's current market cap is $1.7 billion.

LEXIN乐信

LexinFintech Holdings, a leading Chinese microlending platform that targets China's young consumers went public in December 2017 and reported 3.3 million active users for the first three quarters of the year. The main investors included Matrix Partners China, JD.com, DST Global, China Renaissance Capital, K2 Ventures, Huasheng Capital, and Bertelsmann Asia Investments. The company's current market cap is $1.59 billion.

ʊIANPU.AI
融360

Jianpu Technology, a Chinese online financial planning platform, filed for a $200 million IPO in November 2017 and has a current market cap of $958 million. The main investors included KPCB China, Zero2IPO Capital, Lightspeed China Partners, Sequoia Capital China, Temasek Holdings, Sailing Capital, and Yunfeng Capital. The company is wholly-owned by Rong 360, and it generates revenue from fees for its recommendation services on loan products and credit card products.[13]

adyen

Another payments unicorn which went for an IPO is Amsterdam-based **Adyen**, which provides a payment platform accepting different methods and forms of transaction. Founded in 2006, it boasts Facebook, Uber, Netflix, Airbnb, and SoundCloud as customers. Its IPO was done in June 2018 with shares surging 90%. Its market cap is over $20 billion.

In the lending arena, **Funding Circle**, founded in 2009 provides business loans through a peer-to-peer marketplace. Since launching in London, it has funded $5 billion worth of loans. It went public in September 2018 raising $392 million and valuing the company at around $2 billion.

iZettle

iZettle is a Stockholm-based firm established in 2010 and purchased in 2018 by PayPal for $2.2 billion. Known as the social payments company, it facilitates person-to-person and business-to-consumer commerce. It is an MPOS (mobile point of sale) manufacturer, which offers low charges on transactions and even nanopayments.

Atlanta, GA-based **Green Sky**, offers technology to merchants and banks to provide loans to customers for healthcare, solar, home improvement, and other purposes. It raised over $800 million in its IPO in May 2018 and had a market capitalization of $2.5 billion in October 2018.

Let's Get Started

In the next chapter, we will look at how digital banks are strongly moving into the financial services arena and analyze whether it is likely that they have enough strength to change the industry dynamics.

Chapter 2
New Entrants to Banking

New Banking Entrants in a Flash

Traditional banking has remained unchanged for a long time, with most clients using big, stable banks. This has generated a high level of complacency among these banks. However, technology advances, combined with the relaxation of regulations, has led to the emergence of new players who are now threatening the status quo. Incumbents are beginning to understand that if they don't change, they might not survive.

New operating models are emerging. Some players are betting on providing banks with infrastructure. Others are looking to provide customers with more options by aggregating products, and some are trying to provide an open banking interface while still maintaining a wide range of products.

The usage of APIs is seen as a key enabler in improving the quality of the products offered, as well as increasing competition in banking. New categories of banks are being created, such as neo-banks, challenger banks, and iBanks. These are mostly concentrating on being purely digital and specializing in specific niches. While no outcome can be predicted, it is clear that a greater degree of competition will emerge.

The Traditional Banking Landscape

For both consumers and businesses, banking hasn't changed much over the last few decades. We consume products in a similar way to previous generations. Checking accounts, saving accounts, credit cards, and mortgages are all, in essence, still the same. Traditional banks have two types of customers: depositors and borrowers. The bank acts as an intermediary, using money entrusted to them by depositors to lend to borrowers at a higher interest rate. Banks have two main revenue streams, one is income from interest and the other is the fees they charge. On top of this, they can earn additional revenue from cross-selling other products such as insurance.

Traditional banking has thrived for years because customers trust the system. The strength of these banks lies in their large datasets and customer bases. They can generate a large amount of capital from customer deposits at a low cost because customers accept quite low interest rates on their savings accounts. Traditional banks profit because of the large volume of funds that they manage, and the spread that they make on the interest rates between borrowing and lending. So far, it has been difficult for new entrants to compete with them because of their size, barriers to entry and capital requirements.

DOI 10.1515/9781547401055-002

The Effect of Digital Technology

Digital technology challenges banks in two ways. First, it is transforming traditional businesses. An example of this is the number of financial transactions that have shifted from traditional channels to mobile and web applications, thereby providing customers with more choice. Another is how financial processing is being sped up, and transaction costs are being reduced. This generates a big threat for incumbents who have had easy profits in the past, due to lack of competition.

Technology is reinventing businesses, and new business models are being introduced. Most disruption in the future is likely to come from outside the banking world. Traditional banks are struggling to fuse their physical and digital assets together to transform their present businesses. New entrants might be able to reach customers more effectively since they are starting with a clean slate.

It is important for retail banking to ride the wave of digital technology because new, innovative financial service start-ups are popping up every day, supported by accelerator hubs and incubators in various major cities worldwide. Traditional banks have to defend their positions against these start-ups to stay current and profitable.

Retail banking will face big challenges in the near future. Some people believe retail banking may even soon disappear, as digital technology is slowly eating up revenues. An estimated 30% of banking revenues from Italy, France, and Germany are being lost due to digital technology.[14] Some start-ups are now earning significant revenues from their operations, and more companies will soon be operating with a profit margin. These companies earn by charging low fees for a large number of transactions, instead of the usual business model which involves high transaction fees.

In the past, banks just copied their competitors' innovations. However, they are now finding it difficult to imitate these innovations because their competitors are entrepreneurs or technologists, not bankers, and the rate of change has accelerated dramatically.

The Case for Change

The number of start-ups is growing, and established retail banks must be able to implement their own digital reinvention if they want to thrive in the future. Retail banks must be able to transform their business models as the old ways to make money will become commoditized. Digital transformation programs need to be set up that can react as quickly as start-ups do. Changes need to be made to the banking culture, which has until now been characterized by fear of progress. Stakeholders have to understand that change needs to happen fast, and they need to be adaptable.

Retail banks must also reinvent by making changes from the outside in. This means that they must cater to their customers' priorities and needs, innovating in a way that may cannibalize their present business. Their culture and processes often do not support reinvention because banking institutions are, by nature, slow and risk averse. As such, reinvention must be handled separately and have supporting funding.

Many banks struggle regarding innovation because their aims are unclear. They lose market share to new entrants or faster-moving incumbents because they do not have discretionary funds and become paralyzed by choice. Some of them implement unconnected initiatives that yield small returns, squandering their investments.

Some bank executives do not know how or where to start when it comes to innovation. The main obstacles that they face are talent management, governance, and funding.

Regarding talent, banks need to appoint executives who monitor the creation of innovative ideas until these ideas are ready for scaling. Hire people with skills in deal structuring, due diligence, and business evaluation and relationship management. Banking institutions must develop a mindset of innovation and disruption.

Concerning funding, bank executives need to be able to experiment but should avoid following the herd and focus on the needs of their particular bank—implementing a carefully planned, long-term program of change.

 ## New Operating Models for Banking

Banks can choose to continue operating their current full-service model by providing corporations and individuals with various products and services. However, banks will find it difficult to compete with some providers because of their legacy software. They may not be able to offer products at lower prices with better customer service and simpler processes.

Because of the emergence of new technologies and regulations, it has become necessary for the banking industry to develop new business models. While there has been little change in banking for the past few decades, there have been radical changes in other industries. For example, it is now normal for people to use Airbnb or Uber rather than traditional hotels and taxis.

In terms of business models, some banks choose to become infrastructure providers to fintech companies or other financial institutions. Solaris and Bancorp are using this business model, and their clients see the benefit of not having to carry out certain activities that are complex and heavily regulated.

Big banks will find this model profitable, especially if they can spread compliance costs across a large number of customers. However, they will not earn large profits from it, as this is a service that is likely to be commoditized. Additionally, they can only cater to local customers because regulators make cross-country (and cross-state in the US) operations very expensive.

Other banks choose to become aggregators or distributors of financial services products. They do not create the products and services but procure them from various partners. They do not incur manufacturing and compliance costs but can offer customers access to different products and services. With this model, customers first allow banks to consolidate their data from different financial services providers. They then offer services to help their clients make better operational and financial decisions. They offer the right advice and/or service to a customer, through the right channel at the right time. These banks receive a small fee for every product or service that a consumer buys.

The problem with this model is the use of customers' transactional data. Banks will find it difficult to offer advice without access to this data. The Payment Services Directive 2 (PSD2)[15] in Europe will soon allow third-parties to access the transactional data of European banks, helping aggregators. Through internet platforms, customers can gain relevant and timely advice by using contextual data; this is data that is appropriate to a specific customer based on their preferences, location, time of the day, etc. There are also sites offering price comparisons allowing customers to search for the best deals.

The aggregator model allows banks to offer customers added value by working with them and understanding their finances, thus providing options for them to make a decision. It can be very profitable for banks, especially if they have economies of scale that can service millions of customers with just one application platform.

Perhaps the ideal business model for banks would be a hybrid one. Banks that are vertically integrated have the advantage of being able to provide superior customer fulfillment and have better execution capabilities. However, they can only offer a limited number of self-produced products and services as these will require a high degree of specialization. These products and services must be open so that third-party providers can provide them for other banks' use. Using this type of model can mean offering products and services with simpler processes and faster delivery.

Some of the competitive advantages that banks have include large customer bases, trust, strong execution capabilities, large data sets, large amounts of capital, and access to cheap funding through deposits. Banks that decide to shift to the aggregation model may lose all these advantages. Thus, the best course of action may be for them to assume an open yet vertically integrated model.[16]

Banking as a Service and Open APIs

Banking as a service and APIs have been hot topics recently—everybody seems to be talking about them, and for good reason, because they are transformational. We will cover these topics in simple terms. An API (Application Programming Interface) is a collection of functions that developers can use to create applications. Instead of developing interfaces from scratch when working with third parties, developers can

[handwritten top: Fintechs]

[handwritten right margin: API's speed up banks ability to build systems]

take advantage of these APIs. They request the use of this code through the syntax made available in the partner's documentation. Once they have access, they can interact with the partner's platform through the API.[17]

In the past, banks took a long time to build systems. They spent millions coding them, and integrating them with third parties was a laborious task. Currently, the approach is changing, thanks to APIs. New financial service start-ups want to build solutions quickly and at a low cost by collaborating with other firms.

They create APIs, symbolically saying, "Here are the keys to my service, please help yourself, and together we can create something bigger." For example, if I sell e-commerce platforms and I want to offer a cheap payment system using multiple currencies, I could decide to use an API from a provider such as Stripe. This would save me a lot of hassle with coding and having to establish partnerships with several merchants in different geographical locations. By using their API, I could offer full multicurrency payments by following Stripe's reference guide to help me use their account balances, charges, customer details, transfers, and refunds functions. I could even skip reading the reference guide if I decided to use an off-the-shelf connector from a firm such as Mulesoft, which makes the process even easier. By using the API, I would still be able to fully control the way that my customers see my web page and mobile app, but I would not need to create complex code or even involve a big team of IT developers in my project.

Benefits of Offering APIs for Fintech Providers

Fintechs offering APIs demonstrate that they are open to collaboration. When different services are connected, larger products can be created. Never-before imagined ideas can be brought to life. This is partly why the app stores of Apple and Android have become so popular, as they freely allow people to build apps on them.

Let's suppose you are a small company (such as Nymi) offering a bracelet that has Bluetooth connectivity and a heart monitor. You could work for months coding to incorporate a few credit card providers so that you can pay with the bracelet. This will take both time and money. However, if you created an API, allowing everybody to connect to your bracelet, then many new ideas could emerge. The bracelet could be enhanced by new apps created by those third parties and used to pay fares on the Underground (subway), replace security passes at your office, and even authenticate yourself when you call your bank.

Challenger banks wanting to develop their services fast can use APIs. A great product has been created by Fidor called FidorOs, a solution that does not carry their branding based on API services. Customers can either choose to use their own core banking system or use Fidor's core banking module to set up a bank from scratch. There are also APIs that deal with a wide range of activities, such as analytics, scoring, identity service, loyalty, community, and third-party management.

How Traditional Banks can use APIs

APIs can be used by both banks and their fintech partners. For example, if a bank wants to connect with PayPal on the bank's mobile app, the PayPal API would allow customers to see the funds they have available in PayPal, and details of recent transactions. This would be useful for enriching a statement, which normally just reads PayPal on the transaction line. On the PayPal app, an API created by the bank would allow PayPal users to see their available balance. So before making a payment, the customer would know which account or card to use, based on their available balances. To take this a step further, another company such as Curve, a company that offers a card which can store several cards from different banks, might decide to integrate both the bank and PayPal's APIs, so that customers can establish a set of rules which dictate how a transaction is paid for when they use their Curve card.

Incumbent banks have a double dilemma. On one hand, there is a clear need to upgrade their core banking systems. On the other hand, they need to decide how much the use of APIs opens them up to the rest of the world.

Core banking systems have been built over decades, and are highly complex. If they had been created today, a completely different framework would have been chosen for their development. Upgrades to and maintenance of these systems are costly, and every change to the system requires a lot of testing, due to the huge risk of getting things wrong. Some banks consider these systems to be a competitive advantage. They have invested more than others and given epic names to their systems, such as Santander's Partenon system and Lloyd's Galaxy. The issue is, there are companies right now that are prepared to build better systems, that are future-proofed and more flexible. A good example of this is the operating system called VaultOS, built by ex-Googlers, which keeps a ledger of transactions using blockchain technology, a system that records all transactions on a permanent online database. Also, new fintech giants such as Alipay have a strategy of upgrading all of their IT architecture every four years.

Banks have been reluctant to open up, and only started to do so because of new regulations being introduced. In the United Kingdom, from 2018, banks have been mandated to allow registered third-party providers access to information about customers' transactions, as well as the ability to execute payments on behalf of customers. The main fear they have is that banking may become commoditized. A third party that connects all banks could check the best interest rates and fees and propose the best current accounts, savings, and lending deals. The third party could create an app with a great user experience and remove the need for customers to even contact traditional banks. Banks would, therefore, be losing their relationship with the customer, which would translate into a loss of profits.

Sooner or later banks will need to upgrade their core banking systems and open up to third parties, but this will take courage. The future is looking brighter for customers as things become more transparent.

Neo-banks, Challenger Banks, and iBanks

Different terms are used in the fintech community to describe new banks. There is no official definition of what each bank does, but I've laid out some categories below, which will help you to understand how different banks operate.

What Are Neo-banks?

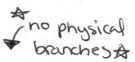

A *neo-bank* is a company that provides an upgraded and updated version of a traditional bank, without holding a banking license. It uses websites and mobile applications rather than physical branches to provide its customers with banking services.

A neo-bank offers traditional banking services like accounts and transactions, asset management, credits, deposits, investments, and so on. Some neo-banks also offer crowdfunding, P2P lending, cryptocurrencies, and robotic financial consultants. Neo-banks minimize costs and aim to speed up services. The key factor is that since they don't possess a banking license, they need to work with a partner bank to provide services. This is comparable to a Mobile Virtual Network Operator (MVNO) in the mobile industry. They are using one of the big provider's networks, while offering the customer a different experience.

With the increase of global investment in financial technology, neo-banks show a lot of promise in the United States and Europe. Popular neo-banks include Moven, Simple, and GoBank. Moven offers direct-to-consumer products, in collaboration with CBW Bank. It offers a bundle with an app, a debit card, and a contactless payment sticker. Simple, on the other hand, offers surcharge-free ATM STAR network access and current accounts, while GoBank offers a checking account to customers who want to pay low fees.

The neo-banking model is facing some problems, mostly due to its reliance on another bank's infrastructure and license. In fact, GoBank in the United States announced that it would stop allowing accounts to be opened through mobile devices. Customers would have to buy a kit from a store to open an account instead. Another neo-bank, Simple, had issues with payment scheduling and service delays. Moven, on the other hand, had to expand internationally to attract more customers.

Recently, large banks are taking an interest in neo-banks. Spain's BBVA acquired Simple. It has also invested in Atom, a challenger bank which will be discussed below. These acquisitions have allowed BBVA to foster a culture of innovation, align internal resources, and establish a customer base in different geographical areas.

What Are Challenger Banks and iBanks?

Challenge traditional banks

Lately, a new breed of banks has emerged, and some have called this the evolution of the neo-bank. These can be compared to no-frills airlines, offering banking at a lower cost. It is questionable whether they will be as successful as low-cost airlines.

A *challenger bank* is a new bank that competes with large national ones for business. It has the potential to offer better deals and superior service. Instead of having physical branches, it offers online and mobile banking; although there are challenger banks that collaborate with other banks to accept money over-the-counter. It relies on customer deposits and lends money to individuals with lower interests.

A challenger bank does not have to deal with legacy issues as it starts with a clean slate. Many customers may have reservations about them because these banks are relatively unknown, and people are often loyal to their traditional bank. A challenger bank may not be as big as a traditional bank, but it typically needs to comply with the same rules and regulations.

Aside from being mobile-only, challenger banks also have other common characteristics. Their apps reflect changes in customer behavior. Aside from peer reviews and peer referrals, consumers also rely on social interactions to test the functionality of challenger banks, which offer a different visual experience.

Challenger banks offer everyday banking experiences by becoming more relevant in consumers' lives. They don't just provide monetary transfers and transactions, they provide a meaningful context by offering a concierge-based approach that traditional banking don't usually offer. Challenger banks are focused on their API layer, thereby giving them agility and flexibility to expand their products and services through strategic collaborations.

Challenger banks have various specializations. For example, Aldermore and Shawbrook Bank cater to small- or medium-sized enterprises and individuals, while Clydesdale and Metro Bank offer credit cards, checking accounts, and other traditional banking services and specialize more geographically.

Most of these banks have private equity backing. For example, JC Flowers, a private equity firm, provided OneSavings Bank with capital in 2011. AnaCap Financial Partners backed Aldermore, and Pollen Street Capital backed Shawbrook Bank. Some challenger banks are very profitable. In 2014, Shawbrook Bank reported £18.6 million[18] pre-tax profit during the first half of the year, while Aldermore reported £50.3 million profit.[19]

However, challenger banks face potential problems. First, they must prepare for the effects of increases in interest rates and the tightening of monetary policy. Since they began, after the financial crisis in 2008, they have experienced supportive monetary policies and steady growth. They remain untested in a more hostile environment.

Some people identify *iBanks* as another emerging bank category. They look at monetizing banking in a different way. Instead of making a profit through fees and interest, they try to gain revenues from monetizing data. An example of this is the niche bank, Loot, which focuses on students. Loot aims to profit from non-traditional revenue streams, such as advertising and cross-selling. Another example is Secco-Bank. Their subsidiary SeccoAura is looking for an alternative way of monetizing personal data, and it allows members to earn tokens through referrals done through social networks when people buy items that have been liked by SeccoAura's members.

Challenger Banking in the United States

The United States have created amazing fintech companies such as Stripe, Square, and SoFi. However, they haven't launched banking start-ups. This has been mostly linked to the regulation that is set up. In short, there has been an absence of a federal regulatory regime that fintech firms could use, which means that fintechs would need to apply for a license in every single state in which they want to do business.

However, the Office of the Comptroller of the Currency (OCC) has cleared the way for a light banking license that can be issued to fintech start-ups. This was cleared by the US Treasury in 2018 after dealing with significant opposition from state regulators. This means that if all goes well, new banks will start emerging in the United States very soon and many overseas companies have already expressed interest in launching.

Key Players

In this section, we look at interesting companies that are making important progress in this category. Fintech is a very volatile industry, so by the time you read this, these companies may have changed substantially.

In 2009, the digital bank Fidor started operating in Germany. Its focus is to re-establish the confidence of customers in banking by allowing them to participate actively in the bank's decision-making. At present, their portfolio of products includes business and retail banking, covering checking and savings accounts, lending, and bonds. It has more than 100,000 customers and 300,000 community members.[20]

As one of the pioneers in innovative banking, Fidor received various international awards for being transparent and disruptive in its approach. Its use of social media is innovative. It provides a space for individuals to share their knowledge and experience with finance. It does not use financial advisors to sell its products. Its digital framework is interactive, fun, connected, and transparent, and their motto is that money management should be enjoyable.

It has a banking license similar to that of a traditional bank, but it does not act like one. To encourage customers to sign up and liven up the user community, it offered €50 to customers who created a video with the theme of "user-help-user." It raised its interest rates on savings and lowered its lending rate by 1% when its Facebook account generated 2,000 likes. Fidor Bank's customers can also transact foreign currencies online and use its currency cloud. Customers can apply for a loan in just a matter of seconds. They can also interact with other customers online to seek advice and give opinions.

In Q3 2016, Fidor partnered with Telefónica Germany to launch O2 Banking, Germany's first mobile-only, full-service bank account. It has been highly successful as people have enjoyed only needing a phone number to do business.[21]

 Rocketbank

Rocketbank is an iBank from Russia. Because of the style of their customer service and viral marketing app, it has been dubbed a "bank for hipsters." Alexey Kolesnikov co-founded Rocketbank with three of his friends in 2012. They wanted to let young Russians manage their finances through an app. It became famous for recommending its own users to move their money away just hours before Interkommerz, its servicing bank, went under. Despite this, Rocketbank survived, thanks to a Russian bailout, and in December 2015, Rocketbank signed a deal with Otkritie, the fourth largest Russian bank in terms of assets.[22]

N26

N26 is a Berlin-based start-up, that is trying to reinvent banking. It collaborates with Wirecard, and operates as a full bank with a license to operate around Europe. It has more than 2,000,000 users. Launched in Germany, N26 is now available in six countries.[23]

N26 can offer products in real time and supports an aggregator model. Expense sharing is one of the interesting features that allows its customers to split bills with friends. This is similar to Uber's fare splitting. N26 is also collaborating with other fintechs to build its own products since it already has a license to become a full-fledged bank. Since February 2016, N26 uses TransferWise, seeking to offer an enhanced, seamless experience to its customers.[24] The company launched in UK in 2018 and also announced its plans to enter the US market in 2019.[25]

 LOOT

Loot bank, a money management start-up for students launched by young entrepreneur Ollie Purdue, links to a prepaid card. It lets students monitor how much money they can spend, based on projected spending, outgoings, and total balance.

Purdue developed the idea with London's Fast Forward, a pre-accelerator program. He showed a prototype to Charles Tyrwhitt's founder, Nick Wheeler, hoping he would invest in the project. Wheeler and seven other investors invested £200,000 each in Loot, which earns revenue from Mastercard transaction fees[26] and plans to focus on monetizing their data. In December 2017, Loot Bank raised $2.2 million in seed funding, totalling $6.2 million in financing.[27]

 **monzo**

Monzo is probably the hottest UK challenger bank based on popularity and awards won. It reached the 1 million customers mark in 2018, although most of its customers use Monzo as a secondary bank account. This mobile banking app from the UK, which achieved a record for fastest crowdinvesting, getting one million pounds in just 96 seconds from more than 1800 investors. It provides purchase tracking in real-time, geo-location transaction viewing, purchase viewing by category, and a graphical timeline of overall expenditure. The app has received impressive feedback. It has an API to connect to external companies and has been built by an entirely British team. It started as a prepaid card, but once regulators granted Monzo a restricted banking license it became a full fledge current account provider. Monzo switched its beta testers to a checking account and became a full bank in April 2017.[28] It also secured a further round of funding at around £71m, seeking expansion to Europe, Asia, and the US.

 Atom

Founded in Durham, UK, Atom Bank is one of the digital-only banks offering financial products for consumers between 18 and 34 (the so-called millennials). Users can perform transactions through the app. Its products include fixed saver accounts as well as mortgages. Up till 2018, Atom raised £369m in five funding rounds.[29]

TANDEM

Tandem is a British challenger bank. It received its operating license in November 2015. Tandem allows customers to add bank accounts from other providers and monitor their spending. The bank's goal is to engage customers and help them manage their habits and behaviors. It started rolling out its app to customers at the end of 2016. Tandem will offer checking accounts, loans, and credit cards in 2017; currently, it provides savings accounts.[30] In August 2017, Tandem acquired Harrods Bank for £80m thus gaining access to a banking license.[31] In 2018 Tandem launched a credit card aimed at customers that have non-existent credit histories.

STARLING BANK

The Financial Conduct Authority and the Bank of England granted Starling Bank, a mobile-only business, its banking license. Former Allied Irish Bank Chief Operating Officer Anne Boden heads Starling Bank.[32] The bank launched a current (checking account) in 2017 and business account in 2018. Its focus is on making the most of big data, and it allows customers to analyze their spending habits and keep a clear view of the state of their finances. Starling has also started offering white label banking services for clients such as Ditto and Raising UK.

Monese caters to expats and immigrants, who may have a difficult time opening a bank account in another country. It takes about three minutes to open a Monese current account. It also offers a Visa debit card and low-cost international money transfers, and it's also possible to deposit and withdraw cash, as well as store various currencies in the account. Monese earns money by charging a fixed monthly service fee per account.[33] Monese is present in 20 different European countries with available options in local languages and the ability to operate as a local Euro bank with a unique IBAN number.[34] In 2018 it scored a $60 million series B investment led by Kinnevik.

The Future in a Flash

In most regions of the world, there is space for more competition, and it is likely that some of the new entrants will end up being profitable in the long run. Challenger banks that start in a specific niche have swiftly started transitioning into other product offerings in order to increase their profit per customer. This can either be achieved through partnerships, or in-house developments.

It is also very likely that some of the traditional banks won't manage to adapt well enough to the new environment, which requires constant modernization and change. Hence, some of these might disappear, or have to change their models radically.

The concept of banking will change and integrate a lot more with our daily lives; however, a Kodak or Blockbuster killer is not expected in this industry. The same big brands that we are used to seeing will retain a lead in this space, thanks to their experience dealing with regulation and their strong financial positions.

Chapter 3
Rethinking Payments and Remittances

Payments and Remittances in a Flash

Fintech has made a strong entrance into the payments arena. Consumers can make the most of innovative methods of sending and receiving money using mobile apps, peer-to-peer payments, and cryptocurrency transfers.

We will look into how migrant workers send money to their families through fund transfers or remittances. In 2011, the amount transferred was at least $483 billion,[35] and this figure is steadily increasing, which represents a great opportunity.

Mobile money transfers are popular in developing countries because citizens often find it easier to send text messages than to physically go to a money transfer operator or branch. Peer-to-peer money transfers allow users to send and receive money through a network not controlled by any central authority. Each transaction occurs in an online marketplace where one person sells a currency and another one buys it. Cryptocurrency is also another innovative way of sending and receiving remittances. It is inexpensive, and senders and recipients maintain their anonymity. However, users have to have a digital wallet—a device or an online service used to make electronic transactions—before they can initiate transactions.

Other interesting payment trends are social media and nanopayments. Social media networks allow users to send and receive money through peer-to-peer transfers. Nanopayments are used for monetizing online content through charging small fees.

Traditional Remittances

It is useful to understand how remittances traditionally work to identify inefficiencies. A typical transaction is done in three steps. First, the customer sends the money through a sending agent via the internet, phone, or email. This sending agent instructs its operations team to send the remittance to the recipient's country, and the recipient receives the funds from the paying agent. In general, settlements between the sending and paying agents are not done in real-time. The agents settle the transactions periodically through a commercial bank.

The sending agent charges a fee for the remittance transaction, and the sender also pays for the currency-conversion fee so that the payment of the remittance can be made in the recipient's local currency. Small money transfer operators also require the recipient to pay a fee to receive the remittance to cover unexpected movements in the foreign exchange rate. Remittance agents also earn interest because they invest the funds overnight before they deliver them to the recipient.

DOI 10.1515/9781547401055-003

Traditional Delivery Methods

There are three traditional ways to send remittances: through money orders, checks, and drafts; through wire transfers; and through ACH transfers.

The safest and most common way of sending remittances internationally is using money orders, checks, and drafts. International money orders are the most secure and convenient mode. Recipients can go to various locations to cash them or deposit them directly into their bank accounts.

Wire transfers involve financial institutions who agree to process the money through the Society for Worldwide Interbank Financial Telecommunication (SWIFT) messages. The remittance transaction takes place between two financial institutions, so both the sender and the recipient can expect to pay fees.

In a wire transfer, money moves from one bank account to another through money transfer operators (MTOs). The MTO gathers the information from the sender, and then triggers the wire transfer message to the receiving financial institution. For the wire transfer process to be successful, the sender must provide the recipient's name, address, account number, and bank information.

Aside from bank-to-bank transactions, wire transfers can also be through a cash wire transfer, a service usually offered by MoneyGram or Western Union. Using this method, the money transfer company uses its own funds for the wire transfer process. An individual goes to one of the company's branches to give the company representative the cash that he wants to send to another person.

Wire transfer fees vary depending on the money transfer service. For faster service, the money transfer company typically charges a higher fee.

Another way of transferring money is through the Automated Clearing House (ACH), an electronic network for batch processing of transactions by financial institutions. This is an intermediary who receives the payment, clears it, and informs the financial institution.

Banks offer ACH transfers to their clients, who want to transfer money anywhere in the world. Unlike the wire transfer, the ACH transfer goes through its own network, which is a financial hub composed of various financial institutions. The National Automated Clearing House Association (NACHA) manages ACH transfers for all financial institutions in the United States. The Single Euro Payments Area (SEPA) is NACHA's counterpart in Europe.

In ACH transfers, the sender sends a direct payment through the network. Their bank sends their transaction, together with others, at regular intervals throughout the banking day. Then, the ACH operator sorts the batch and sends the transaction to the receiving financial institution. The recipient's bank receives the funds transferred by the sender. ACH transfers take more time than wire transfers and are less expensive.

Initiating Online Transfers

An online money transfer is any fund transfer that is performed through the internet and does not require the sender to visit a money transfer operator or bank. Currently, most money transfer operators and banks allow online money transfer services.

This type of funds transfer is safe, convenient, and fast. Many bank customers have online access to their bank accounts, so they can easily transfer money to anyone around the world, as long as that recipient has a bank account. The back-end process for the money transfer can be either ACH transfer or a wire transfer.

Independent companies, on the other hand, have websites on which users can create their own account. These users have to provide a debit card, a credit card, or a bank account to initiate a funds transfer. They also need to provide the bank account details of the intended recipient. These companies, such as Moneygram, collect the fee from the users' bank accounts.

PayPal revolutionized the remittance process by using an email address as a unique identity. A PayPal user can transfer money by paying into a PayPal account from a credit card or bank account. Once the money is in the PayPal network, transactions occur instantly between PayPal users. However, the recipient needs to withdraw the money from their PayPal account to their bank account or to a PayPal credit card.

 ## Size of the Remittances Market

In 2016, remittances, money sent by migrant workers back to their country of origin, amounted to $573 billion. In 2016, these grew by 7% to $613 billion. Payments to low income countries were $466 million in 2017, growing by 8.5%.[36] According to the World Bank, remittances are about 300% higher than the Official Development Assistance given to developing countries and more stable than private capital flows.[37] Additionally, remittances are worth more than portfolio equity and private debt flows to these nations. In about 14 developing countries, they exceeded the foreign exchange reserves. Remittances are also at least equal to 50% of the reserves in at least 26 developing countries.[38]

Due to consumer demand, money transfer start-ups are emerging around the world. The disruption of the banking industry could mean it will face tough times since there is a huge opportunity for these start-ups to absorb the market share once belonging to the top banks and money transfer specialists. Peer-to-peer payments have enabled individuals to send money to their intended recipients in just minutes using cloud technology. According to Forrester Research, this type of payment scheme could generate at least $17 billion in transaction volume by 2019. With advances in technology, the global community expects the process of sending and receiving remittances to become more efficient, safer, and generate a positive impact.

In 2017, the average cost of sending remittances globally went down to 7.1% from 10% in 2009. This saved migrant workers $54 billion. The World Bank estimates that cutting prices by at least 5% can save workers up to $16 billion a year.[39] Digital payment products can cost as little as 3.4%, and technological innovations in the payment infrastructure and payment instruments improve the safety and efficiency of remittances.

 ## Upcoming Trends in Remittances

The first notable trend in remittance technology relates to infrastructure expansion. Automated Clearing Houses and card payment schemes have established procedures, policies, and standards, so it makes sense to invest in them. They are often reliable and widely used.

The second trend involves combining payment instruments and current infrastructure. Most countries have pre-existing payment systems already set up. Using this infrastructure with innovative products and services can prove to be less expensive than completely rethinking the process. Some financial institutions, in both sending and receiving countries, have created card-based products that allow the families of migrant workers to withdraw remittances at ATMs or use them for payments. The use of the card infrastructure is cheaper, safer, and more efficient than cash. However, regulators in some countries do not allow dual-purpose cards.

A third trend entails combining domestic and international payment mechanisms. In some countries, citizens increasingly prefer to use electronic payments instead of cash. Some even use this type of payment to transfer funds to another person locally. Nonbanks and banks issue electronic money based on arrangements with the country's regulators. Payment service providers and international money transfer operators use the existing electronic payments structure to send the funds to a particular receiver in that country.

A fourth trend is around new players that are making the most of the current payment infrastructure. New companies have started to operate within the remittance market to enhance the potential of the existing network. Some of these companies provide cross-border services that also enable financial institutions to maintain ownership of the consumer base. They offer efficient and transparent cross-border payment products. There are also companies, often banks, that allow interoperability between Automated Clearing Houses, mobile money, and the internet. They have created a hub that allows for both domestic and international remittance transfers. Online remittance providers like PayPal allow senders to try various options. Senders can pay using their bank accounts, credit card, or debit card, and they can choose how they want the money delivered to the recipient.

A fifth trend is around non-remittance companies offering remittance services. Retail stores and import businesses can become remittance companies. Some online companies are even offering remittance services to their clients through their current payment infrastructures. For example, a business offering online foreign exchange information can offer remittance services. A customer can provide online instructions for their bank account to be debited and the money to be credited to the recipient's bank account.

Innovative Ways of Sending Money

Mobile Money Transfers

Companies now offer money transfers using a mobile phone. The introduction of smartphones allows users to use different online services and apps, even in rural areas. In several countries, it is now possible to send money via text message. Large banks and money transfer operators offer mobile apps to their clients to make it easier for them to send money.

Mobile apps are a convenient, secure, and fast way to remit money internationally. In 2015, international remittances using mobile technology grew by as much as 52% compared to the previous year. In that same year, US migrant workers sent about $600 billion to their families overseas.

Cryptocurrency Transactions

As digital currencies, cryptocurrency transactions, such as bitcoin, do not need to pass through banks. They incur no hefty fees and parties to the transaction also remain anonymous. Digital wallets act as storage for these currencies. They can reside on the user's computer or in a cloud. One problem with this method could be the risk of fluctuations in the exchange rate, as well as the lack of banking protection in the case of problems such as hacking or fraud. However, as the currencies mature, insurance against these problems is emerging.

The main models for these remittances are the pure cryptocurrency model, the cryptocurrency-to-fiat model, and fiat-to-fiat model. In the pure cryptocurrency model, the currency is transferred directly from person to person. In cryptocurrency-to-fiat, a cryptocurrency operator is used to convert the cryptocurrency into the target currency. This assumes that the originating country has easy access to cryptocurrency and is typically the case of developed countries. This is the model likely to have the highest degree of success. In the third model, both sender and receiver use a physical currency, but the remittance operator uses a cryptocurrency for the transfer.

Peer-to-Peer Payments

In a traditional foreign exchange trade, a company can sell or buy a particular currency from another person online and earn money from it. In a P2P transaction, a person trades currencies with other persons in a marketplace. The platform offering the service earns a small amount of money from each transaction.[40] Boston Consulting Group estimates P2P payments to grow by 30% through 2020.[41]

A peer-to-peer money transfer company offers almost complete transparency. A customer understands the fees they have to pay for each transaction, and, compared to a traditional foreign exchange company, they benefit from a lower exchange rate and a small fixed fee. Registering with a platform is easy, and a user can send any amount of money. Online platforms are secure and easy to use.

However, P2P money transfers also have their disadvantages. First, they are relatively recent, which might make customers feel uneasy. Second, some P2P currency exchange companies allow prices to fluctuate unless a user locks in the rate. Traditional money exchanges lock the price at the agreement date. Third, some P2P companies also charge fees on money transfers.

Key Players

In this section, we look at interesting companies that are making important progress in the remittance category. Fintech is a very volatile industry, so by the time you read this, these companies may have changed substantially.

↗ TransferWise

Founded in January 2011 by Taavet Hinrikus and Kristo Käärmann, TransferWise is a peer-to-peer money transfer operator with its headquarters in London. It currently has offices in Estonia, Singapore, Sydney, and New York, among others. With at least one million clients and at least £800 million worth of transfers each month, it supports 47 currencies.[42]

TransferWise does away with costly cross-border transfers and currency conversion by rerouting payments. It does not send money directly from the sender to the recipient but redirects the funds to another recipient of an equal transfer in the opposite direction. The original recipient receives the money from another sender who initiated a transfer of the same amount. TransferWise either charges a fee of 0.5% or €2, or the equivalent, depending on which is the larger amount.

Estonia deserves a special mention. It became the Silicon Valley of the Baltics because, during the Cold War, the Kremlin halted the independence movement in Estonian universities by restricting the teaching of social sciences and philosophy.

Students focused on information technology and computers instead. These people became Estonian software developers, who played a central role in the KGB spying efforts and the Soviet space program.

Estonia gained independence from the Soviet Union two years after the fall of the Berlin Wall in 1989. When Netscape introduced their internet browser three years later, Estonia became an entrepreneurial e-republic. Most of Estonia is decentralized and digital. Estonians rarely visit a government office and have access to broadband WiFi. They have been using mobile phones as identification and for voting online since 2007. Estonia was responsible for developing Skype and the P2P music service Kazaa.

TransferWise's Hinrikus and Käärmann still live in Tallinn, Estonia. Käärmann developed the Scandinavian and Baltic version of Yahoo Finance. He had a consulting deal with Deloitte in London, where he met Hinrikus, a fellow Estonian. Sending money to their families back home, Käärmann and Hinrikus realized that transaction fees were costing them a lot of money. Being software engineers, Hinrikus and Käärmann thought of a solution. From Hinrikus' Estonian bank account, he would transfer euros to Käärmann's Estonian bank account. Then, from Käärmann's British bank account, he would transfer pounds to Hinrikus' Lloyds bank account, saving on international transfer fees. They invited other Estonians to transfer money through their method.

In 2001, Käärmann and Hinrikus resigned from their jobs to build TransferWise using about $1.3 million of their own money. The company now transacts at least $750 million monthly with about one million users in 60 countries. Monthly, it earns roughly $5 million in transaction fees.[43]

In November 2017, the company raised $280 million in a Series E funding round to expand into Latin America and Asia.[44] In January 2018, TransferWise announced the launch of its new borderless account and debit card that can hold 28 currencies in one account.[45] This expands its business model significantly and its ability to earn revenues.

venmo XOOM
A PayPal Service

PayPal aims to remain at the forefront of international money transfers, so it has followed a policy of acquiring the best companies it can find that offer potential and synergy with its business model.

Popular among millennials, Venmo is a peer-to-peer payment technology that has various uses. Users can pay for items quickly through its app. They can post their transactions in the Venmo app for their friends to see. This feature is primarily social advertising, which means merchants are very excited about it. Venmo charges 2.9% per transaction, and there is a 30¢ charge for merchants. In 2017, Venmo users transmitted $6.8 billion in the 1st quarter and $8 billion in the 2nd quarter.[46]

Xoom, acquired in July 2015 for $890 million, is a leading international remittances provider. Xoom enables its customers in the United States to send money to anyone around the world. It prides itself on being able to perform payments at lightning speed and allows customers to reload phones and pay bills in a cost-effective, quick, and secure manner through computers, tablets, and mobile phones.

PayPal is making adjustments to its brands in order to align them to its global business strategy and ensuring that cannibalization is minimized between its products. So for example, it has removed web functionality from Venmo.

Zelle

Arizona-based Zelle is considered Venmo's replacement, and it has already achieved a higher number of users. It is a P2P payment platform that allows for safe payments and banking transactions. Payments can be done using just emails or mobile phone numbers. The key of its success is its integration to US banks, and it provides excellent fraud protection. In its first year it reached more than 100 million consumers proving its relevance to the US market.

worldremit.

UK-based WorldRemit is continuously building its business on a global scale. Founded in 2010, it is, at present, worth around $670 million. It set up headquarters in the US, particularly in Denver, to capture the US market, where 10% of all worldwide remittances originate.

WorldRemit charges a lower commission than Western Union and users from 50 countries can use their mobile phones or computers to transfer money to individuals in more than 150 destinations worldwide. They can send money to mobile wallets, cash pick-up points, or bank accounts. WorldRemit is leading its competitors in the area of money transfers to mobile wallets, with 100,000 transfers each month, 25% of the company's total transactions.

Based in London, Azimo is a mobile money transfer company with more than half a million customers. It is expanding its operation in Europe and targeting migrant workers, who earn less than the average income. Founded in 2012, it can transact in

80 currencies and covers 200 countries. Its target regions are Africa, Latin America, Asia, and Eastern Europe. Azimo is integrated with several messaging apps and has received investment from the Viber owners Rakuten.

Currencycloud

Based in the UK, Currencycloud offers cross-border money transfers and is used by payment and money transfer businesses. Its Payment Engine, a cloud-based platform, connected to an API, is used by companies like Xe.com, TransferWise, and Azimo. Currencycloud boasts at least 500,000 end users and is used by no less than 150 companies like WorldRemit, WeSwap, and MANGOPAY.

Currencycloud's main competitors are banks, but the platform charges less for the same money transfer service. On average, Currencycloud processes $10 billion worth of payments transactions yearly in 40 currencies in 212 nations. It has offices in London and New York, and plans to expand to Asia in 2019. It has raised more than $68 million in funding from investors including Sapphire Ventures, Google Ventures and Anthemis Group.[47]

Remitly

Seattle-based Remitly is a mobile remittance app that allows individuals in the US to send money to the Philippines and India. It has raised more than $200 million in funding. It acquired Talio, a picture-messaging app, to incorporate its features into the Remitly app. Remitly processes an average of $1 billion in money transfers each year. Focusing on its customers, its mobile-first service continues to disrupt the remittance market with its low fees.

ripple

Founded in 2012, Ripple is a US-based company that offers an internet protocol to connect the disparate financial systems of different countries, offering secure funds transfers. It has received more than $90 million in funding and supports two solutions, one for retail remittances and one for corporate disbursals.

Ripple's distributed financial technology enables banks to send real-time international payments across networks, with no settlement risk, and eliminating the need to have separate accounts in different countries. It also enables banks to open new revenue opportunities, lower processing costs, and deliver better overall customer experiences.

Social Media-based Remittances

Social media is a great way to connect with friends and share stories and pictures with them. With the advent of financial technology, as mentioned earlier, it is also possible to send money through them to anyone in the world.

A remittance fintech company can take advantage of social media to make money transfers cheaper and faster, globally. Usually, the company has an app that users can use to send remittances through social networking sites like WeChat, Twitter, and Facebook. At present, Facebook does not charge a fee for peer-to-peer payments through its Messenger app. On the other hand, WeChat, the popular Chinese social media site, charges 0.1% for transfers. Both Facebook and WeChat allow payments between users within the same country; and in February 2017, TransferWise introduced a chatbot to Facebook that allows customers to do international payments.[48] In most cases, a fintech company will also charge a fee for processing a transaction. The recipient can collect the money from cash pick-up points, or it can be sent to their bank account.

Key Players

WhatsApp

WhatsApp is a cross-platform, proprietary, and encrypted instant messaging system for smartphones. Based in California, Facebook acquired the company in February 2014 for about $19.3 billion. WhatsApp had at least one billion users by February 2016, making it the top messaging application at that time.[49]

WhatsApp has huge potential for integrating payments. Axis Bank, in collaboration with WhatsApp, allows users to request and send money—and the transfer is instant. The sender has to enter a sender code and amount to be sent to the intended recipient. After pressing the "Send" button, the recipient will receive a message informing them. They have 15 days to move the money to their bank account. If they fail to transfer the funds, the money will be returned to the sender's account.

Facebook

In March 2015, Facebook announced that it was offering users the option to send mobile payments through its Messenger app. Users of the app can use a debit card to send money to other Facebook users without charge. They need to create a message to the recipient, then tap the "$" icon. Recipients have to open the message and enter their bank details. The money transfer happens immediately; however, it may take up to three banking days for the funds to be available in the recipient's bank.[50]

In October 2016, the Central Bank of Ireland gave Facebook a license to operate P2P payments and charitable donations through its Messenger service all across Europe. With its license, Facebook now allows its users in Europe to donate to registered charities in the European economic area and carry out P2P payments.[51]

WeChat

Developed by Tencent, WeChat is China's cross-platform instant messaging app released in January 2011. As of May 2016, it has at least 900 million active users. It is available for most phone operating systems.[52]

WeChat supports money transfer and payment through peer-to-peer electronic bill payment and transfer. Users must have their WeChat Pay account to use this feature. They can use a debit card to add money to their WeChat account. Those users with credit cards can only use them when paying merchants.

Most retailers in China, including Taiwan, Macau, and Hong Kong, accept WeChat Pay. In 2014, WeChat Pay introduced the "Electronic Red Envelope" instead of the traditional red envelope given to friends and relatives as a form of greeting them on holidays. and this was a huge success. Tencent is looking to extend WeChat Pay globally and has had great success in Finland, where by partnering with local payments firm ePassi it boosted the amount of shopping that Chinese tourists make during their holidays.

Viber

Developed by Israel-based Viber Media, Viber is a voice-over IP and cross-platform instant messaging app that also allows users to exchange audio and video messages, and images. In February 2016, it collaborated with Western Union to allow users to send money to other users anywhere in the world.[53]

Using the WU Connect platform, Viber focuses on sending money, integrating solutions that use foreign exchange conversion, robust technology, data management, and compliance, regulatory, and anti-money laundering infrastructure.

Nanopayments

For the film and music industries, it was a challenge to monetize something that people can get free of charge. Apps created for Facebook and other social media sites also had the same problem. Today, there are strategies that can get people to pay a small amount for these services.

Nanopayments have been in existence in Asia for many years now. In 2007, Tencent in China brought in $523 million in sales and $224 million in operating profits through nanopayments. In this case, almost 60% of the earnings came from digital goods and games, while 13% came from advertisements.[54]

Apple's App Store was successful because of people who pay small amounts of money for virtual goods. Users are willing to pay from $0.99 to $4.99 for various apps that they can download from the App Store. Social networks want to replicate this success, so there is a need to have a reliable, stable, and easy-to-use payment system.

Most users are young, so they do not have access to credit cards. In China, children can add money to their Tencent accounts by purchasing "QQ coins" from physical retailers or charging it to their phone bills. Similarly, Korea's Cyworld and Japan's Mixi use the same system.

X Factor's (a very popular TV show) CEO Tony Cohen believes that charging a user £0.05, for example, to watch an old episode, can help increase demand. Users also avoid illegal file-sharing sites if they can watch old episodes cheaply. According to OneTouch marketing manager Eli Gurock, 90% of people worldwide do not have access to credit cards, and many credit card users do not want to use them online. Nanopayments can bridge that wide gap and address the problems web merchants have with capturing more customers.

The Future in a Flash

In the globalized world we live in, we can expect the use of remittances to continue growing. We can also expect migrants to become more aware of cost effective ways to send money home, and assume that the level of trust in these services will increase. Mobile wallets are also likely to become an important tool for performing these transactions as more people gain access to smartphones in the developing world, especially in Africa and Asia. Transactions will become easier and easier to perform, and the focus will shift toward providing value added services such as cybersecurity and data insights.

Chapter 4
Digital Lending Innovation

Digital Lending Innovation in a Flash

By looking at innovations in money lending, we can see how far we've come, starting with pawnbrokers and evolving into internet-only banks offering immediate loan approval.

The idea of digital lending has been around for many years, but it is only now that innovations that allow for transformation are taking place. Digital consumer lending, student loans, small business loans, and mortgages have all seen unprecedented growth and undergone radical changes in recent years.

The biggest change has probably been the introduction of peer-to-peer lending. A significant amount of funds have gone into this space over the last decade, and even though the business model of these companies is still fluctuating, it appears that this type of lending is more than simply a trend. The use of advanced analytics to inform credit scoring and eligibility for lending is another significant innovation. We will examine in detail how these and other technologies are being applied to different requests for lending.

 **A Short History of Lending**

Pawnbrokers were the first people to begin lending money. They asked for items as collateral to minimize their lending risk. This was the first time the world saw secured lending. In the Middle Ages, Christians were banned from lending money while charging interest. However, non-Jews could borrow money from Jews with interest. Moneylenders used to sit on benches, known as "banca," which gave rise to the word "bank." When a lender stopped lending money and smashed his "banca," this was known as "banca rupta," which led to the term bankrupt.

In the 18th century, Mayer Amschel Rothschild invented international banking. His five sons ran a network of banks in five European cities. Within the century, his family became the wealthiest in the world. In the late 18th century, building societies started to emerge in taverns and coffee houses in the United Kingdom, particularly in Birmingham. In 1775, a property owner founded Ketley's Building Society, where member subscriptions financed the construction of houses for members. Founded in the early 1800s, the Philadelphia Savings Fund Society provided a means of saving and access to loans for average Americans. In 1932, the creation of the Federal Home Loan Bank system by the US Congress paved the way for residential mortgage lending by US banks and other financial institutions.

DOI 10.1515/9781547401055-004

In 1950, businessman Frank X. McNamara invented the credit card and was the first person to use a Diners Club Card to pay a restaurant bill. In 1958, Bank of America followed suit by launching BankAmericard, which later became Visa. Barclaycard was the first credit card in the United Kingdom, released in 1966. In 1973, Visa reduced transaction times through the computerization of the credit card system. Prior to computerization, payment between credit card issuers, banks, and retailers was manual and slow. It usually involved phone calls because checks had to be made against credit balances and a list of stolen credit cards.

Lenders in the US started using FICO scores to make informed credit decisions in 1959. The first reverse mortgage was granted in 1961 when Nelly Young of Portland, Maine, lost her husband. She needed to keep her house and was helped by Deering Savings and Loan's Nelson Hayes. In 1970, the US Congress chartered the Federal Home Loan Mortgage Corporation (Freddie Mac), to create a secondary market for traditional mortgages.

Online lending specialists grew up between 1980 and 2000. Quicken Loans, a Detroit-based mortgage lender, launched its online application and review process in 1985. First Internet Bank started its online-only banking in 1999, offering banking services and home mortgage loans.

Peer-to-Peer Lending

Peer-to-peer is an interaction between two parties with no intermediary. This was a term originally used in computer networking, but it now has various uses, from peer-to-peer file sharing to peer-to-peer lending.

In finance, peer-to-peer lending started with the launch of Zopa in the UK and Prosper in the US, which match borrowers and lenders in a central marketplace. In a nutshell, a borrower goes to a P2P marketplace to borrow money. If approved, they get a risk classification, which determines how much they will need to pay in interest. The loan then gets funded by one or more private investors. This turns out to be a good deal for both sides as they get better interest rates than banks offer. To be successful, credit scoring and fund diversification processes need to be well architected.

In 2016, Prosper had at least two million members, and about $6 billion in loans were taken out. Zopa, on the other hand, was used to make roughly £1.4 billion in loans and had at least 114,000 members.

During recent years, peer-to-peer lending has grown rapidly, and some believe that it will continue to do so. Peer-to-peer lending is more profitable than keeping money in savings accounts, though it is riskier. Peer-to-peer lending is perceived as having better social value and being more responsible than traditional banking.

P2P Marketplace Lending Business Model

Peer-to-peer platforms take both the depositor and borrower businesses away from traditional banks. They transfer income and the associated credit risk to the loan investors at the point of origin and earn nothing from loans held on their balance sheets. Most of their revenue comes from fees charged when new loans are taken out, so they need to be making sales continuously.

Consequently, if there is no appetite for lending and risk in the market, their performance is heavily affected, which is in turn reflected in their revenues and company valuation. As a result, some believe a purely P2P market is unsustainable. Some companies, like Ratesetter, have changed their model and now charge fees throughout the life of the loan. This provides a more stable business model.

Standard marketplace economics indicate that loans are normally originated at a 5% premium. Assuming a loan length of four years, this would mean a 1.25% transaction fee. Platforms would also charge an annual maintenance fee of around 0.8%, which would make them an average of around 2% all inclusive. A bank would make a lot more than this, as they generally have margins of around 7% net interest, after deducting credit losses.

So far, peer-to-peer lending has not been very profitable. The top lenders in the UK, Zopa and Funding Circle, lost £50 million in their first decade. They've been on a steep learning curve and have had to spend significantly to attract new customers. Sales and marketing, and origination and servicing expenses have taken up roughly 50% of the operating revenue of these companies. Referral schemes have been very generous. Ratesetter, for example, rewards referrals with £50 and gives new lenders £100 if they keep an investment of at least £1,000 for one year. Funding Circle customers earn £40 if they recommend a friend who goes on to invest at least £1,000. Zopa customers get £50 if a friend lends £1,000 with the platform and £100 if the friend lends at least £2,000.

There are different approaches to dealing with unpaid loans. Some lenders spread their investment over many different loans so that their eggs are not all in the same basket. In these cases, interest rates are indicative and depend on the number of unpaid loans. Other firms set up provision funds, which mean that they put money aside to cover potential default on loans.

P2P loans are still looking for an optimal business model to sustain profitability. A path to stability could be to have P2P lending as just one line of business and offer other banking services as well. This would allow them to have loans on a balance sheet and earn a profit from them. A hybrid model could help them navigate the difficult lending times in a better way. They would be required to get a banking license, and some have already started to go in this direction.

Key Players

In this section, we look at interesting companies that are making important progress in this area. Fintech is a very volatile industry, so by the time you read this, these companies may have changed substantially.

⠿ LendingClub

Founded in 2006, Lending Club raised $10.26 million from Canaan Partners and Norwest Venture Partners. It became a peer-to-peer lending company in 2007. In December 2014, after several rounds of investment, Lending Club completed its initial public offering (IPO) at $900 million. In June 2015, it collaborated with Opportunity Fund and the Clinton Global Initiative to provide $10 million in funds to small businesses in California. In April 2016, it collaborated with Funding Circle and Prosper to build the Marketplace Lending Association.

Lending Club facilitates business and personal loans and finances elective medical procedures. It is one of the world's largest online credit markets, where borrowers can obtain loans quickly and easily and at a low-interest rate. Investors inject funds so that the company can provide the loans. In return, they earn interest on their money. Lending Club operates online and has no physical branches.

A borrower can obtain an instant quote without damaging their credit score. If they agree to the offer, investors can start funding their loan. A lender can create a portfolio of loans for quality borrowers. They can open an account quickly and receive their repayments and interest monthly, with the option of reinvesting or withdrawing them. A person looking for medical financing can apply through Lending Club's network of providers around the country or online. A bank facilitates the loans, so lending activities are subject to fair lending practices, consumer protection, and disclosure requirements.

Lending Club's founder, Renaud Laplanche, ended his tenure as CEO in May 2016. An official audit showed the company had knowingly sold an investor $22 million in loans that the investor did not want, falsifying documents. This led Lending Club's stock price to tumble to $3.5 from an initial high in its IPO of almost $26. Lending Club's fluctuations show how quickly successful businesses in this area can fall from grace.

Launched in 2005, Zopa is Britain's biggest peer-to-peer website. It broke even in 2016 and has at least 50,000 lenders with £1.6 billion of loans, at an average rate of 0.8%.

Borrowers pay around 5% interest, depending on the loan term, loan amount, and credit rating. Typical borrowers include homeowners who want to consolidate their debts, make home improvements, or buy a new car. Lenders earn an average return of 5% on a minimum investment of £10. However, Zopa recommends that new investors invest £500. Lenders can receive repayments monthly and have the option to reinvest them.

Zopa recently obtained a banking license in the UK in June 2017, allowing a move toward bank launch. It raised £44 million in July 2018 to fund the creation of a traditional bank, which will initially have a focus on saving products.[55]

PRO$PER.

Founded in San Francisco, Prosper is a marketplace for lending with at least $7 billion in loans. It matches borrowers and lenders in a socially and financially rewarding manner. Borrowers can apply for a loan of up to $35,000, and lenders pool their funds to lend the money. Popular investors in the company include Credit Suisse NEXT Fund, Institutional Venture Partners, Francisco Partners, and Sequoia Capital.

Prosper uses pre-set rates determined by a system that considers the borrower's credit risk. Lenders have the option to invest or not at the rate set by Prosper's algorithm. The company profits by charging a fee per transaction, which can range from 1% to 5%, with an annual servicing fee of 1% charged to investors.

In 2017, Prosper signed an agreement with a group of institutional investors to purchase up to $5 billion in loans through 2019.[56] Also, Prosper partnered with Clarity Money to enable eligible customers to apply for loans.[57]

Rate%Setter™

Established in London in October 2010, RateSetter has at least 33,000 active lenders who have lent at least £2.7 billion. Their default rate, quoted at 0.71%, is extremely low, and none of their lenders have lost money. Lenders do not pay a fee, but borrowers have to pay a risk-weighted fee that covers costs and management of loans, as well as contributing to a provision fund against bad debts. Lenders can earn as much as 4.56% on a minimum investment of £10. They can lend money for whatever period they choose. If they choose to lend for a longer period, they receive a higher return on their money.[58]

陆金所
Lufax.com

Lufax is a Chinese P2P lending marketplace. Its official name is Shanghai Lujiazui International Financial Asset Exchange Co. It was founded in 2011 and raised almost $500 million in 2015. It is owned 49% by Ping An, China's largest insurer. It's got an American CEO, Gregg Gibb. It not only does P2P lending, but also investment in equities. Its intention is to offer Chinese investors the opportunity to diversify their assets by investing worldwide. Lufax already has partnerships with Saxo Bank and with eToro, a social trading platform. It also hired five banks (Citic Securities, Citigroup, JP Morgan, Morgan Stanley and Goldman Sachs) as joint sponsors to work on a forthcoming IPO which has been delayed due to changes in regulation aimed at reducing risk in this arena. In May 2018 they had $24.55 billion in loans on their books.

www.yirendai.com

In December 2015, CreditEase floated Yirendai on the NYSE at $10 per share and raised $86 million in the process. Yirendai is a peer-to-peer company owned by CreditEase and is China's largest P2P company. Launched in 2006, it became a full-service financial company offering wealth management and finance products and services. It now offers consumer loans, small business loans, mortgages, rural loans, car loans, and student loans. Aside from peer-to-peer lending, it also has wealth management products including insurance, alternative investments, credit, real estate, and equities.[59]

◆ LendingRobot

Established in 2012, Seattle-based LendingRobot is a loan comparison engine that uses algorithms to help lenders search for the most profitable loans. As a cloud-based service, LendingRobot has at least 40 various filtering criteria for Prosper and LendingClub. It automates and simplifies peer-to-peer lending investments so that lenders can increase their profits while saving time. It aggregates various data and evaluates different loans based on each investor's criteria. It offers a unique proposition to individual investors due to its automation services.[60]

In January 2017, LendingRobot launched an automated hedge fund to facilitate investment exclusively in loans on P2P platforms.[61]

Consumer Lending

An unsecured loan is one that doesn't have any assets or securities against it and so is riskier for lenders. However, it is less risky for the borrower because they have no property that serves as a guarantee if they fail to repay the loan. Because of this, the lender charges higher interest rates to offset the risk.

An unsecured loan can be of many types: signature or personal, credit card, student, or a peer-to-peer loan. A borrower can secure a personal loan from credit unions and banks. They can use it for any purpose and usually pay off the loan monthly. If they have good credit standing, they can expect to pay off a loan at a lower interest rate.

A credit card is another type of unsecured loan provided by credit card companies. A credit card holder uses it to pay for whatever they need. Normally, they pay a high interest rate on their credit card balance if they fail to pay their balance in full and on time. A credit card company may offer a 0% interest rate for a time to encourage people to apply for its card.

Digital lending allows customers to get an unsecured loan through online lenders. In the United Kingdom, this lending market is worth around £2 billion.[62]

Customers utilize digital lending for convenience, simplicity, transparency, and flexibility and personalization. They do not have to go to a bank branch to apply for a loan. They can use a mobile app anywhere and anytime to gain access to credit. They are only required to provide some information and answer a few questions. Usually, they simply have to select the loan maturity and value. The system's algorithms will take care of the rest of the complex process using a collection of past data.

Lastly, digital lending can provide borrowers with incentives for keeping a good loan repayment record so that they can get preferential terms and better rates the next time they apply for an online loan.

In a study by SAP Value Management Center and Bain & Company, only about 7% of traditional banks' products are compatible with digital transactions, making them vulnerable to competition.[63] Financial technology start-ups, telecommunication providers, and incumbent retailers have recognized this opportunity and are taking advantage of it. These new digital entrants can offer loans at a better price because they assume a lower base cost and are better able to target specific risk markets.

Banks need to invest in digital lending if they don't want to lose market shares. They have to create better customer experiences, remove avoidable and bad interactions, make the loan application process easier, and create an agile operating model for a cheaper, better, and faster lending process.

Key Players

In this section, we look at interesting companies that are making important progress in consumer lending.

PayPal's Max Levchin in 2012 unveiled another start-up, Affirm, an online company offering credit with more transparency and lower fees. Affirm is slowly making its way into physical retail stores, offering loans with low payment installments, very much like traditional credit cards. The loans can be agreed on at the cash registers of select merchants in collaboration with First Data, another payment-tech giant. Additionally, Affirm loans are also available for over-the-phone purchases with the retailers Coleman Furniture and Modloft.[64] Its current valuation at the beginning of 2018 was close to $2 billion.

Affirm does not charge late fees and offers low Annual Percentage Rates (APR). It targets individuals such as millennials and immigrants without credit cards to use its loan facilities. The company was able to raise $275 million in June 2015. Popular investors include Lightspeed Venture Partners, Khosla Ventures, Andreessen Horowitz, Jefferies, and Spark Capital Growth.

Affirm offers an annual sliding markup from 10% to 20% to help its customers pay back their loans. Its algorithm considers the borrower's name, mobile number, social security number, email, birthday, and behavioral factors when granting a loan.

In October 2017, Affirm launched a new application to enable payments for large purchases.[65] It also raised $200 million in funding led by GIC with the participation of Khosla Ventures and Spark Capital.[66]

AVANT CREDIT

Avant received more than $325 million in equity funding in 2015, with a valuation of about $2 billion. General Atlantic, Balyasny Asset Management, JP Morgan, DFJ Growth, August Capital, Tiger Global Management, and RRE Ventures led this round of investment. According to Avant's CEO and Founder Al Goldstein, the company wants to become a leading provider of loans to low- and middle-income customers.

Avant tries to be different from its competitors by targeting below-prime customers and providing its own funds for the loans. This means that it can collaborate with new industry players and not be in direct competition with P2P companies such as Lending Club. Avant provides unsecured credit in the United Kingdom, Canada, and the United States.

.⊪*Kreditech*

Established in Germany, it built a wide array of banking and credit products for individuals with little or no credit history. PayPal's Peter Thiel also invested $44 million with other investors like Amadeus Capital Partners. Since its inception, the company has raised $497 million in equity.

Currently, Kreditech operates in Russia, the Czech Republic, Poland, Mexico, and Spain. It is using its platform to reach out to individuals who lack credit history. Its algorithms consist of 20,000 various data points that assess a single loan application. To date, about 850,000 customers have taken out loans with the company. Kreditech is planning to launch in Brazil next year. Instead of offering loans in the USA, it is focusing on developing economies. All products will be sold under one brand, Mondeo.

In May 2017, Kreditech raised €110 ($120) million from Naspers' PayU following a strategic partnership financing, reaching a valuation between €300 and €500 million.[67]

ZestFinance has built algorithms to provide customers who cannot acquire credit from banks with loans. Recently, it received $150 million from Fortress Investment Group. Based in Los Angeles, its popular investors include Northgate Capital, Peter Thiel, Matrix Venture Partners, Lightspeed Venture Partners, Eastward Capital Partners, and Kensington Capital Holdings. It was formally known as ZestCash.

The Fortress investment will fund ZestFinance's Basix loan, a product for near-prime consumers. The technology used by ZestFinance uses non-traditional factors to determine whether to lend to consumers who have no access to credit provided by banks. In a study carried out by credit-scoring company Credit Karma, it was estimated that Basix could serve at least 42.2 million people who have FICO scores between 600 and 680. Borrowers can use the loan facility to pay back a large loan or consolidate their debts.

In February 2017, ZestFinance launched the Zest Automated Machine Learning (ZAML) Platform to enable credit underwriting. Lenders can use ZAML to analyze huge amounts of non-traditional credit data to increase the approval rates and lower the risk incurred in advancing credit.[68]

LendUp

US LendUP is recasting the payday loan business so that high-risk borrowers learn their lesson and become more responsible with their credit. Its app can process short-term loan applications of up to $1,000 in just a few minutes, and borrowers cannot roll over these loans automatically. LendUP also provides opportunities for the riskiest borrowers to get the lowest rates by learning from online classes, referring others, and repaying loans on time.

In June 2017, LendUP raised strategic funding from PayPal to expand into credit cards and other online services. The terms of the deal were not disclosed.[69]

Digital Lending for Students

A category that stands on its own inside the consumer lending space is student loans. Many students need loans to fund their university studies. Some countries, such as the United Kingdom, have a good support system for students, as governments can fund loans at extremely low interest rates. This doesn't mean that student loans in the UK earn a good return on investment, since student loans are about £70 billion, or 16 percent of UK's GDP, and many of these loans are never repaid.[70] However, rules are different around the world. For example, student loans are big business in the US, with $1.5 trillion in loans outstanding as of February 2018. After mortgages, student loans are the next largest debt market. Taking advantage of this market, many companies and start-ups have started lending to students online.

Peer-to-peer lending companies offer two types loans to students: consolidated loans after graduation or traditional loans for qualified graduate program students. Each loan is linked to a particular degree, program, and school, reducing the risk for companies, and building relationships between students and lenders. Of course, different degrees imply different levels of risk, and going to a certain university does not guarantee that people will end up earning enough to repay their loan.

Peer-to-peer allows investors to contribute money, together with other investors, to fund student loans in a qualifying school.[71] An investor earns money from the interest paid by a student and assumes the risk if a student defaults on a loan. However, they are also doing society a great favor by helping students secure their future.

Key Players

SoFi

In 2011, James Finnigan, Mike Cagney, Ian Brady, and Dan Macklin established Social Finance or SoFi. As Stanford Business graduates, they used it to offer more affordable student loan options to fund a student's education. With $2 million initial capital, they funded 100 students, with an average loan of $50,000.[72]

Since then, SoFi has raised millions from investors like Baseline Ventures, Discovery Capital Management, Wicklow Capital, Peter Thiel, and Third Point Management, among others. It also raised money through loans from Morgan Stanley, Bancorp, and Barclays. SoFi also started offering personal loans and mortgages in 2015. As of October 2016, it has funded at least $12 billion in loans and helped 175,000 individuals.

Sofi aims to disrupt the financial services sector by providing borrowers with more personalized financing options, mobile access, and better service. Although the loan process is digital, it has hundreds of employees who assist member-borrowers.

An innovative disruptor, SoFi targets high-end customers with specific degrees from particular schools, offering them refinancing of student loans. Social Finance or SoFi invites its borrowers to free parties at cocktail lounges, attempting to build a community, and it thanks its customers by throwing parties. SoFi has refinanced more than $9.76 billion in student loans.

Sofi has also established its own hedge fund to purchase its loans. To accelerate its growth, it also offers personal loans, as well as insurance products, wealth management tools, and a savings account. Sofi is planning to file for an IPO in 2019.[73]

CommonBond

Established in 2011 by Jessup Shean, Mike Taormina, and David Klein, CommonBond aims to solve frustrating problems in the student loan industry by offering exceptional customer service, simple and tech-enabled loan experiences, and competitive pricing.[74]

CommonBond focuses on bringing together investors and student borrowers. It has technology that can speed up and simplify the entire loan process, and its focus is on the customer. It also offers students hosted dinners, career support, panels, and networking opportunities. Its Net Promoter Score[75] system considers customer feedback from various student borrowers and loan applicants and helps the company focus on its products and pricing, as well as over-deliver on customer service and technology to keep CommonBond growing.

CommonBond's average borrower is 33 years old with an annual income of $159,028 and $5,996 in monthly free cash flow. It has refinanced more than $2 billion in loans.

earnest

Earnest, a lending company, has at least 80,000 data points to assess prospective borrowers with little or no credit history. Based in San Francisco, it offers personal loans to students and refinancing of student loans for indebted graduates, with rates of 2.47%.[76]

According to Earnest's CEO and co-founder Louis Beryl, Earnest received $17 million in funding from Maveron, a venture capital company. Unlike its competitors, Earnest considers credit card details and banking history when deciding whether or not to approve a loan.[77]

In October 2017, Earnest was acquired by student loan leader Navient for $155 million in cash, seeking to create and deliver customer-centric credit products to educate consumers and offer them advanced digital services.[78]

loanhero

Student Loan Hero, a student loan management tool, has at least 2,000 borrowers and $63 million in managed debts. It has a proprietary platform for its algorithms. Expansion Venture Capitalist, Socratic Labs, and Start-up Chile were among those who invested in the company. Founded by Andrew Josuweit, it first focused on app recommendations, but then shifted to providing student loans.[79]

When he graduated, Josuweit had $104,000 in student loans. He had to keep up with all the loans by using an Excel spreadsheet. He created Student Loan Hero in May 2012, and the public beta debuted in October of that same year. A prospective borrower has to enter loan and banking credentials on the website and answer some questions so that the algorithms can decide what programs they qualify for. Student Loan Hero also provides an amortization schedule and other government programs that a borrower can use.

Matt Lenhard and Nate Matherson started LendEDU to help graduates refinance their student loans. They discovered that graduates who wanted to refinance their loans had to fill out lengthy application forms and they wanted to simplify this process.

A prospective borrower fills out one application and gets access to various student loan refinancing options, without doing any damage to their credit score. On average, they can save about $12,000 through loan refinancing.[80]

Digital Lending for SMEs

Since the 2008 recession, well-known banks have been awarding fewer loans to small and medium-sized enterprises (SMEs), and other firms have started appearing to fill the void. Three interesting business models that are worth exploring are innovative short-term working capital, peer-to-business lending, and invoice financing.

Short-Term Working Capital

For companies looking for short-term loans with quick delivery, fintech is good news. Up until a few years ago, there were no suitable alternatives to banks. Companies would end up having to request merchant cash advances, receiving a lump sum in exchange for a share of their daily credit card sales. Effective interest rates would be over 100 percentage points, making them very expensive. Companies such as Kabbage, OnDeck, and PayPal Working Capital have introduced low-cost alternatives.

These companies require a certain number of months of credit history, a certain amount of credit turnover, and they will also look at the personal credit score of the owners. The good thing is that there is almost no paperwork, and everything is done online. PayPal is the easiest company to qualify for and has good rates. However, borrowers need to be selling through PayPal. Kabbage is the next easiest, and OnDeck is the most restrictive of the three. OnDeck requires personal guarantees, meaning that you are pledging your personal finances to pay back the loan.

The companies will tap into applicants' sales details from different sources such as Shopify, eBay, Amazon, Xero accounting, and the like, to gain a clear view of your profitability.

Traditional banks are taking note of these innovations. For example, JP Morgan Chase collaborated with OnDeck to add an online lending platform to its conventional underwriting process. Kabbage also forged a similar partnership with Spain's ING and the UK's Santander to provide the platform for the banks' delivery and underwriting services.

Peer-to-Business Loans

Because of banks' restrictions on lending, some businesses do not have access to credit. Peer-to-business structures offer an alternative to this problem by providing an opportunity for investors to earn money. At the same time, it allows for businesses to acquire much-needed funding. Businesses get funds quickly and at a lower interest rate, while lenders receive a higher profit from their investments. Banks cannot offer the same high margin to depositors, because of their costly structures.

In April 2014, the United Kingdom's Financial Conduct Authority started regulating peer-to-peer lending, including business lending, to protect consumers and supervise and guide related anti-money laundering measures, promotions, and other activities. Peer-to-peer lending firms now have base capital requirements that have to be reported monthly to the FCA.[81] The FCA also requires peer-to-peer lending platforms to follow the Client Money Rules in the FCA Handbook to protect lenders' money and comply with disclosure requirements.[82]

In an auction P2B lending model, a borrower can initiate a loan by specifying the amount and the date of repayment desired. Then lenders try to outbid each other, offering an interest rate they feel will mitigate their risks. At the end of the auction period, the borrower can decide whether or not to accept the loan, depending on the average interest rate. They pay for the loan monthly with the added interest.

If the borrower does not repay the loan on time or defaults, lenders lose their money. Thus, necessary precautions must be taken by scrutinizing each loan and having the borrower answer specific questions. They can also spread their investments by funding several small loans. Investors can opt not to lend their money if they feel that a borrower is too risky. From a borrower side, missing payments on a P2P loan will affect a business/person credit rating. A defaulted loan will be passed to a collections agency and may even lead to court.

In the United Kingdom, Octopus Investments entered the peer-to-peer lending business in April 2016 with at least £5.5 billion in assets. It offers investors a discretionary portfolio of asset-backed loans from Octopus Property.[83] Established in 2009, Octopus Property (formerly Dragonfly) had about 3,500 borrowers with a loss rate of 0.1%. Octopus's loan origination is of the highest quality, and it has a reliable underwriting process. Octopus views the peer-to-peer lending model as having strategic value because of the innovative investment model.

Invoice Financing

Invoice financing, that is, getting financing for as-yet-unpaid invoices, can consist of invoice factoring, invoice trading, or invoice discounting.

With factoring, an invoice financier will manage the sales ledger to collect money owed to a company. Factoring allows companies to grow by generating funds to keep a business afloat while waiting for customers' payments. Usually, a third party (a factor) pays between 70% and 90% of total accounts,[84] and customers make their payments to the factor. Then the factor remits the balance to the business less its service fee.

The factor will first assess the creditworthiness of the customers before it accepts the accounts. It is not a collection agency, but customers must have good credit standing. It may also consider yearly revenues and how many years the business has been in operation before agreeing to provide the factoring service.

The factor will request payment from customers after checking the accounts receivable for completeness and accuracy. Upon receiving payment, it will move the balance of the invoices back to the business owner. Other factors charge fees and pay a business owner 100% of the total value of the invoices. Some factors allow the business to collect payments and receive the repayments plus fees when customers pay.

Before technological disruption, banks were the only ones providing factoring. However, the introduction of technology allows for a different product, *invoice trading*. Instead of managing the entire sales book, companies can select which invoices are sold to financiers. By placing these invoices on a platform, individual investors can invest in a similar fashion to peer-to-peer lending. Players such as Market Invoice and Platform Black have entered the market, bringing in crowdsourcing platforms to provide invoice factoring, invoice trading, and invoice discounting services.

Supplier chain finance is another option for fund purchasing. In this type of financing, a company registers with a platform, provides information about invoices that require payment to suppliers, and issues a promise to pay. The platform will then look for funders to pay the invoice in a competitive bidding process. Suppliers will receive immediate payment, and the company gains breathing space.

Key Players

Founded in 2009 by Marc Gorlin, Rob Frohwein, and Kathryn Petralia, Kabbage offers a technology and data platform for business loans.[85] It can connect directly to QuickBooks, PayPal, banks, and even social media to assess the creditworthiness of a prospective borrower. A borrower only has to wait about six minutes to find out if they qualify for a loan. However, the convenience and speed of approval come at a price.[86]

Kabbage can provide a borrower with a maximum of $100,000, payable in six months. On average, a borrower might take out eight loans yearly for a total of $50,000. Kabbage is one of the top alternative lenders in the US. It attracts investors because of its low loan default rate. It offers loans to established businesses using an automated model that assesses character, capacity to repay, and business stability and consistency. It also uses some non-traditional metrics like a prospective borrower's online reviews and social media followers.

In 2012, Kabbage became part of Red Herring's Top 100 North American private enterprises. In 2014 and 2015, Forbes Magazine named it as one of Top 100 Most Promising Companies. In 2016, CNBC name Kabbage as one of its annual Disruptor 50 companies for being ambitious and forward thinking, revolutionizing markets and industries worldwide. The company has already lent more than $5 billion to its customers, and 20% of this was requested during nights and weekends, times when standard banks are not in operation. It raised $490 million in equity funding mainly from Softbank ($250 million) and other investors. Kabbage is expected to use the funds to expand into Asia, offering insurance and payroll products and services while positioning for an IPO for 2019.[87] The company is also developing new payments processing technologies which could compete with PayPal and Square.

OnDeck>

OnDeck is a financial platform that provides loans to small and medium enterprises. It was founded in 2007 and went public in the NYSE December 2013, when it raised $200 million. With its headquarters in New York City, it has provided more than $10 billion in loans since its inception. The company has got a proprietary small business credit evaluation software and is focused on marketing its cloud platform to banks. It has an agreement with JPMorgan Chase and are looking for further partnerships. In 2017 it reported revenue of $351 million.

PayPal Working Capital is for PayPal users who want a fixed and affordable business loan. A borrower pays the fees and pays back the loan through their PayPal sales. However, they do not pay any penalty fees, pre-payment fees, late fees, monthly bills, or interest charges. The maximum amount they can borrow depends on the sales history of their PayPal account. Loan approval only takes minutes, and the money goes to their PayPal account instantly.

PayPal ensures that the borrower repays at least 10% of their loan, plus a fixed fee, every three months for the 18 months of the loan term, or until the borrower has repaid the loan in full. Only one loan can be taken out at a time. The borrower needs to pay their loan in full before applying for another loan.[88]

PayPal Working Capital started as an invite-only pilot in September 2013 and later collaborated with WebBank to expand the business. According to PayPal's VP for SMB Lending, Darrell Esch, the fact that its customers' sales histories drive credit decisions in approving instant business loans makes it unique.[89]

In September 2017, PayPal acquired Swift Financial, a company that provides cash advances and loans to small U.S. businesses, to expand its credit business and be able to offer small loans to merchants seeking working capital financing.[90]

◘ Square

San Francisco-based Square Capital is a fast-growing lending company founded by Jack Dorsey, also a co-founder of Twitter. In 2014, it launched a cash advance service for merchants that use POS systems. It used the merchant's cash flow and sales data to determine if the merchant qualified for a loan. It is now expanding its services to include online loans with fees of between 10% and 16% of the total loan amount.[91]

Collaborating with Upserve, a start-up offering software and POS in the restaurant sector, Square uses Upserve's cash flow and anonymous sales to analyze which restaurants qualify for a loan. Eligible restaurant businesses can take advantage of a personalized loan through the Upserve software, paying a fixed amount of their everyday sales. In the 2nd quarter of 2016, Square provided at least $189 million in loans to about 34,000 businesses.

In October 2017, Square Capital expanded its customer base by creating a formal partnership program with BigCommerce, a prominent e-commerce software company, to make loan offers to its small business customers. In addition, the company is extending its loan offerings to restaurants that work with Caviar, Square's own delivery service.[92]

Levi King and Brock Blake started Lendio in 2011 as a financial service that simplifies the process of obtaining a loan through matching. Instead of applying for a bank loan, a small business owner can use Lendio's platform to look for lenders who can provide them with a business loan. Instead of competing with companies like OnDeck, Lendio collaborates with lenders so that business owners can receive pre-approved loans. Well-known investors in Lendio include Highway 12 Ventures, Tribeca Venture Partners, and Runa Capital.[93]

In July 2017, Lendio provided more than $500 million in loans to over 21,000 small businesses across the US.[94]

Ant Financial

Ant Financial is the consumer lending arm of Alibaba. In 2018 they exceeded $95 billion in consumer lending. In just one year, it doubled the amount of lending. Its interest rates can go as high as 15%, though in general they are below those numbers. Ant Financial's valuation is calculated in 2018 at $150 billion, after they raised $14 billion in funding. These funds are destined for global expansion and developing new technologies.

Digital Mortgages

MortgageTech has not grown at the rate of other products, mostly because mortgages are a very complicated and heavily regulated product. However, this area represents one of the biggest opportunities in fintech, as worldwide mortgage debt is estimated at $15 trillion.

In a 2015 National Association of Realtors Home Buyer and Seller Generational Trends report, for the second consecutive year, 32% of recent homebuyers were millennials. However, these millennials used the services of real estate agents, and 45% of them had difficulties with the mortgage process.

In a US Primary Mortgage Grid/Nation Satisfaction Survey in 2014, about 25% of borrowers felt dissatisfied with the origination procedure. They still value personal guidance but prefer the accessibility offered by online mortgage services. Market participants may move away from push regulators and proprietary platforms, allowing for innovation and disruption, which can overturn old market models and business practices.

The mortgage industry could benefit from disruptors because the disruptors could quickly replace vendors and/or platforms. Regulators must allow marketplace innovation to offer a more interactive, proactive, flexible, and faster approach to mortgages.

Some innovators are searching for novel ways to meet consumer demand and increase profitability at every stage of the mortgage process. Currently, mortgage companies tend to view technology as an important requirement for doing business but aren't necessarily prioritizing it. This mindset differentiates current mortgage companies from emerging innovators.

Because of the housing crisis, purchasers and lenders of mortgage-backed securities have learned that the ability of a borrower to repay a mortgage can be unreliable. Emerging innovators correlate and simplify the multistep and multiparty processes and validate and compile information sources to have a more accurate measure of a borrower's creditworthiness.

The automation of validation and verification functions reduces subjectivity and costs and hastens decision-making. The use of various data points determines the value and quality of collateral, borrowing capacity, and cash flow, and performs analysis to identify possible misrepresentations and fraud. Some newer models use new technology that considers employment markets, household cash flow, infrastructure investment, demographic trends, and personal preferences.

Mortgages are a rich source of data on borrower employment, income, credit and usage, assets, and property, but many mortgage companies limit their use of this data.

However, new tools and technologies in business analytics and intelligence can help mortgage companies with credit-driven data to better identify prospective clients.

Fintechs in this area can be divided into three groups. The first offers platforms and IT solutions to originators, the second supplies or aggregates data to be used by originators and services, and the third offers disruptive end-to-end origination.

Key Players

HABIT<u>O</u>

Founded by Daniel Hegarty, Habito is an online mortgage broker in the United Kingdom offering brokering services to help customers find and apply for the best mortgage. The company uses technology that can perform mortgage analysis across more than 100 lenders to determine the best deal based on the requirements and circumstances of the borrower, who can then apply for that mortgage in less than 30 minutes.

According to Hegarty, Habito has at least 15,000 mortgage products and can make intelligent decisions based on interest rates, eligibility criteria, product features, and affordability.

Habito raised £1.5 million from Mosaic Ventures as seed funding, and well-known angel investors include Paul Forster, Tom Stafford, Yuri Milner, Samir Desai, and Taavet Hinrikus. Habito does not charge borrowers anything; it profits from the commission taken from the chosen lender. In 2017, Habito raised £1.5 million in a Series B funding led by Atomico and the participation of Ribbit Capital, Mosaic Ventures, and Revolutionary (Ad)Ventures. The total funds raised were over £27 million.[95]

SoFi, like the other marketplace lenders, is growing fast, but it will be a very long time before it becomes a threat to present mortgage giants like Bank of America, JP Morgan Chase, and Wells Fargo. In a 2nd-quarter 2015 report by the Mortgage Bankers Association, it showed that mortgage origination during the period was at $395 billion, and the biggest lenders were these three banks.[96]

However, according to the report by Inside Mortgage Finance, non-banks closed 37.5% of US mortgages in 2014. PwC believes that marketplace lenders could grow at an annual rate of 33%, to $150 billion by 2025. This forecast could prove to be true because it is easier for a prospective homebuyer to apply for an online mortgage from non-banks.

SoFi entered the mortgage market with about $50 million worth of mortgage originations monthly that it sells to Federal Home Loan Mortgage Corporation (aka Freddie Mac) and the Federal National Mortgage Association (Fannie Mae). Instead of using debt-to-income ratio to determine how much money to lend, it looks at the free cash flow of the borrower.

Lenda is a start-up founded in October 2013 that operates in Washington, California, and Oregon. It makes online mortgage refinancing available quickly and easily. With at least $1.54 million capital from Structure Capital, Winklevoss Capital, and 500 Start-ups, it removes mortgage brokers, telemarketers, and loan officers from the mortgage process and offers a less expensive and more streamlined mortgage refinancing procedure.[97]

Lenda can cut the whole refinancing process down to two and a half weeks for a fee of $2,000. According to Lenda's CEO Jason van den Brand, consumers are tired of telemarketers who offer them low rates even if they do not qualify for them.

Lenda's algorithm can find the most appropriate mortgage out of a pool of 200 products with 10-year to 30-year fixed rate terms. It will present a maximum of four options so the potential borrower can make a choice. The whole application process can be completed in 45 minutes, and Lenda charges the lender.

loanDepot®

Founded by Anthony Hsieh in 2009, loanDepot is now the US's fifth largest mortgage lender, according to Inside Mortgage Finance. In 2015, it was the seventh largest in terms of volume. Since its launch, it has grown by 70% on a yearly basis, with about 400% yearly market share growth.[98]

According to CEO Hsieh, the company's platform delivers high-touch human and high-tech digital experiences through its network of lending officers and its website. Its technology digitizes the mortgage experience by considering how potential borrowers want to have access to credit on their own terms. The company has funded at least $150 billion mortgages since it began in 2009, and has got more than 6400 team members.

sindeo®

Sindeo, an online mortgage broker, offers a new platform that makes it possible to approve mortgages in just five minutes. SindeoOne offers at least 1,000 mortgage products to potential borrowers.[99]

According to its CEO and co-founder Nick Stamos, it combines a new service model with technology for a more educated and happier borrower. Customer satisfaction is three times higher than industry averages. Stamos further claimed that the company's customers had saved about $17 million since they are getting better mortgages.

SindeoOne offers guides and tips every step of the way and helps its borrowers understand the options. In addition, it produces a credit report and begins the underwriting process upon verification of eligibility. For borrowers who want a personal touch, Sindeo can provide a mortgage advisor to guide them and answer their questions.

The Future in a Flash

Lending is about temporarily giving money with the expectation that it will be repaid, and the key variables are risk and return. Technology allows improvement in both areas.

On the risks side, technology allows to calculate risks more precisely. This is really necessary especially in emerging markets, where people and businesses typically have no credit history or traditional financial documentation. By introducing new sources of data, people can be assessed better and more people can be assessed.

On the return side, new opportunities are generated by the introduction of new players: different types of lenders, and different types of borrowers.

Even though we will never be able to deal fully with uncertainty, what we are moving toward is a more efficient market in which there are fewer losses during the lending process and more satisfaction with the products on the market. Innovations such as better credit scoring driven by big data, peer-to-peer marketplaces and blockchain will be the enablers of this move toward efficiency. By standardizing the way that lenders and data providers connect, the process of lending will become more efficient.

Chapter 5
Commercial Banking Transformation

Commercial Banking Transformation in a Flash

Commercial banks have realized that profitability is strongly dependent on innovation. New entrants are forcing commercial banks to quickly adapt to change and offer innovative solutions to SMEs and larger enterprises. Although it is hard to accurately estimate the exact market size of SMEs, it is certain that they are the backbone of most economies across the world. Therefore, new "sharing economy" players are developing business banking platforms to inherently link fintech start-ups, payment service providers, and SMEs.

Fintech start-ups are acquiring a larger market share due to their customer-centric approaches. Currently, the main areas of commercial banking that fintechs are helping to improve include the introduction of specialized platforms, the improvement of pricing and customer selection, cost reduction, and the optimization of processes. Other services offered by fintechs include payroll, online accounting, expense management, and benefits management.

In some cases, partnerships between banks and fintechs are an effective way for banks to gain an insight into the world of digital innovation and position themselves at the core of the fintech industry. Nevertheless, banks have the competitive advantage of being more familiar with regulatory requirements.

 ## How Commercial Banking Works

The traditional commercial banking model covers business banking, which caters to the needs of small and medium enterprises (SMEs); and corporate banking, which provides corporations with custom banking and financing services. In both cases, their customers are depositors and borrowers. Commercial banks accept deposits from trusted customers and lend them to borrowers at a higher interest rate. They also offer fund transfers, credit creation, and other general services.

Commercial banks' profits come mainly from their net interest income, that is, the interest income on loans, minus interest expenses on deposits and other funding sources. For example, a loan portfolio of $2 billion which earns 6% interest generates an interest income of $120 million. If the expenses of a customer deposit portfolio of $1.3 billion, earning 2% are $26 million, the net interest income is $94 million. At the same time, banks diversify their income sources and ensure higher liquidity through non-interest income, which includes income from areas outside their lending operations, such as deposit fees, transaction fees, annual fees, and so on.

DOI 10.1515/9781547401055-005

 **SME Market Size**

Although it is hard to put a number on the exact market size of SMEs, according to McKinsey and the International Finance Corporation (IFC), there are approximately 365 to 445 million SMEs globally, of which between 55 to 70 million are formally established as micro-businesses and between 25 to 30 million are formally established as SMEs. The remaining 285 to 345 million are informal enterprises.[100] In 2012, SMEs accounted for 99.8% of all enterprises in the European Union, employed almost 67% of the total workforce, and contributed 58% of gross value added (GVA).[101] Additionally, it is estimated that of the 5.5 million private sector businesses in the UK, 99.9% are SMEs, employing nearly 60% of the private sector workforce.[102] EU SME employment has picked up recently at a 5.2 % growth between 2013 to 2016, almost 50% faster than overall employment in the EU-28 economy over the same period.[103] In China, SMEs contribute around 80% of GDP and 60% of national employment.

A report by BBVA shows that 80% of European banks see the SME Market as an important growth area, and loan balances in the region are over £120 billion. 63% of SMEs appear satisfied with the banking service they are getting; however, they would welcome a decrease in their fees.[104]

The Impact of Fintech on Business Banking

Fintech start-ups are acquiring a larger market share due to their customer-centric banking propositions. Overall equity investment in fintech start-ups has grown from $4 billion in 2013 to $12 billion in 2014,[105] $19 billion in 2015,[106] and almost $20 billion in 2016.[107]

Five main areas exist where fintechs can provide improvements in business banking: introducing specialized platforms, servicing underserved sectors, improving pricing and customer selection, reducing costs, and optimizing processes.

Introduction of Specialized Platforms

The creation of full-fledged service banks can be a big challenge, especially if a bank wants to cater to specialized lending opportunities. However, if fintechs focus on specific services, they can be successful, offering better portals than the ones offered by incumbents. Advanced offerings such as foreign exchange and supply chain finance are obvious examples, but improved day-to-day services such as payments are also redefining business banking.

More than 70% of fintech companies are focusing on banks' most profitable ser-vices—personal and SME banking accounts—which account for nearly 50% of the banking industry's profits.[108] Focusing on individual services and products offered by traditional banks allows fintech companies to provide cost-effective services with new technologies, such as artificial intelligence, that can better identify the individ-ual needs of consumers and SMEs.

Business lending is a big opportunity. Today, almost 60% of income for banks comes from granting loans to retail customers and SMEs. The biggest fintech lender in the United States, Lending Club, has offered nearly $9 billion in loans since 2007, and it accepts higher default rates because it capitalizes on efficiencies.[109] The main areas of business lending that are being invested in are marketplace lending, merchant and e-commerce finance, invoice finance, supply chain finance and trade finance—we cover these in the lending chapter.

Apart from the lending opportunities, electronic payments solutions can also be lucrative. The evolution of fintech has led to the circulation of virtual money, which beats the time-consuming processes of traditional business banking and facilitates the seamless payment of expenses. Although these amounts may be relatively small compared to corporate banking, people are starting to use these services en masse, because they are convenient and efficient.

Servicing Underserved Segments

Established banks commonly exclude a significant amount of the population. Based on IFC data, 45–55% of SMEs globally don't have an overdraft allowance but would benefit from one. While 21–24% have accessed loans, they are still severely limited. Worldwide, another $2.4 trillion in demand for credit exists, according to IFC data. In the US, 44% of SMEs' requests for lending were rejected. In the United Kingdom, there is a funding gap as large as £59 billion. On top of this, about 30% of British SMEs did not manage to get the funding they attempted to obtain.

By offering alternative lending services, fintech companies provide innovative approaches to segments, such as subprime loans, which are not served by tradi-tional corporate banking. Funding Circle, Kabbage, Lendio, OnDeck, and Swift Capital are some of the players that have capitalized on the 20% decline in bank lending to SMEs since 2007. Lending to larger businesses has risen by about 4% during the same period.[110]

Improvements in Pricing and Customer Selection

The data that banks hold is as valuable as gold—especially all of the transactional data. By combining this data source with other external ones, commercial banks can improve their pricing strategies, which can sometimes be very complex in the corporate space.

This wealth of information can also be used to decide how to categorize customers and what products to make available for each different type of business. A company that has a good solution in this space is PrimeRevenue. Data processing can also help with underwriting practices. Some of the new fintechs in the US use more than 2000 different data points from more than 100 sources to make their credit decisions.

Enabling Cost Reductions

Fintech can create services, platforms, and products on a budget. As they start from a clean slate, there are no legacy issues to be resolved. Legacy issues are mainly connected with the IT systems that support an operation, but other concerns such as culture and workforce character carry legacy issues, too.

Different innovations can be used to reduce costs in banking. For example, in the servicing space, virtual assistants can enhance customer service while simultaneously reducing costs. When looking at back office processes, several tools are being introduced, including robotic process automation, which can replace human intervention by using algorithms, electronic identification solutions, and optical character recognition.

Optimizing Processes

The use of technology is automating transactions, and customers can make payments using mobile phones and tablets. Therefore, bank staff are now required to play more of an advisory role rather than actively carrying out transactions. According to Citigroup, numbers of US bank staff are expected to shrink by 30% between 2015 and 2025, from 2.6 million to 1.8 million people. In Europe, bank branch employment is expected to decline by 38% from 2.9 million to 1.8 million.[111]

Fintechs provide digital features that can improve these processes. For example, advanced decision-making engines such as the ones developed by Kabbage allow for quick credit approval. Platforms such as the one developed by Earthport can allow international payments to be settled in real time. Finally, a platform such as Ripple can encourage live international payments, cutting costs significantly.

How Traditional Banks Can Catch Up

The use of ground-breaking technologies that accelerate business banking transactions is forcing business banking to quickly adapt to change. Some business banks have already started partnering with fintech players, but doing so involves risk that needs to be managed.

Another strategic course of action is that of investing in strategic development and gaining a better understanding of what fintech start-ups really do. Either way, traditional business banking needs to reshape its model to accommodate change. Otherwise, their customer portfolios are likely to be taken by companies making better use of technology.

The Impact of Fintech on Corporate Banking

Fintech hasn't been seen to be a big threat to corporate banking so far, perhaps because of the more complex needs of corporate clients. Sophisticated corporate portals have already been built, with advanced functionality such as treasury management, cash pooling, and the ability to check balances and sweep from different banking institutions. They exist both locally and internationally, using the SWIFT payments system—a vast messaging network used by banks and other financial institutions to quickly, accurately, and securely send and receive information, such as instructions for money transfers. Additionally, large corporations have gained and still retain sizable economic and customer relationship advantages. They know their customers and how they like to do business.

This doesn't mean that corporate banks can rest on their laurels. The biggest threat for corporate banking comes from other banks already present in the corporate sector. Fast-movers that have integrated fintech innovations into their business models may become game changers. Specialized customer service and efficiency improvements can change the value chain and offer corporate clients a superior customer experience. Also, given that the fintech services remain largely unregulated, they may deliver sizable revenues along with customer insights, based on big data analytics and refined risk modelling practices.

A recent study by McKinsey finds that growth in the developed markets of Australia and New Zealand, Hong Kong, and Singapore is mainly driven by the mobile channel. In these markets, customers are shifting to mobile banking, seeking a seamless and swift banking experience. Growth in emerging markets is driven both by secure site and mobile banking.[112] To improve customer relationships and anticipate the increasing threat of fintech players, corporate banking needs to accelerate its digitization. Strategic alliances with fintech companies have already taken place: BBVA with Holvi Bank,[113] CIBC with NAB and Leumi,[114] and Santander UK with Kalixa Payments and Monitise,[115] with the aim of achieving higher profits and improved risk management.

In developed markets, banks should improve their digital sales, thereby expanding their customer base. The integration of diverse technology platforms, the use of big data analytics across multiple channels, and the analysis of customer behavior can help corporate banking identify customer needs and provide suitable services. In emerging markets, corporate banking should capitalize on the opportunity that arises from high smartphone penetration, especially in Southeast Asia. Fast movers that adopt digital technologies are more likely to increase their customer base. However, corporate banking should maintain personal contact with customers.

Key SME Banks to Watch

Cogni, originally known as Bizbaze, is one of the promising players in the fintech field, providing PSD (Payment Services Directive) business banking to European SMEs.[116] The Dublin-based i-banking platform targets SMEs, micro-businesses, and start-up entrepreneurs involved in the sharing economy and provides them with low-cost, customized financial services. The data-driven bank offers multi-currency business accounts linked to artificial intelligence financial tools and assists SMEs in automating their tax and savings, receiving salary payments, or making money transfers without overdraft fees. Cogni is classified as a "High Potential Startup" by the Irish government.

HOLVI®

Holvi is a Helsinki-based online-only business bank for entrepreneurs and SMBs.[117] The bank enables entrepreneurs to manage their businesses efficiently by opening digital business accounts and transferring money between accounts. The service also provides built-in invoicing and paperless bookkeeping options. Holvi was acquired by BBVA, the multinational Spanish banking group, for approximately $100 million on March 7, 2016, as part of BBVA's digital transformation process. It operates in Austria, Germany, Estonia and Finland.

Using Revolut for Business, SMEs in Europe and the UK can manage international payments, payroll, and corporate travel.[118] Seeking to cut back on banking fees and normalize interbank exchange rates, Revolut features an innovative mobile app covering international payments, corporate cards, merchant accounts, and business travel. In June 2017, Revolut for Business launched business accounts in the UK and Europe, enabling businesses to hold and transfer money across 25 supported currencies.[119] It also added fintech partnerships and cryptocurrencies to the platform. The company expanded into the US market in September 2017.[120] Revolut are working hard to create a new acquiring product that will be more effective for merchants.

Business banking start-up Tide offers automated bookkeeping, integrated invoicing, business banking, and banking assistance services.[121] SMEs can open a bank account in less than three minutes with no initiation, monthly, or annual fees and can capitalize on a range of value-added services, including money-saving tools, APIs to build apps or integrate them with Tide, auto-categorization of transactions, integration with Xero and FreeAgent online accounting, 24/7 banking assistance, and secure banking transactions.

In July 2017, Tide raised $14 million in one of the largest Series A funding rounds of the year. The funding seeks to enable small- and medium-sized businesses to find their balance in the wake of Brexit.[122]

точка

The Russian bank Tochka offers an online finance bot for SME customers. By selecting "income for business" from the bank's dashboard, SMEs can keep funds at the point of transaction and run their businesses online via Facebook.[123] The social media network, which has 2.23 billion active users per month, has opened its messenger platform for business, thereby enabling SME customers, both legal entities and private customers, to pay their bills, check their account balances, ask financial questions or apply for a mortgage loan.

Counting

UK based CountingUp provides a business bank account that combines book keeping. Founded in 2017 by Tim Fouracre, who also founded Clear Books cloud accountancy, it has raised £2.3 million in seed funding in 2018. CountingUp claims to be able to open an account in less than five minutes and its accountancy integration includes profit and loss reports, book keeping categorization and ability to attach receipts to transactions.

Online Accounting for SMEs and Integration with Business Banking

As mentioned above, recent studies reveal that 63% of SMEs in the UK are satisfied or relatively satisfied with their banks regarding quality of services and cost, but 45% claim that they would be more satisfied if their bank reduced costs. Evidently, the remaining 37% are totally dissatisfied, which provides fintech with significant opportunities.[124]

Fintech can offer SMEs the added value services they need and are willing to adopt. The use of cloud accounting can help SMEs save time and money through automation and simplified financial reporting. This is an untapped opportunity for banks as well. By offering differentiated, digitized service in a heavily commoditized market, they can drive more growth and re-establish customer relationships.

Tools for SMEs

Payroll

For small businesses, payroll can be an intricate task because it includes hiring new employees, providing them with contracts, managing their vacation requests, and processing their expenses claims. Some business owners do not like the idea of out-sourcing these tasks, considering in-house processing to be more cost-effective than outsourcing and because they want to protect the wage information.

In fact, outsourcing payroll tasks with the use of suitable software can save an SME money because it does not involve employee training, software, hardware, and IT support. Instead, the CEO or the HR manager just needs to ensure that all the paperwork generated by the software is compliant with legal requirements. After all, outsourcing payroll tasks allows SMEs to invest in developing greater value-added products and services that can offer higher profit margins.

Online Accounting

The growing involvement of the fintech sector in providing low cost, less time-consuming, and more customized services puts banks under pressure. Individual customers are seeking to manage their finances on the go, whereas SMEs look at mobile-oriented services to manage their businesses efficiently. Hence, fintech start-ups are taking aspects of traditional banking and offering customers user-friendly solutions.

Online accounting is very important for SMEs since they need to handle invoicing, accounts receivable, accounts payable, and employee expenses. Great cloud-based software has been created for this purpose, such as Freshbooks, Quickbooks, Xero, and Wave. They offer SMEs the tools to record their payroll entries and outsource their accounting, invoicing, and receipt tasks.

Having realized the great potential of the fintech sector and seeking to smooth out the impact on traditional banking, banks are forming alliances with online accounting providers. For example, NatWest has partnered with Edinburgh-based fintech FreeAgent to offer SMEs an innovative sharing-economy capability.[125] With FreeAgent, SMEs can perform accounting tasks online, saving both time and money.

Given the fact that online accounting firms have a lot of information on their customers, it wouldn't be surprising if they tried to take over traditional banking in the short term. To do so, they would need to learn how to deal with the subtleties of banking, such as complex regulatory requirements and risk management.

Expense Management

Expense management is one of the biggest challenges for SMEs. The use of the digital and mobile channels offered by fintech provides SMEs with cashless, paperless, and mobile handling of their expenses, leading to better cost control, increased productivity, and a greater chance for success. It is refreshing to see that expense management is starting to be consolidated in SME bank propositions, for example in Holvi and US Bank.

Benefits Management

Benefits management is important for SMEs as it facilitates the way they manage their resources. Fintech offers competitive benefits management software by equipping SMEs with the tools they need to track demographic data and analyze employee segments to optimize healthcare coverage. SMEs can take care of employee benefits by collecting all the information on the composition and size of a workforce, and then deciding on appropriate group plans and individual coverage. Consequently, they lower the costs associated with recruitment, increase employee loyalty, and achieve a higher rate of productivity.

Key SME Tool Players

Founded in 2009, FinancialForce.com is a San-Francisco-based company offering cloud business ERP (enterprise resource planning) apps for effective resource and talent management, benefits management, sales engagement, project management, financial management, and accounting. Built on SalesForce architecture, Financial-Force.com enables SMEs to share customer records, reporting tools, and revenue recognition analytics by syncing their transactions across one system. FinancialForce.com also has EMEA (Europe, the Middle East, and Africa) offices in Harrogate, UK, and Sydney, Australia, as well as in Chicago, IL, Manchester, NH, Burlington, Ontario, and Granada, Spain. It has been named to the Forbes 2018 Cloud 100, the list of top private cloud companies in the world.

Founded in 2013, Zenefits is an HR platform suited to the needs of start-ups and SMEs. The platform offers broker services, HR advisory services, and tech support, while its online software automates health insurance, payroll, and other key business perks.[126] Zenefits got to a valuation of $4.5 billion in 2015, but two years later it had to lay off almost half of its staff. This was due to aiming to achieve growth targets that were too aggressive. Zenefit's vision is to simplify how organizations with less than 500 employees connect with people to get the right heath, wellness and benefits solutions.

GUSTO

Gusto, formerly known as ZenPayroll, offers cloud-based payroll and employee benefits solutions to SMEs. Founded in 2011, the California-based company integrates with FreshBooks, QuickBooks, and Xero to provide specialized online accounting, including payroll automation, benefits management, and payroll taxes.[127] In December 2015, Gusto raised $50 million in fundraising, thereby reaching a valuation of $1 billion and directly competing with Zenefits.[128] Their partnership with Capital One Spark Business offers SMEs online banking solutions with no transaction limits, monthly fees, or minimum balances and a 1.00% APY (annual percentage yield) for a Spark Business Savings account.

Gusto is part of the unicorns club, with a valuation of over $2 billion. It received $140 million in Series C funding. The funds will be invested to create new direct-to-employee benefits that allow employees to choose how they want to get paid.

Addressing the needs of HR managers, CEOs, and accountants, Hibob features an HR and Benefits platform for SMEs.[129] The Israeli-British start-up was founded in 2015, and in June 2016 it raised $7.5 million from a group of VCs and angel investors to launch an innovative HR platform to meet the needs of SMEs.[130] Hibob offers people management, employee benefits, employee engagement, and pension auto-enrollment solutions. Additionally, it features a very efficient Help Center section, where interested parties can find lots of useful information on using Hibob and getting the best customer experience.

In April 2017, Hibob raised $17.5 million in Series A funding led by US VC firm Battery Ventures, with participation from Arbor Ventures, and Fidelity's Eight Roads Ventures. The firm's total funding reached $25 million.[131]

sproutsocial

With more than 17,000 brands in its portfolio, Sprout Social is a promising fintech in the area of social media management. Founded in 2010, the Chicago-based company offers a range of business solutions for SMEs, including social media management, social media marketing, social customer service, and social media analytics. Sprout Social has official partnerships with LinkedIn, Facebook, Twitter, Instagram, and Google+, and integrates with Feedly, Zendesk, Bitly, Google Analytics, and User-Voice.[132] In 2016, the company was voted the most innovative social media platform[133] and #2 in Crain's Chicago Business List.[134]

Founded in 2006, Xero is widely used by more than 16,000 accounting firms around the globe with a subscriber base of more than 1.2 million people and used by 8800 accounting firms in more than 180 countries. In 2015, the company was ranked #1 in Forbes' Most Innovative Growth Companies List,[135] and in 2016, it generated an operating revenue growth of 67% and subscriber growth of 51%.[136] The New Zealand-based cloud accounting software company leads the New Zealand, Australian, and UK markets by offering online accounting, sales tax, invoicing, bank reconciliation, payroll, and inventory services to SMEs. Through the years it has raised more than $325 million in funding.

The Future in a Flash

Business banking will embrace fintech much more quickly than corporate banking, since the barriers to entry into this area are lower. However, looking at the medium term, all of commercial banking will be impacted by technology.

We can expect to see a massive improvement in account opening and account servicing processes, which can currently be very painful, due to the amount of paperwork and due diligence required. Opening bank accounts and managing them will become easy. It will also be easy and relatively cheap to get the right software to manage all of the mandatory reporting requirements that small businesses have, mainly around tax and accounting. We can expect that the divide between bank accounts and peripheral services such as accountancy and ecommerce will be highly integrated, creating customer centric products that are yet to be imagined.

Only the companies that understand technology properly and invest in it regularly will survive in a new environment with new rules.

Chapter 6
Next Generation Commerce

Next Generation Commerce in a Flash

Technology is changing the way that people shop and is raising customers' expectations. In this chapter, we examine the different areas of commerce.

When we visit stores, we generally pay at point-of-sale (POS) terminals. Fintech is introducing mobile points of sale usable on any mobile device, anytime and anywhere, to process customers' payments. These systems are popular with flea markets, food trucks, tradeshows, sports venues, and the like. They can even process major credit cards if there is a card reader attached to the mobile device.

In the same line, tablet-based POS terminals are helping the retail and hospitality sectors because customers need not line up or wait for their bills. With tablet technology, the POS goes to the customer for faster and more convenient service. Tablet-based POS systems allow retailers and restaurants to gain new revenue streams by having remote sales events or arranging outdoor seating. Staff can engage customers anywhere and complete the sale immediately.

Online commerce is being made easier by several companies that make checking out on e-commerce websites very easy, making it cheap for merchants, and providing customers with several payment options.

Technology not only affects merchants but customers too. The increased usage of mobile phones has led to the emergence of mobile wallets. With these, customers can leave their plastic and paper money at home and just use their mobile devices for payments.

Finally, we explore smart credit cards and TV-based commerce. Let's start by looking at changes in customer behavior.

Changes in Customer Shopping Behavior

The retail industry has set its sights on mobility, and in particular, the growing popularity of mobile devices like tablet computers and smartphones that are Internet-enabled for comparing, researching, purchasing, and reviewing products and services.

As customers become comfortable with technology, merchants have had to adapt. The internet was originally used merely to do research on products and prices, and then the actual transaction was done in person. As people started to feel more comfortable about submitting their information online, they began to buy. The emergence of mobile phones and tablets meant purchases began to shift to these devices. The introduction of near-field technology on phones has also created a trend of people using devices such as phones, watches, and bracelets to pay in physical stores.

DOI 10.1515/9781547401055-006

A Forrester Research report stated that 82% of US consumers buy from stores, while 56% usually use mobile devices to compare prices online. Mobile devices are clearly changing consumers' shopping behavior.[137]

Mobile commerce constitutes a major part of electronic commerce transactions. According to a forecast by Goldman Sachs, mobile commerce will account for almost half of all electronic commerce transactions by 2018. According to a survey of 5,000 consumers, shoppers using mobile devices behave differently to shoppers using computers. Mobile shoppers are more likely to scan the barcodes in stores and read the reviews. As such, retailers must have different services, marketing, and sales strategies aimed at them. There are also differences among mobile shoppers. For example, customers who are ages 18 to 34 use their mobile devices to shop late at night, and most of these are women. Men, on the other hand, are 27% more likely to subscribe to retailer alerts near their location. Mobile shoppers are willing to provide information for a more personalized shopping experience and to enroll in loyalty programs.

Point of Sale (POS) Evolution

In this section, we discuss the evolution of point of sale (POS) terminals. We seldom notice them when paying for our transactions in a store; however, there is a whole industry behind them.

Previously, a cashier had to enter an item's price manually to operate a cash register. The business had no record of the transaction except for a copy of the paper receipt. Computerization allowed the evolution of the POS system, with the product database being stored in the system, on a server, or on a computer.

The POS system evolved to include a barcode reader to minimize manual price entry. Transactions that pass through the barcode reader were then stored electronically without any human intervention. Today, some retailers use cloud-based point-of-sale systems that allow for online data storage.

A modern point-of-sale system has the following components: cash register, cash drawer where receipts and vouchers are also stored, receipt printer, barcode reader, and card machine.[138] The cash register is the POS system linked to a computer or server, and it can even be a tablet or iPad linked to a cloud-based system.

Anyone who wants to set up a retail business today will most likely choose a modern point-of-sale system, which is low cost but very functional. They are likely to choose a cloud-based POS system that allows them to access the important aforementioned POS components.

Modern point-of-sale systems can be integrated with other databases and electronic systems. A POS system can have inventory management and accounting systems for the automatic reconciliation of daily transactions.

Understanding mPOS

A mobile point-of-sale or mPOS consists of a portable mobile device that processes customer transactions. Fixed modern POS systems are most beneficial to retail stores and restaurants. Since most transactions are now done through debit and credit cards, a point-of-sale system must have a card swipe machine attached to it. A mobile point-of-sale system performs the same functions but can work remotely.

The mPOS acts as a bridge between e-commerce businesses and point-of-sale systems. A retailer can use a mobile device as an alternate point-of-sale system if they want to save on upfront investment. mPOS systems are also more affordable to repair.

mPOS systems can help prevent delays and lines at the checkout. In retail stores, long lines at the checkout sometimes mean customers decide not to make a purchase. By having employees armed with mPOS systems, they can serve and charge customers more quickly.

A generic handheld mobile point-of-sale system is a portable register with a slot for card swiping. An mPOS with a card reader, on the other hand, is a mobile device with a USB port or audio jack for attaching card readers. The mobile device can be anything, for example, an iPod Touch, smartphone, or tablet with a POS system that can scan an item's barcode, or the transaction can be entered manually. It must be able to accept card payments, recognize electronic signatures, and generate a receipt through a portable printer.

 ## mPOS Business Model

Large retailers need customizable and robust mPOS platforms and they must be able to integrate these platforms with their present payment systems. Large store owners invest heavily in their mPOS systems and expect to make a return on their investment. Thus, the mPOS platforms must be able to generate foot traffic to their physical stores that convert into sales. Therefore, mPOS providers focus on creating personalized solutions to meet the requirements of these large retailers, like in-store geo-location, consumer data analytics, and omnichannel integration.

On the other hand, small retailers need simple payment systems that accept mobile and card payments. Small retailers or even individuals can use mPOS systems for their business transactions. For example, taxi drivers, local café owners, and small-scale vendors can use mPOS systems to accept electronic payments. Traditionally, POS systems require hardware and charge expensive fees. However, mPOS systems offer a cheaper and more convenient alternative.

mPOS solutions for small retailers can also be customized and simplified. They can integrate various features, depending on a retailer's budget or requirements. Retailers can select the kind of data and features they want for their mPOS system.[139]

Currently, mPOS is popular even outside of the retail industry because it allows businesses to accept non-cash payments anywhere. Courier companies, businesses offering home services, pop-up stores and other similar businesses commonly use mPOS. mPOS providers enrich the customer experience and change the way customers interact with businesses.

Some people may regard card payments as outdated or obsolete because of the popularity of smartphones. However, card payments are still the focus of mPOS systems, which continue to flourish with the introduction of NFC-enabled mobile devices. According to the Bank for International Settlements, in 2018 roughly 273 billion mobile transactions will be carried out in 22 countries. This will be the primary instrument for payments in coming years, so mPOS must be able to support mobile payments.[140]

Developers are focusing on creating next generation payment services involving mobile phones, which now have NFC capability to allow contactless transactions from phones or cards. This flexibility provides for the reconfiguration of newer devices over time. An important strength of mPOS terminals is that they can adapt to an omni-channel and digital payments environment.

When Square introduced the Square mobile card reader, a little square device that attaches to a mobile phone, the payments industry started considering mobile point-of-sale to give small retailers a chance to accept payments from credit and debit cards. Many companies offered mPOS applications, but most of them struggled to find a way to profit effectively from them.

BI Intelligence[141] analyzed retailers' mPOS requirements to discover any concerns about it. Retailers use the term mPOS to refer to many different types of hardware and software—mPOS hardware can include devices like tablets, smartphones, or smart registers; mPOS software can be partially or fully cloud-based and use mobile operating systems.

Small retailers take advantage of mPOS systems, but because of the low volume of transactions, mPOS providers face the ongoing challenge of how to be sustainable. Currently, the mPOS business model is moving toward software-based value-added services. mPOS suppliers upsell to existing customers instead of acquiring more merchants. For example, they sell other business applications like payroll and marketing to small retailers that are accepting credit and debit card payments.

Key Players

In this section, we'll examine interesting companies that are making important progress in this area. Fintech is a very unpredictable industry, so by the time you read this, these companies may have changed markedly.

◙ Square

Based in San Francisco with the tagline "Making Commerce Easy," Square Inc. (SC) markets various hardware and software payment products, like Square Reader and Square Register. It also has a program for financing small businesses known as Square Capital and Square Payroll. Founded in 2009 by Jim McKelvey and Jack Dorsey, it launched its first app in 2010 and commenced trading on the New York Stock Exchange in November 2015.

Square Register accepts offline credit and debit card payments on a merchant's or individual's mobile device. It is available in Australia, Canada, the United States, Japan and recently launched in the United Kingdom. The app enables the user to enter their card details manually or swipe their card through the Square Reader, which is connected to the mobile device through the audio jack.

Square's main business comes from mobile point-of-sale. The $49 chip card and contactless reader that started to be distributed during the first quarter of 2016 already has 2 million sellers. With every new reader, a retailer receives two mPOS devices, one for contactless and chip and pin card transactions, and the other for magnetic stripe payments.[142]

Square's chip card and contactless reader are capable of processing EuroPay, MasterCard, and Visa transactions (EMV). With strong near-field communications (NFC) and EMV sales, Square could change things for small retailers, who are hesitant to use EMV because of the costs associated with terminal upgrades. Many of Square's clients are micro- and small businesses. In August 2018, Square released a new version of its magstripe reader that comes with a Lightning connector, useful for the new iPhones that come without a headphone jack.

It has also built Square Capital, which has lent more than 1 billion to small businesses.[143]

Square also offers Square Instant Deposit allowing retailers to immediately transfer funds from their revenues to their bank accounts for a 1% fee. This feature has attracted at least 58,000 users since August 2015, and at least 600,000 transactions have been processed. Square also has a digital invoicing platform, Square Invoices, attracting 100,000 users in one and a half years. This software competes with Fresh-Books, an invoicing firm in the mPOS market.

Klarna

Klarna is a Swedish payment solutions provider, which is safe and easy to use. It allows buyers to possess products before paying for them. It takes on the risk of fraud and credit, restricting customers from buying if they are too risky. Established in Stockholm by Victor Jacobsson, Niklas Adalberth, and Sebastian Siemiatkowski in

2005, it is active in 18 markets and has more than 1,400 employees. Popular international clients include ASOS, Wish, Samsung, Disney, and Spotify.[144]

In the United States, Klarna decided to offer separate apps for buying and selling. According to Klarna CEO and co-founder Sebastian Siemiatkowski, a user can purchase an item on a Klarna-powered site by merely entering their email and zip code. They can pay Klarna within a month through a chosen payment scheme. Klarna has offices in Columbus, Ohio, New York, and San Francisco.[145]

In May 2016, Klarna unveiled an in-store solution. According to Siemiatkowski, they expect their physical commerce solution to outgrow their online business. With this move, Klarna competes with big banks, Android, Samsung, Apple, and PayPal.[146] In 2017, Klarna got a full banking license to expand beyond financing payments. In January 2018, it partnered with ACI Worldwide, a leading provider of real-time payments, in order to expand to other geographies.[147] It is estimated that Klarna has grown to 500 US online retail partners since launching its first credit product in October 2016.

Millennials like to shop using Klarna as it allows them to buy and pay later, though there is always the danger that not paying for their shopping might negatively affect their credit scores.

After a $20 million investment from H&M in 2018, the company is believed to be worth more than $2.5 billion, and may be targeting an IPO next year.[148]

LifePay is a Russian mPOS company offering SME-lending and online acquiring. By collaborating with Futubank, it launched its online acquiring, allowing its customers to integrate e-payments into their websites. Its loans are initially only available to legal entities or existing LifePay customers. The minimum loan a borrower can take out is 50,000 rubles.[149]

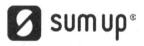

Established in August 2012, SumUp's vision is to become the leading brand in global card acceptance. It has customers in 15 countries, including the United States, Brazil, and Germany. SumUp offers a card terminal with an app that allows small retailers to accept card payments using tablets or smartphones cost-effectively and securely.

London-based[150] SumUp entered the US market offering small- and medium-sized enterprises contactless and EMV compatible devices that work with tablets and smartphones. Its primary target was US retailers, who will have to pay a 2.75% fee per transaction, without long-term contracts. SumUp's products were the first EMV-certified end-to-end mobile point-of-sale payment systems.

The strategy of vertical integration is one of the main reasons why SumUp's valuation has increased. SumUp designed its own hardware, thereby reducing the price of a unit tenfold. By May 2015, at least 300,000 retailers were using its platform.

SumUp charges low transaction fees. The UK Financial Conduct Authority authorized the mPOS company as a Payment Institution, and PCI-DSS and EuroPay, MasterCard, and Visa have certified it to ensure that payments processed meet the highest security standards.

Established on August 30, 2014, by Stas Matviyenko and Anna Polishchuk, Settle offers a restaurant app that allows diners to pre-order their lunch. This way, app users spend less time waiting for their food and finish eating lunch 60% faster than normal.

Settle started in Ukraine, charging restaurants a 20% fee. However, in the United States, it plans to launch a free service for both users and restaurants, only charging restaurants a small commission for every pre-order during off-peak hours. For peak hours, it plans to charge app users a small fee.

Settle has now merged with Allset, a firm established in April 2015 by Ukrainian entrepreneurs. It collaborates with restaurants in Palo Alto, San Francisco, and New York so that busy people can eat at these restaurants during lunch. Using the Settle software since its inception, it aims to help busy individuals save time and enjoy lunch.[151]

In October 2017, Allset raised $5 million in Series A funding led by Greycroft.[152]

One97 Communications offers Paytm, India's largest mobile commerce platform which aims to provide the best consumer experience. Paytm also provides payment solutions to retailers using a semi-closed wallet approved by RBI (Reserve Bank of India). One97 provides services to mobile clients through India's cloud platform.[153]

The introduction of Paytm was very successful. In 2010 alone, the company gained 500 million subscribers. Paytm introduced Marketplace and Wallet to take advantage of its customer base. Wallet is a payment service platform, while Marketplace is for online commerce. At present, Paytm has a turnover of more than 8 bn INR and 300 million registered customers who use the service to pay their bills and purchases. It also holds over 33% market share of UPI payments in India, a system that allows for fast payments.

Tablet-Based Cash Registers

The use of a tablet as a cash register is becoming more popular, especially in chain stores and coffee shops. It is a low cost option, and appeals to retailers and restaurants because of the large display, intuitive interface, and portability. As more retailers adopt them, they are opening doors for the use of contactless payment systems such as Google Wallet and ApplePay.

These tablets are user-friendly and cheap. The app sends sales information to a back office so that managers can monitor sales, manage inventory, and run reports in real time.[154]

Some tablet-based apps also allow customers to add tips on the screen and sign for credit card transactions. Tablet-based cash registers are also popular in farmer's markets, trendy clothing shops, and supermarkets. Big screens allow retailers to view more customer data, and salesclerks can encode customer information electronically.

As with mPOS devices, the operating model is not really geared toward making big profit margins on the sale of the devices. By offering the mPOS service, providers gain access to businesses and information about their turnover. This allows for the cross-selling of other services that will have higher profit margins.

Key Players

In this section, we look at companies that are making important progress in this area. Fintech is an exceedingly unstable industry, so when you get to read this, the companies mentioned may have significantly altered.

⬭toast

Toast is a software company offering POS and restaurant management systems using the Android operating system. It promises to make restaurants mobile and increase the number of guests that can be served. Jonathan Grimm, Aman Narang, and Steve Fredette founded the company in Boston in 2012. The company received Series B funding worth $30 million from GV and Bessemer Venture Partners in 2016.[155] Its software is popular among nationwide chains, small cafes, and restaurants in the United States.[156]

Toast rolled out an inventory management and reporting solution for restaurant operators so that their businesses could experience more profitability, better transparency, and improved operations. The Toast Inventory solution is beneficial to restaurant businesses because it saves time and money as well as increasing revenues.[157]

Shopify is chiefly known as an e-commerce platform, but it offers a tablet-based point-of-sale solution as well. Currently, the iPad POS has the capability to launch various apps that allow retailers to add customized features to their POS solutions. The apps are available through its App Store and allow for upselling to customers, offering wholesale discounts to chosen customers, labels, promotions, marketing tools, invoices, receipts, and so on. These POS apps mean that retailers can dictate their own POS experience. Currently, Shopify has more than 165,000 users.[158]

⊙ POYNT

Established in 2013, Osama Bedier launched Poynt as a start-up company, creating a payment terminal using the Android operating system. Poynt offers an app for tablets and smartphones for businesses such as wine shops, ice cream parlors, or restaurants. It collaborates with banks that have relationships with business owners. Their business model consists of making no profit on the terminal but getting 20% commission on software purchases.

presto

Diners can order and pay for their food using the Presto app by E la Carte Inc. Presto systems include cloud-based software and can be used in casual dining restaurants around the US. However, the restaurant industry has been slow to embrace this payment technology.[159]

Diners like the idea of reviewing the menu, ordering, and paying without interacting with any of the staff. Restaurants experience a 5.3% increase in the average tab and turn tables around at least 10 minutes faster. Tips also increase by an average of 16%.

Founded in 2010 by Christopher Ciabarra and Lisa Falzone, Revel Systems offers an iPad-based POS system. Revel Systems collaborated with Intuit in 2014 to create QuickBooks POS. In 2015, it collaborated with Apple Computers, and in September 2016, the company also collaborated with Shell Global.[160]

Revel Systems has an open API that can integrate with third-party suppliers to allow the latter to customize the point-of-sale system. With its headquarters in San Francisco, it also has offices in Florida and London. Its POS focuses on security, and in January 2013, it became the first iPad-based POS to implement EuroPay, MasterCard, and Visa processing in the US.

Online Acquiring

Online acquiring is the term used for payments for goods and services through the internet. A customer typically enters the required details on the seller's website, actually instructing their bank/financial services provider to pay the seller for a purchase.[161]

Service providers, engaged by a processing center or the acquiring bank, provide for the secure transfer of funds. They use authentication protocols and data protection methods to encrypt customer data on the seller's website. Online acquiring can connect to the acquiring bank directly or use intermediaries such Payment System Providers and Processing Centers.

Some of the fintechs that are emerging are improving the payments process flow of online acquiring. This is the case with Stripe, which removes the need to have a payments gateway and a merchant account. Fintechs can also add more payment methods, including cryptocurrencies, and also make transactions cheaper.

Key Players

stripe

Founded in 2010 by Irish entrepreneurs Patrick and John Collison, Stripe empowers internet businesses using code and design. It offers developer-friendly APIs to allow users to create great products. Famous investors in the company include Elon Musk, Max Levchin, Peter Thiel, Andreessen Horowitz, and Sequoia Capital. It is helping businesses in 25 countries and has nine global offices.[162]

Stripe offers software development kits (SDKs) for Android and iOS that developers and businesses can use to create their own quick and effective mobile commerce experiences. These businesses' customers can pay for purchases easily and securely. Stripe also offers fraud prevention, international support, real-time data access, and modern accounting.

From October 2015, Stripe has offered marketplace sellers the opportunity to receive online payments through Stripe Connect, which can accept debit card payments. Sellers can use Stripe Connect in 25 countries. They just have to add their customers to Stripe Connect, and the system will even automatically update expired credit cards.

Stripe charges small retailers a 2.9% flat rate and a 30-cent fee per transaction. Retailers find it easy to update their payment system with just a few lines of code. Payments are made to their bank accounts after two business days.[163] In October 2016, Stripe introduced various fraud prevention tools that will help developers and retailers curtail digital theft. Radar, a technology developed by the company, uses algorithms and machine learning to process transactions and can pick up warning signs for fraudulent transactions.[164]

Stripe has also introduced Works with Stripe, a directory of hundreds of apps that users can use with the main app. Businesses can take advantage of these services to analyze data. Introduced in the latter part of 2016, Works with Stripe includes Slack, a service app providing transaction notifications in real-time; Card Flight card readers for use with Android or iOS apps; Xero for payroll and accounting of Stripe transactions; Taxjar for tax computations; Shippo for shipping; and Control for business analytics.[165]

Also, Stripe has started testing out a cash advances product, as it tries to expand on the Atlas offering for small and medium businesses.

The company has reached a valuation of over $20 billion, after raising around $245 million in September 2018.

◨ Square

Square has built an online acquisition solution called Square Online. A retailer can accept payments using Square Online in three ways: sell on their own site, sell on Square's site, or sell with a third-party site. They receive their deposits the next day. Square can also integrate inventory and reports with their offline sales and accepts major credit cards. Square earns from the processing fee per transaction.[166]

Braintree

Established in 1998, PayPal is a leading digital payments solution allowing customers to manage and transfer their funds more effectively by providing flexibility and choice in how they send or receive money. It offers a secure and open payments platform that businesses can use both to transact with their online customers and in their brick-and-mortar stores. PayPal's global payments platform has more than 244 million customers, transacting in more than 100 currencies, 17 million merchant accounts, a revenue of over 13 billion, and a market cap of $100 billion.[167]

Established in 2007 in Chicago, Braintree provides commerce tools to users wanting to accept payments from any device in almost every payment method available. Retailers globally can accept, enable, and split payments in at least 130 currencies. Braintree also offers innovative concepts, stellar customer service, and simple processes. PayPal acquired Braintree in 2013 for $800 million having been attracted by the technology developers as well as the internal talent, and integrated the two payments businesses.[168]

The merger allowed Braintree to build, scale, and grow faster to help rewire commerce and improve the connection between retailers and consumers. Braintree offers the mobile-first platform, while PayPal has the reach and power of a two-sided network of merchants and consumers.[169]

Klarna

As mentioned earlier, Klarna had one goal in mind: to make buying easier. Klarna Payments is an e-commerce solution using smart data to give customers real-time credit quickly and easily. Retailers can seamlessly integrate it with their solutions. They can increase their customers' purchasing power, providing them with the option to pay in installments, pay after delivery, or buy now and pay later. They also improve a retailer's average order value and loyalty by using Klarna Payments.[170]

In the US, Klarna collaborated with Overstock.com to provide member retailers with the same features as Amazon's "buy with one click" button. Klarna has more than 60 million customers, 90,000 merchants, and a 10% share of the ecommerce market of Northern Europe.[171]

China's Ant Financial is the financial investment arm of the Alibaba Group, worth more than $150 billion at this time and heading toward an IPO. This makes it the biggest fintech in the world, one and a half times the size of PayPal.

Its payment solution, Alipay, is a mobile wallet that started off by processing payments for Alibaba websites Taobao and Tmall. It is supported in more than 100,000 retail stores and more than 70 countries. Alipay has acquired more than 400 million registered users, almost triple the size of PayPal. The company also has a credit rating service, a money market fund, and a digital bank that lends to SMEs.

The company has big plans for globalization, having already acquired Moneygram and Kakao Pay, a South Korean payment network.

Mobile Payments in Developing Countries

In many regions of the world most people lack bank accounts, credit cards, a credit history, and even a smart phone. In these regions, it is especially important to provide an alternative technology to pay, as this generates a more inclusive environment where business can take place.

A very interesting case is the one of M-PESA. It is a mobile phone based payments system, as well as micro financing system that doesn't require a smart phone or even an internet connection. It allows people to deposit money to an account stored in their phones, receive balances using SMS, make payments, and redeem balances using a network of agents.

It is the most successful mobile phone based system in the developing world, and is present in Kenya, Tanzania, Afghanistan, South Africa, India, Eastern Europe, as well as Mozambique, Lesotho and Egypt.

Being able to store and transfer money digitally opens up doors for millions of people to do more. Merchants can advertise online and collect payments. In the countryside people are even trading solar power using this system.

M-PESA is really popular in Kenya, where 93% of the population have now got access to mobile payments and almost half of the country's GDP is processed through M-PESA.

Mobile Wallets

Traditional wallets were invented in the 1600s as a way to carry identification papers and the newly invented paper currency. Modern wallets, which have slots for cards, quickly followed the introduction of the first credit cards in the 1950s. After that, debit cards, membership cards, and loyalty cards also found their way into the physical wallet.

A mobile wallet is a way of carrying your debit card or credit card information in digital form on your mobile device. Among other uses, instead of using your physical plastic card to make purchases, you can pay with your smartphone, tablet, or smartwatch.

Physical wallets have become one of the most targeted items for pickpockets, although lately, much less cash is being carried in wallets as cash is being replaced by card and mobile payments.

Mobile wallets are also vulnerable to targeting by criminals—in this case, cybercriminals. Establishing good security practices is essential for all providers. Multiple factors of authentication will be set up on devices. This can include PINs, passwords, and biometric information. Combined authentication, keeping some information on a mobile device and some on remote servers, is recommended.

Uses for Mobile Wallets

The main use of m-wallets is to enable payments. They can be used to store credit, debit, and prepaid card details. A customer must download an app, add their card details, and then the wallet can be used to pay in stores using proximity payment technology, such as Near Field Communication (NFC) technology, requiring the user to place the phone close to a reading terminal.

The second use of m-wallets involves commerce. M-wallets can be used to store coupons, offers, and discounts, such as loyalty cards for restaurants, supermarkets, and other shops.

The third use for m-wallets is identification. They can store details of access control cards, authentication, and a person's signature. They can also store the user's biometric details. This field will probably develop the most in future.

Finally, m-wallets are usable for banking—for example, to store cash, pay bills, deposit and withdraw cash from banks and merchants, make transfers to bank accounts and mobile phone numbers, and access banking and investment accounts digitally.

Key Players

A lot of attention has been paid to mobile wallets due to the size of the market. According to Forbes,[172] the mobile wallets market will be worth $4.5 trillion in the US. There are huge numbers of companies involved, but the big names in this area are Google, Apple, Samsung, and PayPal. The fact that the first three themselves offer mobile devices gives them an advantage.

Android Pay

Google Wallet was released in 2011 and became Android Pay in 2015, with Google's acquisition of Softcard. Users can scan their cards and make payments using NFC technology. The device reads a fingerprint to authenticate payments. It also allows for storing credit and sending and receiving payments with no commission. It also receives offers from selected merchants. It is only supported by Android devices.

Apple Pay

Apple released passbook in 2012, which then was renamed Apple Wallet. It allowed boarding passes, event tickets, and coupons to be stored. Then, in 2014, Apple Pay was released, allowing you to store credit and debit cards on your phone and make online payments and NFC payments. It is similar to Android Pay and has been commercially successful from the moment it launched. Apple's technology can also be used to open hotel doors and ride public transportation in many countries.

Samsung Pay

Samsung Pay was launched in the US so that their smartphones had their own payment solution. It allows payments and will soon support the storage of gift and loyalty cards. The main difference to its competitors is that it supports Magnetic Secure Transmission (MST), meaning that it can work with traditional merchant terminals. Instead of storing cards and payment details, it stores secure tokens, ensuring the cards can't be cloned or stolen. It also allows authentication using an iris scanner which is embedded into the devices.

PayPal

PayPal has the disadvantage of not selling hardware, so people wanting to use the wallet need to install it. However, their app can be installed on both iOS and Android. PayPal has been allowing the storage of funds in email accounts for several years, and they recently signed a deal with Mastercard allowing PayPal to have increased presence at point of sale. Mastercard benefits by having its own wallet, Masterpass, as an accepted payment option for PayPal's Braintree merchant network. PayPal also offers a white label version of their wallet for merchants. Another PayPal subsidiary, Venmo, is a payment app that is very successful with millennials.

Smart Credit Cards

While mobile technologies can be a great way to replace cash and plastic, none of these will work when the mobile runs out of power. For these instances, some companies have created intelligent cards, which offer convenience while maintaining security. Curve, founded in London, offers a physical card that can link into all Mastercard and Visa cards, selected using a mobile app. It saves having to carry several cards at the same time. Stratos, a US company, developed a card that uses dual stripe technology and can store all your credit, debit, loyalty, gift and membership cards in one secure and safe place. Other promising companies include Swyp, which is expected to deliver a card that can store and manage 20 debit, credit, loyalty and gift cards at the same time. It will require charging on a monthly basis since it will have a touchscreen embedded.

Will E-Wallets Replace Cash?

Cash is recognized as an expensive, dirty, and not very trustworthy way of carrying out transactions. It leaves room for criminal activity and tax evasion. Governments are keen to move to a better solution. Over time, we have seen transitions from coins to paper money to plastic. Some governments have already announced they will no longer produce coins, so we are already on a journey toward decreased usage of legacy forms of payment. However, bearing in mind the world's size and the number of developing countries, it is difficult to picture a cashless world, at least in the next few decades. It is worth watching the space in India, where the government has ordered demonetization by removing high denomination bills. It aims to increase online payments and reduce the informal economy.

T-Commerce

Television commerce is the term used to describe buying and selling through interactive television. Viewers can review different products and then buy them, and even track their orders. The first attempt at a T-commerce application appeared in 2013, with Samsung Smart TVs. This has evolved to Samsung "Pay on TV," a scheme that allows for payments using major credit cards, debit cards, and even PayPal. It is a simple three-step process that includes entering a PIN code. Television commerce uses various technologies such as NFC (near field communications) and ARC (audio return channel).

It is convenient for the sale of clothing and decor that feature on television programs. During the broadcast, customers can create a wish list of items that they would like to buy.

Brands have a new opportunity here, with the relaxation of strict product placement regulations and growth in sales of smart TVs. They can now take advantage of multiple screen functionality, where a person can shift between a phone, tablet, or screen. The connection speed and screen size can determine the richness and delivery of content.

In May 2013, YouGov research found out that 23% of individuals take advantage of set top boxes as the primary way of accessing the internet through their TVs. At present, Google has Chromecast, a device allowing users to stream media from different devices.[173]

In 2012, American Express collaborated with NBC Universal cable networks and Fox, part of News Corp, to try to convince TV viewers to purchase products shown on screen. It planned to allow viewers to buy products inspired by certain programs on NBC Universal from their mobile devices. Those with Amex cards can get $35 cash back if they used their cards, synchronized with their Twitter or Facebook accounts.[174]

Over at NBC Universal, the social-TV app Zeebox could allow users to speak to friends who are also watching the same show in real time.[175] It could also let users follow related Facebook and Twitter feeds. Furthermore, it offers purchasing information about the items on sale.

American Express and Fox allowed viewers to purchase in real time using their new Fox Now iPad app while they watched "New Girl." Each episode featured a product that viewers could purchase. American Express was betting on the future of television commerce.

More advertisers are finding ways to use content in their advertising strategies, instead of using the usual TV commercials that had nothing to do with the programs. According to NBC Universal's President for ad sales Linda Yaccarino, "context and impact mean everything."

The Future in a Flash

Commerce is about the facilitation of trading in products or services. In a globalized world, technology makes commerce easier and cheaper. The invention of machines such as mobile terminals and tablets helps both buyers and sellers. Specialized payment providers can make purchasing internationally a simpler process. We can expect to see further evolution in this arena to make payments even simpler. The world is moving toward a state in which paper money is used less and less, and one day we may even have economies that are fully digital.

New technologies bring in security and transparency, creating the environment for a world which will be better, safer, and more efficient.

Chapter 7
Crowdfunding and Crowdinvesting

Crowdfunding and Crowdinvesting in a Flash

Getting funding for companies has always been difficult for entrepreneurs and can take a vast amount of effort and time. Crowdfunding helps individuals or entities raise money from other people or businesses for different purposes. It is a means of accessing a pool of funds to finance a project or endeavor. With technological innovation, it is now possible to reach a large number of possible funders, each of whom can contribute small amounts of money.

Individuals or entities can donate money to any cause. Some of these crowdfunding projects offer rewards like an event ticket, acknowledgements on the book cover, or gifts, among other things. Usually, donors expect nothing back, content with feeling good about helping other people. With crowdinvesting, investors invest their money in exchange for equity and share in the profits of the company.

A new type of funding that started in late 2016 is Initial Coin Offerings (ICOs). They have raised record amounts in 2017, challenging venture capital funding, and we will cover these in detail.

How Businesses Traditionally Fund Themselves

It is important to understand funding, since when following fintech start-ups we often see news about the different rounds of investment that they are experiencing. Funding typically has six stages: early stage, seed, growth, expansion, bridge, and IPO.

Early Stage Funding

Initial funding for companies generally comes from savings, and from friends and family, personal bank loans and, now, crowdfunding. Alternatively, angel investors are a good first point of call for a company in its infancy. These invest in young businesses or start-ups that they believe will provide high returns in the future. They search for companies with a strong management team, high growth potential, and a solid business plan, finding other business associates and trusted firms to co-invest with them. They choose their ventures based on the technologies or industries that they are most familiar with, so they can provide mentoring and consultation.

DOI 10.1515/9781547401055-007

Seed Stage

A start-up receives seed funding to get a business off the ground. The business owner usually presents the business plan to a potential investor. If the investor agrees to fund their idea, they receive money to create a prototype or to carry out further tests, and in exchange the investor gets shares in the business. The average amount of funding is $500,000.[176]

Growth Stage

This is the first round in which venture capitalists typically get involved and ends with a type of funding called Series A. Typically, Series A can raise $2–$4 million. Research by J.E. Young and J.C. Ruhnka shows that venture capitalists have a 66.2% chance of losing money at this stage, so it is definitely a gamble. If the idea is feasible, the venture capitalist will ask for a detailed business plan and will sit as one of the company's Board of Directors. The business will start to be professionalized to meet the investor's expectations, and the company will develop and test the solution that will go to market. It will show a prototype to a few clients and ask for feedback. Then, with the venture capitalist monitoring the whole process, the business will arrange for production.

Expansion Stages

The following rounds of funding have successive letters: Series B, C, and D. The business will be growing steadily, producing and selling products or services successfully, and valuation will generally be above $30 million. It will be facing its competitors and endeavoring to capture a share of the market. It will also aim to break even by finding ways to lower costs. The venture capitalist will monitor the management team closely to ensure that they make the right decisions promptly.

The venture capitalist will support the next stage if the management team proves it can hold its own against the competition. However, they may suggest that the team is restructured or that this stage is repeated if the company was unable to satisfy their requirements. They will cease to fund the project if it performs badly at one of these stages.

Bridge or Mezzanine Stage

This stage prepares the business for the Initial Public Offering. The venture capitalist will leave the business, receiving the profit from their investment. The business might merge with another company, eliminate other competitors, or prevent new players from entering the market. Only about 1% of tech firms get to a bridging round of funding.

The business must study its product's market position. It may reposition itself to attract more customers and increase market share. Usually, this is also the stage where the company begins to offer more products and services to attract more customers.

IPO Stage

Reaching the final stage is what most entrepreneurs dream of. Being listed on a stock market allows some of their shares to be cashed in. Private and public equity have different types of investors, and both have their pros and cons. By going public, a business sells its shares through an exchange. In some cases, its Initial Public Offering is of limited interest to the media and the public because it is still small and unproven. However, there are cases, like Facebook's IPO, which became a historical success.

If it wants to go public, the company must first have an underwriter to help it with the sale of its shares. Usually, this underwriter is an investment bank, and its responsibilities include setting the stock price and selling shares to the investors. The underwriter must price the share low enough for investors to take interest.

 ## Crowdfunding Business Model

Crowdfunding is the pooling of assets or capital through the internet to fund a business or project. Communities and societies support these creative or commercial projects. Previously, the vehicle used was a consortium, co-ownership, cooperative, or mutual arrangement. There are four ways in which crowdfunding can raise funds: through donation, reward, lending, or equity.

Aside from raising capital, crowdfunding also provides start-up businesses with non-financial benefits, like pre-sales leads, product validation, a defined shareholder structure, and a gauge of pricing and demand. The business can use its investors to generate feedback and ideas on new products and services, as well as encourage collective decision-making. People who fund the business become its ambassadors and help to promote and market the products through word-of-mouth.

Crowdfunding Motivations

Social motivations have been very popular. Used extensively by non-profit organizations, donation-based crowdfunding funds common purpose or creative activities. It targets smaller campaigns and focuses on community-based or local projects. Funders identify with the cause and gain satisfaction from seeing the project realized. There are crowdfunding platforms that allow individuals to create their own crowdfunding campaign quickly and easily.

Reward-based crowdfunding provides the investor with a product or service. Investors often fund small or creative projects or businesses. Usually, this type of financing serves to test initial demand for the product. Entrepreneurs in the technology, film and music industries use reward-based crowdfunding to generate funds.

Market Size

In 2015, Massolution estimated the global crowdfunding industry to be worth $35 billion. However, this figure included $25 billion from peer-to-peer lending. For equity crowdfunding, it would have been just $1.2 billion. The World Bank also predicted that crowdfunding could be worth $96 billion by 2020.[177]

In the US, investment crowdfunding was worth $1.2 billion in 2015. However, 50% of this was for real estate and the other 50% was for start-ups. The volume of capital for US equity crowdfunding is expected to grow by at least 75% or about $3.5 billion by 2020.

Key Crowdfunding Platforms

US-based Kickstarter is a global crowdfunding platform with its headquarters in Brooklyn, New York. It focuses on raising funds for creative pursuits, and its mission is to make creative ideas a reality. With at least $3.9 billion in pledges, it has funded 418,000 projects, related to myriad things including food, technology, video games, journalism, comics, stage shows, music, and films. Those that fund projects receive rewards in exchange for their money.[178]

Established in April 2009, by Charles Adler, Yancey Strickler, and Perry Chen, Time named Kickstarter one of the "Best Websites of 2011" and "Best Inventions of 2010." *The New York Times* called it the "people's NEA." In October 2012, Kickstarter started operating in the United Kingdom, doing the same in Canada in September 2013.

Project creators do not receive the money if they are unable to raise the minimum funding goal by the deadline. Kickstarter charges a fee of 5% of the total funds raised, while an additional 3% to 5% fee goes to the payments processor. Since there is no guarantee that fund creators will complete the promised projects, it cautions funders to use due diligence. Project creators can be legally liable if they fail to deliver on their promises.

Since 2009, Kickstarter has helped at least 8,800 non-profits and companies and has funded about $3 billion in projects. However, it has faced many challenges since its inception. For example, it was difficult to segregate legitimate project creators from the not-so-serious ones. Many projects failed to deliver results, and project backers felt short-changed. According to a Wharton study, about 56% of the projects failed, and only 25% of successful projects finished on time.[179]

From 2012 onward, Kickstarter has required project creators to list business challenges and major risks and represent the creative process more clearly. This strategy has worked, and since then only 10% of projects have failed to deliver. In 2015, Kickstarter went public, and its board members and stockholders became accountable to the public. In 2016, it introduced Creative Independent to support artists in publishing their essays.

US-based AngelList is for jobseekers, angel investors, and start-ups. Launched in 2010, the platform wanted to democratize the investment process. It began as an online tech-start-up board that needed seed funding. Since 2015, start-ups have been able to raise money from angel investors free of charge. Babak Nivi and Naval Ravikant founded AngelList. In February 2015, AngelList launched its syndicate counterpart in the United Kingdom.[180]

At least $705 million worth of investments has been made through the AngelList platform, in at least 1870 start-ups. Its use of syndicates has generated a venture capital-like hybrid model, in which investors receive carried interest for their part in choosing the most promising investments. Between 2013 and 2015, its Internal Rate of Return was 45% after carried interest and fees.[181]

INDIEGOGO

Eric Schell, Slava Rubin, and Danae Ringelmann founded Indiegogo in San Francisco in 2008. It is open to individuals wishing to raise funds for a start-up, charity, or idea.

It charges 5%, plus any additional fees charged by payment processors like PayPal and credit card companies.[182]

Indiegogo offers a reward to customers, investors, or donors who fund a product or project. In 2016, it collaborated with MicroVentures to provide equity-based campaigns. It launched Indiegogo Life in 2014, a free service for individuals who need money for life events like celebrations, medical expenses, and emergencies. The following year, Indiegogo Life became Generosity.com, which in turn was taken over by You Caring.[183]

crowdfunder

Crowdfunder is a mixture of investment and donation-based crowdfunding. It also encourages collaboration and both offline and online crowdfunding. It follows the all-or-nothing model, with a 5% charge on total funds raised, plus a minimum 1.9% transaction fee. It emphasizes the long-term growth of enterprises. However, Crowdfunder is for for-profit businesses only.[184]

Founded in 2011 in Los Angeles, Crowdfunder connects entrepreneurs with investors. Although most companies are tech start-ups, it can also fund small businesses and social enterprises.[185]

With headquarters in San Diego, US-based GoFundMe provides a platform for individuals to raise funds for life events and challenging circumstances. Although it was established in May 2010 by Andrew Ballester and Brad Damphousse, it started out as "CreateAFund" in 2008. GoFundMe became the new name due to the various revisions made to the website's features. In June 2015, the original founders sold a majority stake to Accel Partners.[186]

Users create their own GoFundMe pages to encourage donors to give money to causes. They need to describe why they are raising funds and how much money they hope to raise from the endeavor. They can also upload videos and photos to their website and share them via their social media accounts and email.

Donors can give money through the GoFundMe website using their credit or debit card. They can also monitor the project's progress through the website. GoFundMe charges a 5% fee whenever a donor gives money. Aside from the 5% per transaction, the payment processor also charges 2.9% and $0.30 per transaction.

ROCKETHUB
The world's crowdfunding machine

RocketHub is for people who want to raise awareness and funds for endeavors and projects. Common project creators include musicians, scientists, philanthropists, photographers, writers, entrepreneurs, game developers, filmmakers, theatre directors/producers, fashion designers, and the like. Vladimir Vukicevic, Alon Hillel-Tuch, Jed Cohen, and Brian Meece were the original founders,[187] establishing the company in 2009 and launching it in January 2010.

Based in New York City, RocketHub was one of the US Department of State's 12 top global partners. It operates in at least 190 countries through its collaboration with the US State Department.

A project creator can keep the funds even if the project fails to reach the pre-established minimum amount. It charges 12% processing fees in such scenarios, and 8% fees if the project raises the minimum amount.

London-based GoGetFunding allows fund creators to raise money for any purpose. It charges 4% of the total funds raised and a 2.9% transaction fee. Anyone can raise money for any purpose. GoGetFunding's platform is also easy to use. However, GoGetFunding is not for entrepreneurial or business projects because fewer people fund such activities.[188]

Launched in 2011, GoGetFunding has the simple aim of helping individuals in need raise funds online. Its crowdfunding platform lets you share your page, track visitors and donate easily. You can either create a private or public campaign and a timed or ongoing campaign. A project creator can add links, pictures, and videos to generate more interest in their crowdfunding project.[189]

StartSomeGood

StartSomeGood is for non-profits and social entrepreneurs. It uses the 'tipping point' model, meaning that after a certain amount has been raised investors receive rewards. It charges 5% for completed projects and 3% transaction fees. It accepts crowdfunding endeavors worldwide and supports non-profits, for-profits, and individuals who have projects focused on doing good in society. StartSomeGood has a smaller reach and is only for social projects.[190]

Launched in 2011 by Tom Dawkins and Alex Budak, StartSomeGood uses crowdfunding to foster social change by supporting change-makers and their initiatives. It provides support, advice, and feedback from its crowdfunding experts.[191]

Top Crowdfunding Campaigns

In this section, we review the campaigns that have raised the most funds for specific projects.

Pebble Funding (Pebble, Pebble Time, and Pebble 2)

Located in Palo Alto, California, the Pebble Company has been the king of crowdfunding: they ran three of Kickstarter's most successful crowdfunding campaigns.

Between April 11, 2012, and May 19, 2012, its first crowdfunding campaign raised $10,266,845, with 68,929 funders. The funds raised were for the production of an infinitely customizable smartwatch that can connect to Android and iPhone smartphones through Bluetooth technology. The smartwatch can also alert the wearer to an incoming call, message, or email.

The second Kickstarter campaign ran from February 24, 2015, to March 28, 2015, and raised $20,338,986 from 78,471 funders. The goal of the campaign was to raise funds for the production of Pebble's second-generation smartwatch (Pebble Time) with a one-week battery life and 20% thinner than the original Pebble smartwatch. This was a crowdfunding campaign that broke records on the Kickstarter platform. First, it was the first project to raise $1 million in just 49 minutes. After just seven days, it had broken the record for being the most-funded campaign ever, with at least $13.3 million in pledges. It broke the record set by Coolest Cooler which is discussed below.

The third campaign was called Pebble 2. It was a Kickstarter campaign to fund the production of Pebble's two new smartwatches with a built-in fitness tracker. The watches have health tools, optical heart rate monitoring, and activity tracking. The campaign ran from May 24, 2016, to June 30, 2016, and raised $12,779,843 from 66,673 supporters.

Coolest Cooler

Coolest Cooler was a Kickstarter crowdfunding campaign that ran from July 8, 2014, to August 30, 2014, and raised $13,285,226 from 62,642 funders. Its goal was to fund the production of a 60-quart cooler with a built-in ice-crushing blender. The cooler also has a waterproof Bluetooth speaker and a built-in USB charger.

Flow Hive

Funded on April 20, 2015, Flow Hive was an Indiegogo crowdfunding campaign that raised $13,255,247 from 38,473 supporters. The money was for the production of a honey-extraction system for all types of beekeepers. Flow Hives makes harvesting pure honey from beehives easier.

Baubax—Travel Jacket

Baubax—Travel Jacket was a Kickstarter campaign that ran from July 7, 2015, to September 4, 2015, to fund the production of a travel jacket with a built-in earphone holder, eye mask, drink pocket, gloves, neck pillow, and tech pockets. The jacket comes in four styles and all sizes. The crowdfunding campaign raised $9,192,055 from 44,949 funders.

Exploding Kittens

Exploding Kittens was a crowdfunding campaign from January 21, 2015, to February 20, 2015, at Kickstarter. Its goal was to raise funds to manufacture Exploding Kittens, a game based on Russian roulette. The player who draws an exploding kitten loses the game. The campaign raised $8,782,571 from 219,382 backers.

Ouya

As a crowdfunding campaign that ran from July 10, 2012, to August 9, 2012, Ouya raised $8,596,474 from 63,416 Kickstarter backers. The money funded the production of Ouya, an Android-powered game console for the television.

Crowdinvesting

Crowdinvesting is crowdfunding used by investors who finance a start-up in exchange for shares. They usually exit the start-up when a large company acquires the business, profiting from the sale. Because of the economic crisis, entrepreneurs find it difficult to access capital. Therefore, they turn to crowdinvesting because it's a faster process.

Crowdinvesting pools together funds from individual investors which are then invested in an idea or project. Like any business, there are risks involved, like loss of investment, lack of dividends, dilution, and illiquidity.

Investors must be careful about investing their hard-earned money in a particular business start-up because they may not receive any return. In fact, the general rule is that they must only invest money that they can afford to lose. Possible investors must also consider the market fluctuations of their investment.

Most start-ups do not distribute dividends because they use the money to expand the business or create more products and services. Dilution is expected if the start-up raises more capital in the future by issuing new shares. Most start-ups raising funds have no operating history, so investors may find it difficult to evaluate their possible performance.

Investors must diversify their portfolio. They can invest small amounts of money in different businesses to spread the risks. They also shouldn't invest all their capital in just start-ups but invest most of their money in safer or liquid assets. Investors also rely on the competence and experience of the start-up's directors, since investors cannot make decisions for the business.

Start-ups may not decide to list publicly in the near future and investors should take this into account. They will find it difficult to get their money back because there are no buyers for their shares, or they may receive less money than they initially invested due to price fluctuations. There is also no guarantee of tax relief. In the United Kingdom, the Financial Conduct Authority allows high-net-worth individuals and sophisticated investors to dabble in crowdinvesting.[192]

With crowdinvesting, a nominee structure may hold the shares for investors, although in some cases, platforms follow a direct shareholding model. There are also instances when investors receive different share classes, depending on the amount they invest. This complexity requires individuals to exercise due diligence before deciding to get involved with crowdinvesting.

Key Crowdinvesting Platforms

EquityNet was the first crowdinvesting site. Established in 2005 in the US, it focuses on investments in social enterprises and consumer products. It attracts single-assisted projects like medical clinics and assisted-living facilities. Company profiles are available to the public but only registered users can view audited financial statements, prospectuses, and disclosures. Registered users can also send messages to companies through the crowdinvesting platform. Transactions occur outside of the platform.

EquityNet has no minimum investment requirement. However, it is common to find companies asking for a $2,000 to $5,000 investment.

▄▆▄ crowd**cube**

Founded in 2011 by Luke Lang and Darren Westlake, UK based Crowdcube is one of the world's top investment crowdfunding platforms. Minor investors or professional investors help businesses grow through debt and equity investment options. Crowd-cube has raised at least £530 million for more than 700 companies in the United Kingdom. Investors can invest a minimum of £10 in a company listed on Crowdcube, and businesses do not get anything if they are unable to raise the pre-established minimum amount. Crowdcube earnings are from commissions for successful cam-paigns.[193]

◯ SEEDRS

As an equity crowdfunding platform, Seedrs is for start-ups and established busi-nesses in Europe. Users can choose to invest a minimum of €10 or £10 in their chosen project.[194] The project creators pool the funds in exchange for equity. Like some other crowdfunding platforms, they do not get anything if they do not reach their target. However, if the money exceeds their minimum expected fund, they can keep it.

The Financial Conduct Authority gave Seedrs its regulatory approval in May 2012. Although its headquarters are in Tech City, East London, Seedrs houses its designers and developers in Lisbon, Portugal. Established by Carlos Silva and Jeff Lynn, *The Guardian* named it as one of "East London's 20 Hottest Start-ups" in July 2012. In August 2012, *Wired* named it "Start-up of the Week." In November 2013, Silicon Valley Comes to the UK included Seedrs in their Top 100 UK Businesses.

Seedrs charges a maximum of 7.5% of the total amount successfully raised by businesses and start-ups. The amount covers administrative and legal costs incurred by the company. Additionally, Seedrs charges funders or investors about 7.5% of the profits they receive from their investments. This amount covers the costs for ongoing investor protection and day-to-day shares management.

In 2017, Seedrs achieved $175 million raised for 168 projects in 8 countries, making it the most active UK funder of private companies. The company also received an injection of $12 million, using their own platform.

In May 2017, Seedrs announced its intention to launch a secondary market in order to enable investors to sell shares in companies they have invested in using Seedrs to other investors.

CircleUp is a crowdinvesting platform dedicated to the fitness, technology, and food and beverage sectors. It shows company profiles, including their business models, retail partners, products, leadership, and revenue. Through its DealFlow feature, investors can easily see which companies are actively raising funds. They can also request product samples and view investment prospectuses. They can purchase shares from a particular company or join a circle that pools funds from investors and manages them. The minimum investment is usually $1,000.[195]

In October 2017, CircleUp announced a $125 million growth fund with a plan to invest in companies directly, including companies in the food and beverage and personal care sectors.[196]

Fundable is both a rewards-based crowdfunding and crowdinvesting platform. A company that wants crowdinvesting can seek help from Fundable in constructing their pitch, building their online profile, and developing their business plan. It can have a low fundraising target of $10,000 to attract smaller customers. Investors, on the other hand, can invest a minimum of $1,000. Transactions take place outside of the Fundable platform.

Wefunder has a minimum investment of $100. It focuses on companies and start-ups in the fields of packaged food, logistics, insurance, green energy, and biotech. Companies have to offer detailed sales metrics, leadership interviews, and summarized business plans. Investors can also send questions to company executives or founders. Currently, all funding transactions take place outside of the platform, but there are plans to change this in future.

localstake

Localstake connects investors and small businesses within a certain area. It focuses on enterprises such as clothing manufacture, food production, or brewing. The minimum investment is $250. Investors can either take advantage of revenue share loans or crowdinvesting. With revenue share loans, they provide loans with fixed rate yet open-ended maturities and receive monthly repayments plus interest on the loan.

COMPANISTO

Companisto is a crowdinvesting site located in Berlin and established in June 2012 by Tamo Zwinge and David Rhotert. The minimum investment is €5, and the maximum is €500,000, and there is no upper limit to the amount a start-up can raise. An investor can become a stockholder of the start-up and can earn profits through dividends or upon exit. Companisto has at least 60,000 investors scattered around 92 countries.[197]

Initial Coin Offerings (ICOs)

An Initial Coin Offering (ICO) is the equivalent of an Initial Public Offering (IPO), but for cryptocurrency. It is done to raise funds without a need to go to a venture capitalist or a bank. It is becoming the most common way to fund new cryptocurrency ventures.

In general terms, a company or group of individuals writes a whitepaper that states what the project consists of, what the key needs are that they are solving, the amount of funding that is required, and how long the campaign will last. Investors that find the project appealing can deposit funds into the crypto wallet of the issuer in exchange for tokens, which will hopefully then be traded on an open market. These tokens will be used to transact in the platform that the company is creating.

There are mainly two uses for ICOs, one is creating a coin that competes with the likes of bitcoin, and the other one is to issue tokens. These tokens can be used to purchase goods and services in a specific platform.

The best way to put this into context is by looking at a specific ICO. For example, Bancor, one of the most successful ICOs, raised $153 million in just three hours in June 2017. People had to preregister to get in. They accepted only Ether, a popular cryptocurrency, so investors had to buy these first in an exchange. Their currency will be used as a way to trade currencies without the need to use an exchange, removing the middleman.

Because of the lack of regulation, many fraudsters have taken the opportunity to publish whitepapers requesting funding with the intention to defraud investors. This is one of the biggest risks when investing in an ICO. As time goes by, stricter regulation is coming into place, from different governments. For example, ICOs have been banned in China until proper regulation is created. Stricter rules are also being implemented directly from the new ICO projects, in a self-regulated way.

According to Coindesk, by end of July 2018, ICOs had raised the staggering amount of almost $20 billion. That is equivalent to the GDP of the US, the largest economy in the world.

The top five ICOs so far have been:
1. EOS, for $4200 million, a new smart contract coin
2. Telegram, for $1700 million, a secure messaging app
3. Filecoin, for $262 million, a decentralized cloud storage system
4. Tezos, for $232 million, a coin that facilitates formal verification of transactions
5. EOS, for $185 million, a competitor of Ethereum, a decentralized operating system
6. Bancor, for $153 million, a currency that helps trade cryptocurrencies in a decentralized way

Blockchain Enabled Crowdfunding

Several companies are currently working on ways to improve the crowdfunding process. The problems that are being tackled include three-fourths of the projects not achieving their target, over 60% of visitors not sure whether a project is legitimate, very little funding going into developing countries, and a quarter of campaigns failing even when they already have some starting capital.

A good example is Acorn Collective, that have organized an ICO in order to launch a next generation crowdfunding platform, that includes the introduction of blockchain, a marketplace for third party services, and early incentives for the raise.

The Future in a Flash

Crowdfunding and crowdinvesting platforms will grow and will begin to incorporate innovations from other parts of fintech, such as big data, blockchain and more efficient payment mechanisms. When looking at the charitable sector, we can expect to see donations being rewarded with small products and offers. Social networks will be integrated so that people can access opportunities easily. We can't expect crowdfunding to replace managed investment funds, but it will become a good option as a starting point, along with angels and venture capitalists. ICOs had a very good year in 2017 and looking at the future, we consider that these are more than a fad, and as the investment model matures, more capital will flow into this financing technique.

Chapter 8
Innovative Wealth Management

Innovative Wealth Management in a Flash

Wealth management is changing: customer expectations are increasing as the new generation inherits and produces wealth, old-school advisors are retiring, and new technologies are simplifying decision-making and opening up information to larger audiences.

Robo-advisors are virtual robots that are used to provide advice at a low-cost. They are forecasted to be managing more than 10% of global wealth in the near future, so this is an important space to watch. The use of analytics provides important insights for wealth management companies, who are working to provide investment recommendations appropriate for their customers. Social investment platforms allow investors to copy successful investment strategies without having to pay for the cost of specialists.

Personal finance management tools allow for the creation of an aggregate view of investment accounts. They are being fused with investment products and other data sources to provide an end-to-end view of a person and their particular financial situation.

 ## How Wealth Management Works

Wealth management is a much-discussed topic, yet not everyone understands its full meaning. For an affluent person, wealth management is a scientific method of enhancing their financial position. For a financial advisor, it is the ability to provide affluent individuals with various financial products and services.

Wealth management incorporates different financial products and services: investments, portfolio management, and financial planning. Families, small business owners, and individuals with high net worth can take advantage of the services of wealth managers to coordinate investment management, tax professionals, legal resources, estate planning, and retail banking.

In theory, a wealth manager can offer any financial product on the market. However, the reality is that most of these managers specialize in certain products and services that they can successfully sell to clients. For quality wealth management, a wealth manager must ensure that they deliver their client presentations in a consultative manner. This means that they must let the client make their own decisions when choosing financial products and services. This is because we live in an uncer-

DOI 10.1515/9781547401055-008

tain world, and nobody can guarantee a certain return on an investment with 100% confidence.

The aim of a good wealth manager is to understand the client's needs. They may involve other experts if a client needs someone with different expertise. The wealth manager must focus on finding out about a client's working environment, life goals, and spending patterns.

Changes in Customer Expectations

The new generation of investors consists of Generations X and Y (millennials), although there are also some baby boomers, influenced by the younger generations. They interact with their financial advisors differently as they want to be treated as unique individuals and receive tailored advice.[198]

These new investors are also in charge of their financial lives. They understand financial advice and make decisions based on that knowledge. They do not purchase a lot of discretionary services and in general conduct their own research. They are less trusting of authority, ask the opinions of financial advisors, experts, and colleagues, and read various sources of information. They use technology as a key tool for accessing financial advice through different devices and channels.

The new type of investor also has a sense of entitlement when it comes to investment strategies and products available to affluent individuals and institutional investors. This means that wealth management companies have to seek new ways to provide access to new asset classes and alternative investments.

With at least two billion smartphones in use and the expectation that this number will jump to six billion by 2020, mobile apps for wealth management are becoming popular with investors, so offering a mobile app is becoming essential.[199]

Changes in Advisors

Technology changes the nature of financial advice and its method of delivery. A robo-advisor is an electronic service that offers algorithm-based and automated wealth management advice that does not involve humans. It mainly provides portfolio management advice and is a low-cost service attracting millennials because it is accessible online and does not require a high balance. Robo-advisors can also use complex algorithms to analyze client data, leading to personalized asset allocations and financial plans. Some financial technology companies have developed methods and tools for providing real-time investment and trade recommendations, catering to an investor's preferences and history.

Robo-retirement is a robo advice system that manages a person's retirement plan with algorithms. Instead of charging 1% to 2% of the total number of assets in the portfolio, as a traditional financial planner would, it charges a fee as low as 0.14% to 0.15% of the total assets under management[200] and has no minimum asset requirement. However, robo-retirement is available only for assets with quantifiable risk. It cannot deal with unquantifiable risks such as a sudden market crash. Clients who need Social Security and tax guidance should use a human financial planner or a hybrid robo-advisor.

Robo tax-loss harvesting, on the other hand, is an automated service for investors who want to pay the lowest possible taxes in non-tax sheltered accounts. Financial technology companies provide financial products and services, making it possible for investors to access them at low cost using smart technology. Robo-advisors can keep track of and rebalance investment portfolios at an affordable management fee.

In December 2014, Corporate Insight, a consulting firm, released the results of its survey, discovering that eleven leading robo-advisors had experienced a 65% increase in their total assets per year. However, this data still only accounted for 0.1% of the total US retail investable assets. Furthermore, the lower fees that robo-advisors charge their clients may not create a sustainable return for venture capitalists.[201]

Robo-advisors have the potential to disrupt the market. Existing wealth management firms with wide distribution capabilities and deep pockets are now collaborating with financial technology companies to develop robo-advisors, and some are developing them in-house.

Even with the dramatic improvement of robo advice capabilities, many investors still prefer personalized service from humans. Reassuring clients during difficult times, persuading them to take action, and synthesizing various solutions still requires human interaction. As such, there must be a unification of robo advice and human capabilities for an excellent client-advisor experience, and wealth management companies need to understand how robo advice enhances and complements customer relationships.

Robo advice can affect wealth management companies' business models. Investors may not be willing to pay a premium if they know they can obtain effective alternatives at a low price by a robo-advisor unless they can understand the real value of human advice and the difference between the two. Wealth management companies can provide value-added services or perform better in investment management.

Human financial advice will not become obsolete. An Accenture survey showed that 77% of clients still trust financial advisors and prefer to work with them. 81% insist on face-to-face interaction, so human advisors still play an important role in wealth management. Robo-advisors, however, can provide new capabilities, especially to human advisors, so wealth management companies need to integrate and adopt them.[202]

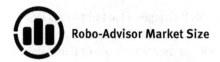 **Robo-Advisor Market Size**

According to A.T. Kearney, a consulting firm, assets managed by robo-advisors may grow by 68% each year and could be worth $2.2 billion by 2020. Because of automation and cost reduction, investors can now take advantage of services such as tax-loss harvesting that in the past was only available to institutional investors. Many of these new investors are young and middle-aged individuals, often ignored by traditional financial advisors who focus on baby boomers.[203]

Another report by BI Intelligence forecasts that robo-advisors will manage 10% of total assets, and it showed that 49% of consumers are receptive to robo-advising.[204] In 2017, the US was in the lead with 200+robo-advisors, followed by Germany (31), the UK (20), and China (20).[205]

Changes in Data Analytics

In 2012, the estimated amount of consumer data created was 2.8 zettabytes (a zettabyte is 10^{21} bytes). Experts believe it will grow exponentially, reaching 40 zettabytes by 2020.[206] The emergence of new technologies has helped find a use for such data. Big data is revolutionizing various industries, and wealth management companies are investing in creating state-of-the-art data management and analytics capabilities.

At present, many wealth management firms use simple analytics to provide important business insights into advisor books, client segments, training program effectiveness, and product penetration. Yet these same companies are creating more predictive and descriptive analytics, combining external and internal data sources, and both unstructured and structured data for more complete and insightful customer profiles. In the future, wealth management companies will also be able to develop algorithmic analytics to support investment decisions in real time.

Changes in Access to Products

With technology, investors can use online wealth management and apps to decide where to place their money, with no need to seek a financial advisor's advice. Financial technology companies, like Wealthfront, Betterment, and Nutmeg, offer an easier and cheaper way for everyone to try their hand at investing. Aside from being accessible to a larger portion of the population, financial technology apps are also paving the way for a shift from active investing to passive. As most of these apps' clients are millennials, it is unsurprising that they opt for passive investing as they have already experienced two market crashes.

Financial technology apps allow financial products to be grouped by themes so that investors can choose a portfolio based on their preferences and values. For example, apps can have groupings like "sustainability," "clean energy," or "sharia compliant."

Financial technology innovators like Wealthfront or Betterment can help reduce information asymmetry, providing customers with value-added products. They are having a major impact on the financial industry by delivering information to investors in a comprehensible and transparent way.[207]

Retail investors now demand access to the same strategies and asset classes once restricted to wealthy investors. For the past five years, financial technology start-ups have been entering the market to provide access to investment solutions for everyone.[208] They offer sophisticated trading strategies by copying those of professional portfolio managers or by using the electronic trading strategies of hedge fund managers.

Some financial technology start-ups also offer alternative asset classes, like becoming creditors in lending platforms. Some companies also provide analytics so that investors can research and test their strategies independently. In a way, we could say that fintech is democratizing access to investment products.

Social Investing

With at least 2.6 billion active social media users around the world, and an estimated 3.02 billion users by 2021,[209,210] wealth management companies must be able to tap these users as potential investors. However, these firms have IT systems that do not allow collaboration through social channels. Thus, financial technology start-ups entering the investment industry are outsmarting larger and more stable wealth management firms. This allowed for several social trading networks to emerge, such as eToro, ZuluTrade, and Ayondo.

eToro, an innovative company offering online trading, provides a proprietary platform for its users so that they can discuss strategies and trades. Users can even copy the strategies of successful and popular users, who allow part of their portfolio to be mirrored. eToro verifies its popular traders and gurus to ensure that these people use their real names and pictures. eToro introduced a customer relationship management app in July 2016 so that well-known investors could communicate with other users.[211]

Some Novel Investment Ideas

Investing Change

California-based Acorns is an app, created by Walter and Jeff Cruttenden, for people who are anxious about and intimidated by investing. Founded in 2012, Acorns is now available for Android and iPhone.[212]

Acorns' users connect all their credit or debit cards, and even checking accounts, to the app. Acorns uses the change from purchases made using these cards and checking accounts to invest in low-cost exchange-traded funds. For example, if a user spends $11.49 on lunch, they pay $12, because Acorns invests the 51 cents difference.

On average, users invest between $30 and $180 per month using this method alone. They can also invest more money by setting up automatic and regular deposits or make one-off large investments using their checking accounts. Acorns charges its users $1 per month plus up to 0.5% of their total investment each year.

This idea is also being followed by banks—for example, HSBC has started offering an app having the same functionality in the United Kingdom. In November 2017, Acorns acquired Vault to enable its customers to automatically invest part of their paycheck into a retirement fund.[213]

Investing as a Game

In the past, the stock market was exclusively for wealthy individual investors and large institutions. However, with the advent of technology, everyone can invest in stocks. Vestly makes stock investing a game. An individual can pick virtual stocks for their portfolio. They earn points based on the performance of these stocks and learn about stock trading without losing real money. They may earn up to $3000 if their portfolio is ranked in the top 100 at the end of each month.[214]

Investments by Women

Ellevest is a new company offering a robo-advisor specifically for women interested in investing. Founded by Sallie Krawcheck, it collaborates with computer engineers, entrepreneurs, and financial analysts to provide an investment app for women.[215]

Ellevest provides hundreds of customized and distinctive portfolios for the female investor. It suggests an investment portfolio depending on the investor's timeline and goals, and an investor can change the portfolio if she changes those goals. She can keep track of her portfolio's progress through the app's daily portfolio-monitoring feature, also receiving an alert if her portfolio goes off-track.

Ellevest provides 21 exchange-traded funds for its investors. These funds have high liquidity, low fees, and tax efficiency. Ellevest charges a low 0.5% of all the assets under management and does not require a minimum initial investment amount. It offers various account types, ranging from the traditional to Roth Individual Retirement Accounts.

Key Players Serving Individual Investors

In this section, we review notable companies that are making important progress in wealth management and focus on individual investors. Fintech is a very turbulent industry, so when you get to you read this, the companies might have drastically changed.

Betterment

Registered in New York as an online investment advisor, Betterment offers its customers a fully automated and diversified investment management solution at a lower price than that offered by the traditional wealth manager. It does not employ any financial advisors or sales representatives.

Betterment invests in fixed income ETFs (Exchange-Traded Funds) and passive index funds. It offers tax-efficient investment accounts that include different retirement accounts. To improve its portfolio, it uses mathematical models that optimize investor returns in various ways, considering the timing of trades, asset allocation, and diversification.

Betterment does not require a minimum investment amount. It charges between 0.15% and 0.35% annually of an investor's total investment. For example, an investor can expect to pay $150 if they have an account balance of $100,000. Betterment is aiming to get wealthier customers.

Betterment launched Betterment Institutional, a B2B offering, in October 2014. It became the first robo-advisor to reach the $5 billion mark in July 2016, and in 2018 had $15.5 billion under management and more than 400.000 customers.

Wealthfront is Betterment's main competitor. Based in Redwood City, California, and founded by Dan Carroll and Andy Rachleff in 2008, it is another automated investment service company. In December 2014, it had at least $1.7 billion worth of assets under management.[216]

Wealthfront was initially a mutual fund analysis company but transformed itself into a wealth management firm. It started offering tax-loss harvesting in December 2012 for customers with an account balance of at least $100,000. Furthermore, it collaborated with the State of Nevada in 2016 to launch a tax-advantaged college savings plan.

Wealthfront doesn't offer its products and services to financial advisors like Betterment does. According to Kate Wauck, Wealthfront's spokesperson, the company aims to create a standalone direct-to-consumer business, so it has no plans to expand to service financial advisors.

Wealthfront's valuation has been in decline mostly because competitors such as Vanguard have been creating their own robo-advisor versions. Wealthfront plans to expand into other financial services such as deposit accounts in order to grow their revenues.

robinhood

Robinhood has positioned itself as a stockbroker for the millennial generation. It has an app that allows its users to transact individual stocks at no cost. Launched in December 2014 through the Apple App Store, it has since launched an Android app.[217] Robinhood aims to encourage the millennial generation to invest by offering a way to transact stocks with minimal knowledge and effort. However, some critics are skeptical about the idea because inexperienced investors could lose money easily. Furthermore, the younger generation has to deal with student loan debt, and they do not typically have high-paying jobs. As such, young professionals cannot afford to lose money in stock trading.

Robinhood may make compromises because it does not charge investors for the transactions, so it may not be able to provide the necessary tools, customer service, and research to its customers. It stays operational because it employs minimal workforce, earning interest on the unused cash deposits from the investors' accounts. Furthermore, it has millions in cash from venture capitalists' investments.

In September 2016, it launched Robinhood Gold, an improved version of the app, for a monthly fee of $10. The new app allows users to trade even when the stock market is closed and provides instant withdrawals, lines of credit, and immediate deposits.

In 2017, Robinhood became the first Unicorn in wealth management after raising $110 million in Series C, which positioned them at a valuation of $1.3 billion. It currently has more than 3 million users, and has recently enabled an option for free options trading.

nutmeg

Based in London and established in April 2011, Nutmeg does not offer a trading platform. It makes investment decisions for its customers based on their risk appetite and investment goals. It invests funds in commodities, securities, cash, and other asset classes like exchange-traded funds.[218]

Nutmeg offers online investment management to its clients. Founded by William Todd and Nick Hungerford, it helps its clients meet their financial goals. It earns between 0.3% and 1% of the total investor's funds. Since its inception, it has already attracted more than 50,000 clients and manages more than £1 billion in funds.[219]

Motif Investing provides a platform for financial advisors to connect with various generations of investors. Financial advisors pay for low-cost yet customizable features for a different tactical approach and client portfolio to help them in strategic investment management.[220]

Motif Investing is a robo-advisor but also aligns itself with brokerage firms. Its users can build a basket or motif of exchange-traded funds and stocks and offer them to investors for $9.95. An investor can invest in a motif offered by Motif Investing, build their own, or invest in a motif offered by a fellow investor. A motif will vary depending on its creator. Each has an index price, a return, a valuation, volatility, and a dividend yield published.[221] It is well funded, with more than $126 million received in investments.

Motif Investing has partnered with JP Morgan to provide retail investors with exclusive access to IPOs.

Rachel Mayer worked as a trader at JP Morgan. When she left the company, she no longer had access to its tools to make investment decisions. Together with two of her classmates from her master's program, she created an investment platform for average investors. Trigger, as an iPhone app, offers real-time data free of charge to investors.[222]

Users can set up financial triggers to help them make investment decisions. For example, they can set up a reminder to sell a particular stock if its price reaches a particular level, a certain percentage, or the one-year high or low price. If any of these things happen, they receive a notification so they can act on it.

Trigger was acquired by Circle in October 2017 for an undisclosed amount, to expand Circle's product portfolio, by creating new investment products for crypt assets.

Key Players Serving Investment Managers

Here, we look at interesting companies that are making substantial progress in wealth management and are focused on investment managers.

Riskalyze, a risk-alignment software company, generated $20 million in funding in October 2016 to fund the expansion of its robo-platform for financial advisors. Based in Sacramento, it provides a platform for financial advisors to obtain a risk score for their clients, enabling them to suggest the right investment strategy.[223]

Riskalyze allows financial advisory companies to rebrand its digital advice platform for their own use. Established in 2011, Riskalyze planned to target small investors and large brokerage firms; however, it failed in this strategy, so instead targeted financial advisors.

Based in Mountain View, California, Addepar is a financial technology start-up offering a wealth management platform aimed at high net worth individuals. Addepar's CEO Eric Poirier is skeptical about the ability of artificial intelligence to encroach upon the work of financial advisors in the near future.[224]

Addepar provides integrated, normalized, and reconciled data through the open API it offers. High net worth individuals worldwide control a significant and increasing piece of worldwide assets, and Addepar plans to tap into this market through technology. Most financial advisors do not understand how technology can help their high net worth clients manage their wealth. Through Addepar, they can grow to understand each of their clients and how they allocate their assets, how they plan their estate, trust, and tax. Addepar's primary clients are financial advisors who can use the company's set of tools, data, and technology to provide services to their high net worth clients.

In May 2017, Addepar acquired AltX, an intelligence platform for the alternative investments market, including hedge funds, private equity, venture capital and real estate. In June 2017, Addepar raised $140 million with Valor Equity Partners, 8VC, and investment manager Harald McPike. The money will be used for research and development purposes and initiatives set to improve the company's technology.[225]

Catering to professional investors, SumZero is only open to people who are part of a research team in an investment banking proprietary trading desk, private equity fund, mutual fund, or hedge fund. At present, it has 40,000 basic users and 10,000 members. Founded by Aalap Mahadevia and Divya Narendra in April 2007, SumZero launched its website in March 2008.[226]

SumZero began as a repository of investment research. Then, it collaborated with Match.com and LinkedIn to connect with new fund managers and institutional investors. Members have to deliver their best ideas so that institutional investors, family offices, pension funds, and Ivy-League endowments will notice them.[227]

Quantopian

Boston based Quantopian, founded in 2011, recruits talented people skilled in writing algorithms for investment. The authors of this code can license it in the platform and get paid a part of the performance of the algorithm if Quantopian decides to allocate capital to it. It uses the idea of crowdsourcing, and the platform can be useful for training in quantitative analysis as well. It is backed by Steven Cohen and has $50 million in funding.

Personal Finance Management

Personal finance management (PFM) includes various services but often refers to tools that assist users in their saving, budgeting, and investing decisions. PFM tools can be bank provided, basic third-party apps, complex third-party apps, and aggregator tools. Aggregators and challenger banks provide the most exciting developments. Major banking institutions often offer poorer aesthetics integrated into their mobile apps, while some of the new providers offer stand-alone apps with greater creativity.[228]

Although banks may not realize that personal finance management tools are valuable only when linked to other services, challenger banks do and put these tools at the center of the user's mobile experience. They provide strong visuals to highlight important points. Generally, these personal finance management tools have higher aesthetic standards and are more intuitive to use.

Yet, personal finance management tools do not provide real insight into a person's financial situation if they are only based on account information. With no aggregate information, their functionality will not mature as users expect or want. In the US, Moven is an exception among banks because its customers can use information from many accounts. As such, it is a market leader in PFM solutions.

Third-party apps aggregate and add more functionality, like Tink, a Swedish PFM app that offers its users credit scoring. In Europe, the second Payment Services Directive (PSD2) is opening up the evolution of PFM tools by mandating open banking. Innovative financial technology start-ups may be able to move quickly to make other mobile apps redundant.

Mint is the leader in PFM. It has more than 20 million customers and helps its customers understand their total financial picture, looking at their expenditures, assets, and income. The app even allows for paying bills, can provide financial advice by linking to other apps such as LearnVest and Credit Karma, and even offers credit cards and third-party loans.

The Future in a Flash

The wealth management industry is progressing toward transparency and openness. This means that more people will get access to wealth services and people will feel more comfortable consolidating their different assets to create a single view of their wealth.

Switched-on investors that put a lot of effort into their portfolios, can achieve more with less effort. Investors that don't have a lot to invest can achieve better returns on their capital without having high-risk exposure.

Open banking, artificial intelligence and big data also mean that robotic advice will get better and better, being able to advise on what is right for us, not only allocating our money between saving goals and expenditures, but also helping us to set and achieve our life goals.

Chapter 9
The Power of Big Data and Artificial Intelligence

The Power of Big Data and Artificial Intelligence in a Flash

"Big Data" refers to large datasets that cannot be stored and analyzed by regular database software tools. Although there is not a predetermined size that makes a dataset qualify as Big Data, the dataset must be large enough that machine learning tools are the only ones that can analyze it. Typically, Big Data exceeds a certain number of terabytes and is stored across many different machines. Therefore, we assume that as technology advances, the size of Big Data will be adjusted accordingly. However, it is not all about the volume of data. To understand big data properly it is also important to understand the variety type, the velocity, and the veracity of the data. The financial services industry is deemed to have the largest datasets because of the nature of the industry.

Artificial Intelligence refers to the use of computer science to create intelligent machines that can work and react like humans. This includes developing tools to reason, plan, process language, perceive and manipulate objects. It is forecasted to replace up to 50% of bank staff and also improve customer offerings.

History of Data

Nearly 90% of available data has been recorded in the 2000s. However, data usage and the need to understand how it worked started in the ancient world with the introduction of the abacus in 2400 BCE in Babylon, Mesopotamia. In 200 CE, Greek scientists introduced the first central processing unit (CPU), known as the Antikythera Mechanism, for astrological purposes.

In 1663, the introduction of the first accounting principles by John Graunt paved the way for the use of Big Data in the modern era. In 1865, Richard Millar Devens used the term "business intelligence" for the first time to describe how the collection and analysis of data can offer a competitive advantage. Then, in 1880, Herman Hollerith, an employee of the US Census Bureau, generated the Hollerith Tabulating Machine, which would become the father of automated computation.[229]

In the mid-1950s, Thomas H. Davenport introduced Analytics 1.0, featuring descriptive analytics and reporting data with structured data analysis. Analytics 1.0 are still used for spreadsheet analysis in Excel. In 1965, the US government released a plan for the first federal data center, aiming to store 742 million tax returns and 175 million sets of fingerprints on magnetic tape.

In the 1990s, the first mentions of "Big Data" appeared, the first one being a paper written by Cox and Ellsworth for a conference on visualization. In 2000, Lyman and

DOI 10.1515/9781547401055-009

Varian released "How Much Information?" the first comprehensive study of information quantification in computer storage terms.[230] And in 2011, McKinsey's "Big data: The next frontier for innovation, competition, and productivity" stated that the financial services and investment sector was leading the pack, with more stored data per firm than any other industry. The study also estimated that, in 2010, 7.4 exabytes (1018 bytes) of data were stored by companies and 6.8 exabytes of data were stored by consumers.[231]

Today, the term Analytics 3.0 is being used by organizations that aspire to integrate Analytics 1.0 (traditional analytics) with Analytics 2.0 (Big Data) to generate measurable business impact.

 ## How Big Data Works

Big data platforms can be thought of as a big engine, such as that of a large airplane. It is very powerful, and it craves information as fuel. Systems will feed information to the platform and can be either functional or operational. Machine logs and sensors can also feed information, as well as external sources such as web pages, social networks, and information providers.

Inside this big engine, data is captured and managed, with the objective of converting it into meaningful insights that management can use. Different big data providers will be specialized in analyzing different cases. The best ones will be able to make sense of both structured and unstructured data. For a system to work well, a good data design and architecture need to be developed. Systems that can provide meaningful insights with little human assistance will be clear winners.

A big data platform will also have a front end used by executives and analysts. This should allow them to manage the business and run a variety of scenarios.

How to Use Big Data Innovatively

The revolution of Big Data is transforming the way businesses organize, operate, and create value. Changes on this scale require effective leadership, and CEOs who capitalize on this opportunity will increase their companies' long-term success.

Customer Segmentation

Big Data is increasingly enabling businesses to empower individual consumers and find new ways to investigate existing markets. Through the use of predictive models, Big Data enables businesses to reach out to their customers and divide the population based on age, sex, location, online purchases, web clicks, social media activities, smart connected devices, and more. Simultaneously, the growing use of social media-enabled platforms allows consumers to connect with businesses and participate in customer surveys that generate useful insights on what customers need. In this way, businesses can customize their products and can run targeted marketing campaigns efficiently.

Customer Personalization and Contextualization

Businesses today are aiming to convert online shopping into a customized consumer experience through the collection and processing of Big Data. Personalization is about providing customers with an experience that is unique to them. Particularly in the retail and financial services industries, personalization is critical due to the wide range of products and services available.

Contextualization refers to providing a different experience depending on the context of the customer, which might include time of day, weather, and location. Banks, brokerage firms, and finance companies, as well as online retailers, use big data analytics to collect information about consumer preferences, purchasing behaviors, geo-locations, and any other information that can be digitally recorded. In doing so, they can identify customer interests as well as predict their current and future needs. This information is then used to provide customers with a personalized experience, helping them locate what they want, when they want it, at the best possible price. Personalization and contextualization also save customers' time and increases customer satisfaction, while saving money for businesses.

Marketing

The use of real-time data enables businesses to adopt a customer-centric approach to marketing. Big data analytics use call center data, transaction data, and customer information to determine customer preferences and needs and deliver the optimal product and/or service.

According to McKinsey, 75% of an average company's revenue is generated by its standard product line, and 30% of pricing decisions fail to deliver the best price. With a 1% price increase translating into an 8.7% increase in operating profits, assuming no loss of sales volume, optimum-pricing offers significant potential for improving a firm's profitability.[232]

According to DataMeer, Customer Analytics are the most popular use of Big Data, utilized for sales and marketing (48%), enabling marketers to employ customer acquisition strategies as well as increase revenue per customer and improve existing products. Customer Analytics are followed by Operational Analytics (21%), Fraud and

Compliance (12%), New Product and Service Innovation (10%), and Enterprise Data Warehouse Optimization (10%).[233]

Online Scoring

Although, in the past, the use of Big Data was not widespread, a number of new players now have entered the field, using Big Data technology and analytics. Online lending services have proliferated as it has become easy to enter the market, while, at the same time, the demand for such services has increased. Online scoring takes into account both traditional data, such as banking history and data from social networks and mobile operators. This offers lenders several ways to cross-check their customers before opening lines of credit.

Several companies are developing processes to rate customers using unconventional data to decide whether to grant loans. We discuss the companies in this space, including Affirm, in the "Digital Lending Innovation" chapter. Other businesses to look at are alternative credit scorers, such as Aire.io and Branch. Aire.io, based in London, is developing a new credit score system targeted at people with a thin file. It uses data from social networks, as well as self-declared information gathered in a virtual interview. Globally, over 4.5 billion people have thin files, so it is a huge market.

China is probably the main contributor to the thin file statistics. The opportunity there is huge as China's centralized database covers only 22% of the country's inhabitants. In addition to this, SMEs only receive 25% of bank-disbursed loans, providing major opportunities to non-bank lending organizations.

China is developing a Social Credit System covering people's entire lives. It will rate all citizens based on commercial, social, and credit factors that will act a bit like a Big Brother, determining what people can and cannot do. It will also include businesses. It will look at everything, including web searches and information shared in chat rooms, as well as data from their jobs, such as performance review ratings. It is expected to be fully operational in 2020.

Risk Management

Big Data technologies present significant opportunities for addressing the risk and regulation challenges in the financial services industry. Comprehensive and real-time data can improve the predictive power of risk models; it can also revolutionize response times and system effectiveness, extend the current risk coverage, and generate cost savings.

According to the Economist Intelligence Unit (EIU), retail banks are more concerned with credit risk than commercial and investment banks (53% versus 43%), and they also tend to be slightly more concerned than commercial and investment banks about market risk (28% versus 23%). On the other hand, investment banks are more concerned than retail banks about operational risk (29% versus 19%) and compliance risk (20% versus 14%).

Out of 208 risk management and compliance executives at retail banks (29%), commercial banks (43%), and investment banks (28%) in 55 countries on six continents, 42% of respondents currently integrate and query Big Data when creating risk profiles, whereas 47% of respondents plan to invest in Big Data. Regarding predictive analytics and data visualization, 41% of respondents are currently using advanced Big Data analytics and 44% plan to obtain them by 2020.

Operational risk is another key area where losses are now bigger than the ones found in credit risk. These include internal and external fraud, system failures, business disruption, and client-related issues. New tools used for applying learning from data to operational risk can become massive cost savers as well as mitigating risks.

Customer Remediation

Big Data initiatives in many firms revolve around improving customer remediation. Banks need to examine their records and review the information they have on millions of customers in order to perform know-your-customer processes. In many cases, they do not need to contact each customer to complete this as external data sources can provide the information required to meet regulations. Some companies are specializing in putting together internal and external data sources to provide a single view of customers, hence minimizing customer contact. This paves the way for a reliable 360-degree view of customers and prospects.

Big Data in the Financial Services Industry

The financial services sector implements business-driven initiatives to accelerate growth, engage customers, and achieve competitive differentiation through innovation. In fact, most banking, financial services, and insurance (BFSI) organizations are striving to adopt a fully data-driven approach to grow their businesses and enhance customer services. Since the financial crisis of 2008, financial services firms have transformed themselves, seeking to reduce their costs and capitalize on valuable insights generated by Big Data across different markets and customers. So, when used effectively, Big Data analytics can improve the predictive power of risk models and the systems' effectiveness while generating significant cost savings. A recent survey by NewVantage Partners, targeting 44 Fortune 1000 and leading firms and technology decision-makers, found that 69.6% of financial services firms view Big Data as critically important to their business success. With regard to investment,

62.5% of firms invested in Big Data in 2015, compared to 31.4% in 2013. The percentage of firms reporting an expected investment in Big Data of greater than $50 million in 2017 is 26.8%, compared to 5.4% in 2014. Finally, 37.0% of firms adopted Big Data to gain greater business insight by capitalizing on a wider variety of information and better data agility.[234]

A key challenge for financial firms is gaining a 360-degree view of their customers through a broad use of Big Data. In this context, a data-driven culture is necessary. Experts believe that big data analytics can be a game changer for financial companies given the growing interest and the increased rate of adoption of analytics. On the other hand, BFSI (banking, financial services, and insurance) companies do not possess the same level of Big Data maturity. Although new technologies are increasingly providing consumers with innovative bank alternatives and many firms manage Big Data quite efficiently, the increasing pace of business requires a faster adaptation to the new challenges. The rapid development of mobile banking and social media banking has raised the bar of customers' expectations on seamless ways to interact with their banks. This means that BFSIs are required to understand customer needs, preferences, and motivation and track client behavior in real time in order to provide the best service at any given moment. In the long term, financial companies will boost their performance and profitability while lowering their costs and sustaining a high level of customer experience.

Key Players in Big Data Analytics

In this section, we look at interesting companies that are making significant progress in Big Data analytics. We had to handpick just a few, as there are several hundred operating in this space.

cloudera

Cloudera is a Palo Alto-based Big Data company that went public in April 2017, and has a market capitalization of $2.29 billion. Cloudera has impacted enterprise data management by offering the first unified platform for Big Data—an enterprise data hub built on Apache Hadoop, an open source software platform for distributed storage and processing of very large datasets. Cloudera offers enterprises a single place for storing, processing, and analyzing all their data, empowering them to extend the value of existing investments while enabling fundamental new ways to derive value from their data.

Most big financial services institutions use Cloudera Enterprise focusing on creating valuable customer insights (building a 360-degree view of a customer), fraud detection, cyber security (using machine learning to predict crime and money laundering), and risk and compliance management (reducing costs and increasing the speed of compliance).

databricks

Databricks is a San Francisco-based company which was created by the inventors of Apache Spark, an open source engine for Big Data processing. It is well funded, having received $247 million since its foundation in 2013. Cloudera already offers a convenient way to store a lot of data, so Databricks is tackling the next problem, which is how to manage this data efficiently.

In the financial services area, it can help assess risk and predict results using hidden insights. It can also help with money laundering detection and product recommendation using a 360-degree view of the customer. Some of their customers include CapitalOne, LendUp, and Haven.

AVANT CREDIT

Founded in 2012, Avant is a Chicago-headquartered personal loan platform. They leverage Big Data analytics to make better credit decisions and provide easy and convenient loans of up to $10,000 to near-prime borrowers. Using Big Data and advanced machine-learning algorithms, AvantCredit analyzes thousands of trends and patterns in lieu of the traditional one-size-fits-all credit model to offer competitive rates on an individual basis.

They offer debt consolidation, home improvement and emergency loans between $2,000 and $35,000 for 24–60 months at a fixed rate that ranges between 9.95% and 36%. Its customer base is estimated at more than 600,000 people.[235]

The borrower needs to have a minimum credit score, show proof of steady income, and be a US resident over 18 years old. Before applying for a loan, borrowers can check the rate that applies to their case. Then, they can sign the loan contract online, and funds will be in their account by the following business day. The platform also allows electronic funds transfers for the loan installments, and there is no penalty fee for prepaying the entire amount.

Avant announced in 2018 that it would spin off its lending infrastructure tech business, with the aim to partner with banks to build savings products, credit decision making technology, and other products.

Founded in 2013, WeLab is a Hong Kong-based internet finance company that uses exclusive risk management technology to analyze Big Data and offer reliable credit services to individual borrowers in the Asian market. WeLab operates two leading online lending platforms, Wolaidai in China and WeLend in Hong Kong, seeking to offer its customers a seamless mobile lending experience. Furthermore, the company has partnerships with traditional financial institutions, which use WeLab's sophisticated credit risk management tools to use Big Data analytics and offer their customers advanced fintech solutions.

In January, WeLab raised $160 million in Series B funding from domestic and international investors, including Khazanah Nasional Berhad wealth fund, ING Bank, and state-owned Guangdong Technology Financial Group (GTFG). This was the first time that funds were raised by a Chinese fintech firm and one of the first times that an international financial institution (ING) financed a leading Chinese fintech player.[236]

In November 2017, WeLab raised $220 million in both an equity and debt financing Series B+ round with Alibaba Hong Kong Entrepreneurs Fund, the World Bank's International Finance Corporation (IFC), and Credit Suisse.[237]

Qualtrics is a Utah-based, leading survey and insight platform that supports data searches and delivers real-time insights. The platform offers customer satisfaction and employee engagement surveys, employee assessment tools, market research, video tutorials, mobile surveys, and more, and it can be used by both novices and those with experience. The platform features a user-friendly interface and innovative tools that can assist users in building new surveys and analyzing the insights gained. Advanced users can effectively customize their surveys to gain insights that will affect their decision making.

Qualtrics support a range of industries, including airline, automotive, B2B, financial services, retail, and travel and hospitality. It also offers a range of helpful resources regarding insight-driven data, including a resource library, blog, innovation exchange, and more. Qualtrics was founded in 2002.[238]

IBM **Watson**

IBM Watson is an artificially intelligent computer system that provides automated data analysis, automatic visualization, and predictive analytics. The software uses DeepQA and the Apache UIMA (Unstructured Information Management Architecture) framework to provide automated reasoning, natural language processing, knowledge representation, information retrieval, and machine learning technologies on open domain question answering.[239]

IBM Watson was launched in 2013 when IBM announced that it was going to be used as a management decision-making tool for lung treatment at the Memorial Sloan Kettering Cancer Center in New York, in conjunction with the WellPoint health insurance company. Since then, Watson's use has been expanded to grow and transform businesses through the combination of cloud-based enterprise searches, content analysis, and cognitive solutions across data insights.

The IBM-specific banking solution contains advanced predictive analytics, with both cognitive analytics and industry-specific models and customizations to those models. The solution helps fine-tune customer segmentation at a very granular level by analyzing customer transactions, spending behavior, and life events.

alteryx

Alteryx is an Irvine, California-based software company and a leader in data analytics. Alteryx's platform interface enables users to process and modularize the software development model efficiently, therefore leveraging data in a transparent way. Analytics are tied into workflows, and they can be used for marketing analytics and machine learning. Furthermore, the company has partnered with Tableau Software, Microsoft, Qlik, Amazon Web Services, Cloudera, and Experian Marketing Services, thereby offering its customers a range of financial, marketing, operational, real estate, and sales analytics. Alteryx was founded in 2010.[240]

Alteryx provides financial services institutions with deeper insights through fast data preparation and blending, easier to use analytics, and simple ways to share analytics with decision makers. They serve retail banks, providing help with product offering and servicing, capital markets, offering segmentation, and insurance, offering risk and price optimization solutions.

GoodData

Founded in 2007, GoodData is a San Francisco, California-based software company that uses Big Data analytics to offer cloud-based business intelligence solutions to a range of industries, including financial services, healthcare, hotels and casinos, media, restaurants, and retail. Through its data-driven guided analytics, GoodData enables businesses and decision makers to realign their business models and gain access to business insights. The company also customizes its analytics applications to the needs of each business to create exponential value for the company.[241]

In the financial services industry, GoodData benchmarks portfolio sales across different locations and agents to gain insights into geographical trends and drive incremental sales. They can also correlate local indicators with purchasing trends to proactively recommend portfolio products to individual agents and branches. Additionally, they can use data to improve the operational efficiency of branches.

Founded in 2010, Domo is cloud-based business management software that integrates with spreadsheets, databases, social media, and any existing cloud-based software solution. The suite offers businesses a wide variety of datasets and delivers a range of social integration features. Domo can be used by small businesses as well as large organizations, since it offers real-time data in a single dashboard that incorporates comprehensible visualizations of data and business intelligence tools.

With its headquarters in Utah, Domo combines all important metrics for banks, allowing them to see deposits over time, set notifications for new account activity, manage credit risk portfolios, and track treasury and non-interest fee income. They have a strong client base that includes Mastercard, Capco, and Lendio.[242]

What is Artificial Intelligence?

The term Artificial Intelligence (AI) is more than sixty years old, even though the term has begun to be used only in the past decade. It is defined in general terms as the use of computer systems to perform tasks that would normally require human intelligence or cognition. This can include recognizing patterns, predicting outcomes clouded by uncertainty, and making difficult decisions.

Over the past years, AI has moved from theory to implementation. A new approach has been developed called deep learning, which uses big amounts of data to identify patterns and make predictions for questions such as: "What language is spoken in an audio?", "Is it a man or a woman in this photo?", "How is a person feeling based on their tone of voice and word choice?". In some way, it imitates the workings of the human brain. Because computers can process almost unlimited amounts of data, they can outperform humans at this job. This has already been demonstrated by computers beating champions at Chess and Go and identifying certain types of cancer in MRI scans. Some people describe this as a new type of electricity, and now people are asking themselves where these tools can be applied next.

Some people like to think of AI.in different stages. In stage one—machine learning—big data models are directed by users. Products such as digital bots, as well as voice assistants such as Alexa and Siri use this type of AI. In the second stage—machine intelligence—an advanced network is used to build models from custom data. This is the stage we are currently at. The final stage is machine consciousness, when machines get the ability to sense and respond to the world, decide where to go, and interact with objects and other machines. This is the case of autonomous vehicles.

Market Size

According to PwC, AI innovations in coming years will contribute 14% to worldwide GDP in 2030. A good portion of this would be generated by replacing human labor, so there will be job challenges for governments to deal with. In banking, former Citigroup chief Vikram Pandit predicted that 30% of banking jobs would be replaced by robots in the next five years. Mizuho Financial Group aim to replace one-third of their workforce using robots by 2027.

International Data Corporation forecasts that spending on AI will grow from $12 billion in 2017 to $57.6 billion by 2021. Deloitte Global predicts that AI implementations will double from 2017 to 2018, and double again by 2020.

Artificial Intelligence in the Financial Services Industry

Several big banks have started investing in artificial intelligence, and these investments vary in size from small proof of concepts to serious investments of more than $10 million. JP Morgan has introduced a contract intelligence system of machine learning to analyze legal documents and extract important data points and clauses. This system could save 360,000 hours of manual review annually. They have also developed an engine for identifying customers that are best positioned for follow-on equity offerings, and a virtual assistant for dealing with internal service tickets from their employees, which can add up to two million tickets annually.

Wells Fargo has a Facebook chatbot that can provide customers their balances and reset passwords.

Bank of America has a virtual assistant called Erica. It can perform day-to-day transactions, provide smart recommendations and anticipate financial needs of customers.

CitiBank has invested in Feedzai, a data science company that works in realtime to identify fraud using big data and machine learning.

Uses of AI in financial services

Chatbots
Customers can interact with their banks, get their queries answered, and solve problems without any human interaction. This is based on natural language processing combined with biometrics recognition for authentication.

Profiling and targeting customers
Customers can be treated as individuals, by personalizing their communications, recommendations and decisions. This is based on big data analysis of unstructured data and machine learning.

Optimizing processes
Middle office and back end processes that are repetitive and add little value could be handled by AI bots. This can include clearing, settlement, and operational processes. By scanning documents, these could then be analyzed and processed. By using robotic process automation, machine learning and image recognition, documents can be interpreted and processed based on procedures and regulations. Referrals to humans would be made in special cases.

Spotting patterns
AI can identify patterns in transactions, which can indicate the occurrence of fraud or money laundering. Opportunities and risks can be found in trading patterns that can lead to investment opportunities. This is enabled by machine learning, parsing big loads of unstructured data.

Companies Specialized in AI for Financial Services

There is a long list of companies that claim to be focused on artificial intelligence, and we cover many in different chapters. In this section we include themes and example companies that are innovating in the field.

–   RegTech AI companies improve compliance workflows by detecting abnormal financial behavior. Examples include Trifacta and DataRobot.
–   Financial AI companies focus on improving accounting, financial reporting and expense processing. Examples include Appzen and Fyle.
–   All purpose AI companies can deal with a varied set of use cases using semantic and natural language applications. Examples include Ayasdi and CognitiveScale.
–   Collections AI companies focus on personalizing and automating communications so that collecting debt becomes more efficient. Examples include CollectAI and TrueAccord.
–   Personal finance management AI companies help customers manage their money better by analyzing their spending and presenting suggestions. Examples include ClarityMoney and Penny.
–   Asset management AI companies utilize algorithms to drive trading and investment tactics. Examples include Alpaca and Alpine Data.
–   Market research AI companies focus on researching customer trends and sentiment in order to produce value out of public social media data and content available online. Examples include AlphaSense and Dataminr.

The Future in a Flash

The use of Big Data and artificial intelligence is expected to become key for competition, fostering innovation and growth. The growing volume and detail of information gathered by enterprises, combined with the rise of social media and the internet of things, is expected to further fuel the exponential growth of these technologies over the coming years.

As data continues to multiply, it is expected that tools to analyze data will improve, and intelligence will come standard with business analytics software such as Business Objects or SAS. It is also expected that real-time insights will improve their quality, and more and more use cases will emerge.

Monetization of data will also become a profitable area. Banks have a plethora of information on customers, and new technologies will allow them to strike the right balance between valuable insights and anonymization.

Managing data is always complex, and we can expect more regulations to be introduced to ensure that it is treated properly. Having an experienced Chief Information Officer (CIO) leading the way will certainly help, so we can expect more companies to create positions of this type.

Artificial intelligence is meant to become as common as smart phones have in a very short period of time. Future generations will grow with it and expect it, as we nowadays expect to have electricity and household appliances such as a fridge or an oven at home. Robots will not take over the world, but they will serve us in ways that we are yet to imagine.

Chapter 10
The Internet of Things

The Internet of Things in a Flash

The "internet of things" (IoT) is fast gaining recognition in many industries. In the financial services industry in particular, which has long capitalized on the intangible, the IoT offers great opportunities for transforming businesses, and IoT applications have great potential. Although there is not one single definition of IoT, put simply it is a suite of technologies and applications allowing devices with embedded sensors to be connected to the internet and exchange data using the same Internet Protocol (IP). Such devices may be electronics, software, pacemakers, kitchen appliances, and cars.

Given its vast potential, the internet of things has a wide variety of uses in a broad range of industries. These include retail, manufacturing, health, hospitality, waste management, and, of course, financial services. These connected devices are used throughout the physical world, seeking to improve quality of life as well as making industries more productive. The IoT network is building not only thing-to-thing relationships but also people-to-thing relationships.

What Drives the Growth of IoT?

According to Gartner, the internet of things will explode by 2020, with more than 26 billion connected devices.[243] Other reports suggest that there will be 34 billion connected devices by 2020, of which 24 billion will be IoT devices, and 10 billion will be smartphones, tablets, and other traditional computing services.[244] Businesses have been the first to adopt the IoT, implementing it to lower their operating costs and improve their productivity. This has enabled them to expand into new markets or develop new product lines. Simultaneously, consumers are adopting IoT technologies to improve their quality of life, and governments are increasingly using the IoT to reduce spending. We discuss the drivers of growth for the IoT below.

Urbanization

Urbanization is a key driver of IoT growth. As cities become more populated, consumer spending increases. For example, in Southeast Asia alone, there are 26 cities with over one million residents, and an estimated 49.7% of the region's total population is expected to be living in urban areas by 2025.[245] The world's most densely populated cities can be found in this region such as Tokyo-Yokohama (37.8m), Jakarta (31.3m), Delhi (27.8m), and Seoul (23.6m).[246] Regarding population distribution by

DOI 10.1515/9781547401055-010

continent, Asia leads with 56.6%, followed by North America, 12.9%, Africa, 10.7%, and Europe, 10.2%, with South America accounting for 8.1% and Oceania 1.4%.[247]

The growth of cities requires the development of efficiencies and strategies for them to remain viable. The IoT can make cities more sustainable and adaptable. Placing devices on objects can help public security and safety departments, transportation departments, and can be a valuable aid in managing infrastructure.

The IoT can become very handy when managing scarce resources—mainly water, power, natural gas, food, and healthcare. By using models that optimize the utilization of these resources, a city can improve its quality of life.

Smartphone Penetration Growth

By 2020, smartphone penetration is expected to reach 2.87 billion users, an increase of 54.3% from 1.86 billion users in 2015.[248] The highest smartphone penetration is in United Arab Emirates, where it is 80% of a total population of 9 million.[249] In terms of absolute numbers, China, India, US, Russia and Brazil are the countries with the highest amount of users, and their penetration percentages are 55%, 28%, 77%, 64%, and 41% respectively. Arguably, the IoT has an even higher potential for growth in smaller hubs, that is, fast-developing countries, that are leaders in smartphone penetration and teledensity.

Smartphone growth drives the internet of things. These devices have three-axis accelerometers, gyroscopes, magnetometers, compasses, and barometers embedded. Investment in smartphones ensures that the quality of these components improves with every release, and the IoT benefits from this. The smartphone is the logical remote control for all connected devices, storing data from fitness trackers, and managing intelligent homes, as well as other uses.

Rising Demand for Connected Devices

Connected devices are being invented at a very fast pace, and this drives consumer demand. An estimated compound annual growth rate (CAGR) of more than 24% until 2021 is expected as a result of increasing smartphone and Internet use, industrial IoT adoption and smart city projects across the world.[250] Government IoT initiatives and the growing number of connected devices that generate and exchange a greater amount of data also explain much of the estimated growth. Internet penetration of 54.6% is expected by 2020.[251]

Increasing Need for Inventory Management

Inventory management is important for businesses because it allows them to control their ordering and storage costs and their use of products. The real-time tracking of inventory using radio-frequency identification (RFID), which uses the IoT, is the next big thing in inventory management. In fact, applications can help businesses track their products in real time by recognizing the barcode label of the product and using the embedded GPS location. Organizations can instantly check their product location and inventory levels and forecast demand. An estimated $13.2 billion RFID tags are expected to exist by 2020.[252]

Cloud-Based Platform Growth

More and more businesses, governments, and consumers are becoming connected, or expect things to be connected. In this context, cloud-based platforms gain a competitive edge. An estimated total spending of $173 billion on public cloud infrastructure is expected by 2026, up 355% from $38 billion in 2016.[253] Additionally, Amazon Web Services (AWS) turned over $5.44 billion in Q1 2018,[254] whereas Microsoft's cloud-based products such as CRM, Azure, and Office365 generated $6 billion in the same period.[255]

The Impact of IoT on Businesses

Firms are producing smarter and more technologically advanced products. This impacts IoT on businesses in several ways. Perhaps the most visible effect is the business landscape itself, as many industries are adjusting or have already adjusted to the new norms. The IoT comes with mainstream technology and, from this point of view, some industries may not be able to keep up with the new developments, while some may simply follow the lead of others.

The logistics industry is one of the first areas expected to face a lower demand for their services due to the IoT automation. The growth of the internet of things and the proliferation of social networks, mobile operators, and "smart" devices have changed business models.

Real-Time Data

Digitization of information as well as instant exchanging and reporting of data between interconnected devices facilitates control and optimizes processes. Companies are now able to check their inventory levels and report inefficiencies and will know if there is a shortage or a surplus of a product. In fact, the IoT shifts waste management to a new level by introducing real-time control, thereby lowering companies' costs dramatically.

Remote Access

As the IoT becomes increasingly popular and a growing number of businesses start capitalizing on the vast network, cloud-based software will make it easier to manage a production line or an entire business remotely, leading to faster processing. For example, a gas company needing to perform regular checks on its tanks and spending enormous amounts of money on travel and wasting hours sitting in traffic can save on commuting and effectively control business costs. Ultimately, this could mean higher profits due to lower operating costs and improved return on assets (ROA).

Increased Productivity

The IoT allows a business to be run remotely and more productively. In this context, real-time data, remote access, and faster processing are likely to increase the productivity of businesses using the IoT. Although there is a cost for shifting from the tangible to intangible, mostly related to the upgrade of the business' devices, eventually, the shift will pay off with more efficiently produced products and services.

The IoT in Categories

There are roughly nine categories in which companies are developing IoT:
1. The wearable category captures any device that is attached to the body—these are mostly fitness trackers and smartwatches, although it includes smart clothes and infant trackers such as smart socks
2. The connected home category is about digitizing the home—lights, sound systems, heating, opening doors, and even smart doorbells
3. The infrastructure category looks at providing the right networks and sensors so that devices can work properly
4. The healthcare category deals with medical instruments such as sugar level trackers, pacemakers, and thermometers
5. The utilities category deals with technology to track the use of electricity, gas, and water to optimize usage
6. The industrial category looks at uses for the IoT in industries where expensive assets are required, such as mining or agriculture

7. The retail category focuses on creating more interactive shopping experiences, using connected sensors and mobile apps
8. The drone category aims at using drones to become more autonomous and helps to capture data for construction and other projects
9. The automobile category uses IoT to transform the car insurance market and improve driving habits

Combining IoT and Blockchain

IoT is often associated with blockchain. Blockchain is a distributed ledger discussed in detail in the "Blockchain and Distributed Ledgers" chapter; but, in essence, it is an immutable database that is hosted through the internet. Blockchain can expand the use of cryptographic data in the IoT space, making customer information more secure and transactions faster. Businesses can also capitalize on the digitization of IoT to manage complexity and lower costs using blockchain, which has a proven record of virtual, cost-effective, decentralized networks. In doing so, they are more likely to build trust in customer relationships, eliminate potential points of failure, and ensure more flexible and secure transactions.

One concrete application for combining these technologies is tracking a history of unique devices and the interaction with others, which could help with auditing and insurance purposes. Another is empowering smart devices to become independent agents that perform their own transactions. A typical example is a vending machine managing its stock and reordering, or a smart car that can identify when it needs maintenance, schedule it, drive to the garage, pay for it, and record its inspection. Commonwealth Bank of Australia, Wells Fargo, and Brighann Cotton have made the first global trade transactions combining the IoT and blockchain technology. In the sharing economy of the future, the integration of IoT and blockchain may enable the full automation of day-to-day operations.

The IoT in Financial Services

The internet of things will transform the financial industry in an unprecedented way. Today's chief financial officers (CFOs) are faced with non-financial responsibilities, especially technology-related, including IoT. A survey by McKinsey showed that less than 33% of CFOs questioned believe that there is a growing need to digitize their businesses and be more competitive.[256] Simultaneously, data analysts expect an added economic value of between $300 billion and $15 trillion by 2020.[257] As the financial services industry becomes more active in the IoT, the benefits derived from it will increase. Remotely-accessed, comprehensive data embedded into connected devices is used in insurance, peer-to-peer lending, and real estate, providing great examples of an industry that is being renewed.

Insurance

Insurance companies are adopting the IoT to integrate policies, premiums, and customers into a comprehensive, readily accessible database, which can lower coverage costs. For instance, in auto insurance, the IoT is employed in calculating the actual mileage covered and the driving behavior of the policyholder through a tracking device. In home insurance, smart embedded devices can detect fire, water leaks, or high levels of carbon monoxide, thereby lowering insurance premiums as the risk undertaken by the insurer will be lower. In healthcare, large companies like Apple or Samsung are tracking the health of individuals through sophisticated monitoring devices, and Vitality offers rewards based on the level of activity undertaken by policyholders. In claims, IoT drives evolution toward active loss prevention, for instance, sensors that can monitor fire, wind and water damage. The integration of IoT in the insurance sector and the increasing number of fintech start-ups is expected to further drive the growth in this sector in new areas including agriculture insurance, car insurance, and health insurance.

Real Estate

Fintech start-ups are employing the internet of things to create new opportunities in commercial real estate. With IoT technology, start-ups collect data about repair, maintenance, and energy use, thereby being able to better assess the value of a property. Also, through occupancy sensors, energy costs can be regulated, and building maintenance can be lowered by up to 30%, especially in industrial zone areas. Should this data go public, it could create a trading market, providing investors with higher transparency and accuracy when bidding. This means the involvement of IoT in real estate could also revolutionize real-time bidding markets.

Other use cases for IoT include determining appropriate places for branches and ATMs, using sensors to track foot traffic, and personalizing services in branches by identifying customers through sensors and wearable devices.

O2O and IoT in Fintech

E-commerce giants such as Alibaba and Amazon worked really hard to disrupt the retail industry. However, after a while, they realized that operating exclusively online is not feasible for long-term dominance. Amazon has started opening 2,000 Amazon

Fresh stores, and Alibaba is investing more than $300 million in a discount supermarket in China.

Online-to-offline (O2O) commerce is a commonly used business strategy seeking to shift prospective customers from online stores to brick-and-mortar businesses. With the correct software and by operating in the IoT network, O2O identifies prospective customers online through internet advertising and email marketing campaigns and shifts them to the offline business. Hence, customers, who are enticed into viewing the actual product, visit the online store, select the product they want and are directed to a brick-and-mortar store, where they make the actual purchase. Companies with both an online and offline presence employ the O2O business strategy as a means to cross-sell.

In the fintech industry, O2O is becoming increasingly popular. As identified, the IoT related statistics are mostly favorable for Southeast Asia due to large populations, swift urbanization, and high smartphone penetration growth. China, Indonesia, Singapore, and Seoul have become fintech hubs. In actual figures, fintech growth in Asia reached $4.5 billion in investments in 2015 and is expected to attract more investment with a focus on new technologies like the internet of things.[258]

China is a leader in O2O due to its large population and the openness to using technology. Unlike the UK and the US markets that are mostly focused on click-and-collect services, the O2O market in China includes on-demand services, daily deal sites, and click-and-collect services. Chinese consumers can use Kuaidi's Zhuan Che taxi app and get a 60% discount on their taxi ride or use 58 Daojia's home services to earn a rebate. Ping An's Good Doctor app has had more than 70 million downloads and allows for diagnosis and support, appointment booking, and consultations with doctors using SMS, pictures and video. Dmall app turns supermarkets into warehouses, where customers can browse from their phone, order, and get their deliveries within one hour within a 2 km radius.

This revolution is enabled by WeChat and Alipay, as their apps include mobile payment systems, QR codes and Instant Messaging.

Hence, the O2O market in China has gone beyond online grocery shopping, including travel, transportation, laundry services, or food delivery. Although it is hard to accurately assess the size and growth of China's O2O market, statistics show an increase of 35% in O2O sales and services in 2015 with a projected growth of 28% in 2016 and over 20% by 2018.[259]

Challenges Faced by the IoT

Although the internet of things presents enormous opportunities, especially in the banking, insurance, and healthcare sectors, there are challenges that need to be addressed.

High-Frequency Trading

Algorithmic and high-frequency trading (HFT) can be further automated with the use of the IoT. By eliminating human involvement and allowing the more comprehensive use of real-time algorithmic data, high-frequency trading can be swifter and more accurate. However, although the entire system will become more efficient, HFT can push the markets up technically based on the momentum that global economic and political events create. Hence, although algorithms do not account for real-world events, they follow the noise generated by these events, creating an unprecedented barrage of trades, which, combined with the IoT, can be impossible to catch up with. Ultimately, IoT data, if not handled properly, may create a bubble.

Data Management

Another major challenge that any business will face is the management of the enormous amount of IoT-generated data. Failing data management, especially in the financial sector, which requires integrity and careful processing, may cause disruption of the stream of information. Also, the validity of data is at stake, considering that the financial sector is highly regulated and, as such, each case requires a careful approach. Distributed ledgers and Big Data might help to tackle this challenge.

Successful IoT Use Cases in the Financial Sector

The financial sector has been struggling to integrate innovative solutions into their services, seeking to improve customer service and work innovation into their customer-centric approach. Following the 2008 financial crisis, large financial institutions, as well as smaller commercial banks and insurers, are experimenting with new technologies. The IoT, with its vast potential, paves the way for the successful integration of technology into the financial sector, lowering risks and enhancing customer value.

Ingenico Group, a global leader in seamless payments, and Intel Technology joined forces in April 2016 to bring secure payments for the IoT. The collaboration required the joint development of a mobile tablet that will support EuroPay, MasterCard, and Visa (EMV) payments as well as NFC (Near Field Communication) payments, thereby preventing credit card fraud.

Groceries by Mastercard is an app that enables consumers to do their grocery shopping using IoT. The application connects consumers to leading grocery stores through the WiFi-enabled touch screen of the Samsung Family Hub Refrigerator, allowing them to manage their grocery shopping and select their favorite brands. The app is developed by Mastercard in cooperation with Samsung and e-commerce platforms FreshDirect or ShopRite and is expected to revolutionize grocery shopping, allowing for better control of household finances.

Mastercard Start Path

Start Path Global brings together start-ups from all over the world, allowing them to gain access to Mastercard's network and enter new markets. The program requires physical and virtual engagement, and it looks for start-ups in several sectors, including banking, logistics, wearables, and more.

VISA

Visa Mobile Location Confirmation is an IoT app developed by Visa, which instantly records credit card transactions and compares them with the real location of the cardholder. The app eliminates the risk of credit card fraud and reduces the possibility of cards being declined while traveling. The IoT app uses mobile geo-location data in real time in collaboration with Finsphere Corporation, a leading company in geospatial analysis.

A Alfa·Bank

Alfa Activity is an IoT app launched by Alfa Bank, a leading Russian bank in cooperation with 42 Agency, a marketing consultancy and advertising agency in Moscow. The app allows customers of Alfa Bank's retail branches to connect their online accounts to tracker devices. The bank rewards customers who work out with higher interest rates on their savings accounts. The app runs through Fitbit, Jawbone Up, and RunKeeper platforms.

The Future in a Flash

The IoT could be the next industrial revolution. It is clearly here to stay, and as new generations are born, they will take to it as naturally as they do to mobile phones. Devices will spread everywhere and will need management and high security. Interacting with robots and connected machines will become normal. They will be able to manage our profiles and check our identities. This means that less manual work will be required and that processes will be increasingly efficient. Work that humans do will become more high value as we live in a world with a higher efficiency.

Chapter 11
Blockchain and Distributed Ledgers

Blockchain and Distributed Ledgers in a Flash

Blockchain is seen as the next revolution to happen around the world, not only for financial services but overall. We will go back to basics to understand what the components of blockchain technology are and how they work. The technology promises to be used in several ways in our daily lives, for example, the creation of smart contracts, improvement of payments, maintenance of medical records, and digitizing our identities.

Cryptocurrency is one of the applications of blockchain. This new form of currency has the potential to make payments cheaper and eliminate the need for fiat (physical or paper) money. We will also look at the story of bitcoin, the most popular cryptocurrency, and Ethereum, the second most important one.

About Distributed Ledgers

In recent decades, we have seen how banks can take wrong turns. Trust in investment groups has been proven to be prone to exploitation. As a result, people have been looking for a system of transacting money that is fraud-proof.

A disruptive technology that could help solve many of the financial system's current problems is the Distributed Ledger. One of the reasons why banks get into trouble is lack of trust in each other, since trust is vital to the success of financial transactions. Distributed ledgers allow people to trust each other unreservedly.

Distributed ledgers are a type of database. Their key features are that they hold data that has been replicated and shared across multiple sites, countries, or institutions. This data has been stored with consensus, meaning that there is no doubt about its authenticity, and it is typically public. Instead of grouping transactions into a block, records are stored consecutively in a continuous ledger, and new transactions can only be added after a quorum has been reached by participants.

The use of distributed ledgers is great for real-time, secure data sharing. There are different types of distributed ledgers, and the main difference is the way in which consensus is achieved. Examples of distributed ledgers are Ripple, MultiChain, and the Hyperledger project.

Ledgers can be either public or private. Public ledgers allow anyone to contribute data, and all participants can see an identical copy of the ledger. This is the case with bitcoin, a database that goes against censorship. Private ledgers allow the distribution of identical copies of the ledger, but only to a limited number of participants. This is the type of ledger that banks are considering when investing in the technology.

DOI 10.1515/9781547401055-011

What Is Blockchain?

A blockchain is one type of data structure that can provide consensus and security when sharing data. It is the most secure database model upon which financial transactions in the digital world can be built.

The common notion about traditional databases is that they are stored in a single server with that server entrusted to manage that database. In a blockchain database, however, there is a decentralized system and there are many interdependent computers involved in managing the database. This makes it virtually impossible to hack the database because no single computer is trusted.

However, the immutability of blockchain-based currencies has been called into question after Ethereum was attacked on June 17, 2016. The hacking began at around 4 a.m. when someone found a way to use bugs in the code to withdraw money from the decentralized autonomous organization (DAO). In less than four hours, the hacker had withdrawn $45 million, which resulted in a 40% drop in the price of Ether and 70% in the DAO token.

In principle, distributed ledgers are inherently harder to attack because a cyberattack would have to attack all the multiple shared copies of the same database simultaneously to be successful. This is not to say that distributed ledger technologies are invulnerable to cyberattack because if someone can find a way to 'legitimately' modify one copy, they can modify all the multiple copies of the ledger.

Blockchain systems are typically comprised of two major components. These two components are a peer-to-peer network and a database.

Regarding the network, blockchain compromises a group of computers connected through a communication model known as peer-to-peer network. This is the mechanism by which computers communicate new changes to that database.

The second major component of the blockchain system is the database itself. The database is an accumulation of the transaction history. The system allows for transactions to be recorded in the order in which they occur.

The Components of Blockchain

Let's take a more detailed look at these components.

A peer-to-peer network is a network consisting of many computers which are called "nodes." These networks of nodes simply connect to each other. There is no limit on how many nodes are allowed to connect within a network. In fact, today there are networks with thousands of nodes connected in a chain, and the total number either climbs or falls on a daily basis.

Having this number of nodes interconnected means there is no single point of failure, so a failure in a transaction cannot be caused by one sole computer. No single node in the network can hack the database or sensor information in the database because all of the other nodes could simply propagate the information in the database.

When a new message appears, it could be sent to any of the nodes, and it does not really matter which particular node it is. The message is usually sent to many nodes to start with and is difficult to trace. When the nodes get the message, they send it on to all of their neighboring nodes, and so on. The message will then propagate rapidly throughout the entire network, which is how a peer-to-peer network works in a blockchain.

These nodes are located in various places, and messages appear in several places at once, making it impossible to tell exactly where the message came from. In this manner, the transaction is free from censorship.

Now let's dissect what is inside the database, the other component of blockchain. The database is a set of historical transactions. These transactions are additions to the database.

Some people might ask, if a database is a history of transactions and there is an existing web of databases, where does the transaction history begin? The first block of a blockchain is called "Genesis" block, which is basically empty. People begin submitting transactions to allow modifications to the Genesis state.

Someone carries out a transaction and propagates it through the network. It is very difficult to tell who made the transaction due to peer-to-peer network technology. That transaction or message will be added to the previous transactions that have been undertaken.

As transactions accumulate, we begin to create blocks of transactions. Transactions in each block are grouped together, creating a consensus of the order in which those transactions occurred. In the same manner, when a new block is added to the network, it connects to the previous block. To secure these transactions, a cryptographic signature is embedded at the end of the block.

A cryptographic signature is very important in a blockchain system. Several properties of the cryptographic signature secure the database, and the signature is what establishes a link to the previous block. The first block establishes a link to the Genesis block. All subsequent blocks, through cryptographic signatures, link to the block that preceded them. The signature essentially enables these blocks to create a chain.

How reliable is the cryptographic signature? It is a mathematical technique used to validate the authenticity of a message. If someone tried to change the information in the transaction history within a block, the signature would become invalid. When it is no longer valid, it sends signals to every node in the network letting them know that someone tried to interfere with or make alterations to that particular block.

When there are already a number of blocks in the network, and someone goes back into the history and makes changes to the old transactions or directly alters the Genesis block, the signatures on all blocks will be deemed invalid.

Simply put, the blockchain system is a collection of unchangeable, permanent records of changes to the database.

Top Cryptocurrencies

Money is one of the basic pillars of society. It is the lifeblood of the economy. It exists to facilitate trade, and through the centuries trade has become complex. Trade occurs between and among peoples, companies, and across borders. A record of transactions is kept in a ledger, and information in a ledger is often isolated and closed to the public.

This is why we need third parties or middlemen such as banks, governments, paper money, and accountants to facilitate our transactions.

With the advent of digital technologies, physical cash will be used much less. The essence of cryptocurrency is to digitize the transfer of money. The underlying technology behind cryptocurrencies is blockchain. With blockchain, networks of computers maintain collective bookkeeping on the cloud.

A cryptocurrency is a medium of exchange. This is designed for exchanging digital information. The process by which exchange of information occurs is made possible by the principle of cryptography.

Cryptography is used to secure the transactions. Moreover, it is also a tool to control the creation of new coins. The first cryptocurrency to be created was bitcoin, way back in 2009. Two years later, the first alternative coin to bitcoin was created, Namecoin. It was created for the purpose of forming the decentralized Domain Name Service (DNS) and making censorship a lot harder. As of July 2016, there were more than 700 cryptocurrencies available for online transactions.[260]

Digital currencies are currently not bound by the laws, rules, and regulations that regular bill-and-coin (fiat) currencies are directly linked to. The lack of governance is a problem as it can allow terrorists and money launderers to transact. Cryptocurrencies, like any other assets, may rise and fall quickly in price, which makes them highly volatile and risky.

In this section, we look at some of the top cryptocurrencies in circulation.

This is the cryptocurrency that started it all. It was first defined in a paper in 2008 and then released in 2009 by Satoshi Nakamoto. Satoshi Nakamoto is actually not a real person, but an online profile, whose physical identity is unconfirmed. The coins are created or 'mined' by solving complex mathematical problems through the use of computer power.

Bitcoin breaks new ground in the way transactions can be conducted. It was created to provide an alternative to the banking system. It is an open accounting system that allows computer networks globally to track ownership of digital tokens, bitcoin, as part of purchasing.

Despite Nakamoto's cryptic online presence, his creation has been widely recognized among programmers and developers around the world. The first known transaction with bitcoin took place in October 2010. A resident of Florida offered 10,000 bitcoins to anyone who would order him a pizza. Someone living in London took him up on the offer and made a long-distance phone call to Papa John's. Today, the amount paid for that pizza has grown to about $5 million.

Bitcoin needed to be more widely accessible for it to thrive and gain more market capitalization. This is because, unlike physical currency, the value of a cryptocurrency is determined by its utility or adoption by merchants and other users. Initially, the currency was traded in forums. Slowly, other organizations such as Wikileaks started accepting donations and payments in the currency.

The first bitcoin exchange was Mt. Gox in Tokyo. By November 2010, the total value of bitcoin was already $4 million. The exchange rate had risen to 50 cents (US) a coin. Bitcoin's value continued to climb, and by February 2011, it was already on par with the US dollar. This gave rise to more users and speculators coming in and investing in bitcoin.

The Mt. Gox system was hacked in 2011, driving the price of bitcoin downward—significantly. However, in 2012, after suffering from stagnation, hacks, and online theft, bitcoin managed to claw its way up again. As of mid-February 2017, bitcoin has the biggest market cap, at around $213 billion.[261] Its price surged by more than 900% in 2017.[262] By December 2017, the price of bitcoin reached an all-time high of $19,783.06. In 2018, the price has gone done by around $6,500, even though it is still highly volatile.

There used to be several players operating within the bitcoin ecosystem that provided wallets, exchanges, and payment processors. There are now platforms that provide a full suite of services, including insurance on payments. Top platforms are Coinbase, Xapo, Circle, and itBit.

This cryptocurrency is similar to bitcoin, but it allows for decentralized organizations to be built on top of the blockchain, and for smart contracts to be executed automatically when certain events have happened. Ethereum blockchain was founded by Vitalik Buterin and launched in July 2015. Vitalik Buterin is a former bitcoin miner. He founded Ethereum to promote and support decentralized tools and apps. Ethereum houses Ether, its cryptocurrency. The platform executes peer-to-peer "smart contracts"

to make automated transactions over its blockchain. This means that by using its built-in algorithms, users can transfer Ether over the blockchain to other users.

Smart contracts written in code make Ethereum more than just a distributed ledger. Ethereum allows developers to create projects powered by smart contracts on the Ethereum blockchain. The most notable Ethereum project was the decentralized autonomous organization or DAO.

The DAO was a leaderless organization, written in open source, that consisted of contracts saved into the Ethereum database. By 2016, the DAO had collected $150 million worth of contracts in Ether. However, an attack in June meant a loss of 3.6 million Ethers, which equated to a loss of $50 million.

Following the attack, the Ethereum community held a vote. The majority of participants were in consensus to change Ethereum's code to get the stolen funds back. However, a minority of users disagreed with this. The minority asserted that to provide a sound history, a blockchain has to be free from tampering. So they continued to mine the old version of the blockchain. This is how the platform was split into two: Ethereum (ETH) and Ethereum Classic (ETC). Ethereum Classic is a continuation of the original Ethereum blockchain; its history is untampered with and free from external interference. Ethereum (ETH), by contrast, is a blockchain that took action to restore funds to their owners. This is the blockchain that moved those funds to another address.

In January 2018, the market capitalization of Ethereum was standing above $124 billion, 2017 was a fantastic year for the cryptocurrency, and the value of the currency grew from $1 to more than $700. By October 2018, the price of Ethereum had gone under $200 and its market capitalization was just over $20 billion.

The value of Ethereum has been great for Initial Coin Offerings (ICOs), as the platform allows for the establishment of smart contracts, which have been thoroughly used by crypto-entrepreneurs.

ripple

Released in 2012, Ripple is a real-time gross settlement system, a currency exchange and remittance network. A few banks, such as Santander, have integrated the system into their operations. As of October 2018, its market capitalization was $18 billion. Ripple is attractive for investors as big financial institutions are committed to using it.

BitcoinCash

Bitcoin Cash is a hard fork of bitcoin. It allows an increase in the number of transactions its ledger can process. Everybody that had bitcoins received one bitcoin cash token at the time of the fork. The market capitalization of this currency stood at $7.6 billion in October 2018.

EOS, by block.one, is a blockchain-based, decentralized operating system, designed to support commercial-scale decentralized applications by providing all of the necessary core functionality. It is based on a white paper published in 2017, and released as open source in June 2018. It operates as a smart contract platform. Its ICO raised over $4 billion. Its market capitalization in October 2018 was $4.8 billion.

Released by former Google employee Charles Lee in October 2011, Litecoin was created as an alternative to bitcoin, though it integrates to bitcoin APIs. Its benefit is faster transaction confirmation that bitcoin. In October 2018, Litecoin was capped at roughly $3 billion.

STELLAR

Stellar is an open source, decentralized protocol for digital currency to fiat currency payments which allows cross border transactions between different currencies. It has been used by reputable companies such as IBM, Deloitte, and Stripe. It was started by Jed McCaleb, the founder of Mt Gox. Its market capitalization in October 2018 was $4.4 billion.

Cryptocurrency Wallets

In the physical world, paper money is stored in a wallet. In the digital world, cryptocurrencies are stored in a "client." Cryptocurrency wallets allow digital money to be stored, giving users control to move money to anyone anywhere. An electronic wallet comes with security features to keep digital money secure.

A cryptocurrency wallet can be kept in several places. It can be installed on any device such as a laptop, a desktop or a mobile phone. In case the user loses the device on which their wallet is kept, the password of the wallet can be backed up and saved on a separate memory device.

There are also online cryptocurrency wallets where users can register and create an account and put money in them. The advantage of online wallets is that users can always access their money anywhere and from other devices.

Some of the top cryptocurrency wallets include Mycelium, HolyTransaction, Cryptonator, and Jaxx.

In terms of physical wallets—devices that look like USB sticks—there are two that are the leading ones to store your crypto offline. These are Trezor and Ledger. They provide an extra level of security, as tokens will be safe even if an exchange gets hacked.

How Blockchain Will Impact Financial Services

Blockchain promises to democratize the global financial system, which means that everyone with mobile devices will be given equal access. Financial institutions should realize the significance of blockchain in the financial industry.

As the technology evolves, financial authorities will end up trembling at the enormous impact of blockchain in every facet of daily life. Truly empowering, blockchain could eventually render traditional methodologies of carrying out transactions obsolete.

Whether it is the trading of assets, values, shares, options, or any derivatives, this technology may create a more efficient and flexible financial system. It may also help prevent depressions.

Common inefficiencies faced by current financial systems will be addressed with blockchain. For example, a lot of redundancy and mistakes in post-trade settlements will be removed. Not only will it save huge amounts of money paid to trusted third parties, but it will also help to make the global financial system more efficient.

The ultimate disruption will not come from blockchain alone, but from a combination of different blockchains (e.g., identification blockchain, security blockchain) with other technologies, such as APIs.

Investment in Blockchain

In the report released in August 2016 by World Economic Forum (WEF) entitled "The future of financial infrastructure," WEF says that awareness of blockchain technology has grown rapidly, although significant hurdles remain.[263] In the same report, it states that over US$1.4 billion has been invested in blockchain technology over the past three years. It has also been discovered that 90 central banks are engaged in distributed ledger technology discussions worldwide, and around 80% of banks are predicted to initiate distributed ledger technology projects by 2017.

Currently, the banking sector has been actively engaged in the opportunities created by blockchain. It is unsurprising that the banks are putting their resources into blockchain because they will have to adopt major changes in the way financial services are delivered in the future.

The blockchain market is expected to grow from $200 million invested in $2017 to $16 billion in 2024, according to Global Market Insights. In 2017, blockchain related companies raised more than $2 billion through over 250 ICOs globally.

Use Cases for Blockchain

Blockchain allows for many uses. Through blockchain, our ability as end-consumers to make transactions is being taken from the physical world to the digital world. This revolutionary system will solve inefficiencies in various industries. Below are some of the first use cases currently being worked on.

Smart Contracts

Standard paper contracts are characterized by their legal wording and rely on third parties for enforcement; and, in the case of problems, on the public judicial system. Smart contracts use a computer code that has been programmed to allow facilitation, execution, and enforcement of agreements using blockchain. Smart contracts can eliminate the need for middlemen, as they can be automated and self-executing. By programming certain conditions, the contracts can self-execute; for example, charging a penalty if certain events have taken place. This is seen as the biggest area where transformation is taking shape. By using blockchain as a part of contractual instruments, a great deal of changes will unfold. With blockchain, something can be recorded on a shared ledger and, once recorded, the transaction will appear in the database and will be irrefutable digital proof that the transaction happened on a particular date between two parties.

A good application of smart contracts is the music industry. Setting up a public blockchain of music allows for music to be sold and benefits distributed in real time between the different parties in the value chain. In addition, there are use cases in many areas such as securities, syndicated lending, trade finance, swaps, and derivatives.

Ethereum was one of the first public blockchain companies to implement smart contracts using *bytecode*—sets of instructions that are interpreted by the Ethereum system.

Payments

Payment transactions traditionally involve using trusted third parties such as banks and remittance centers. However, with blockchain, payment transactions could become hassle-free and save payment transfer fees, which are usually charged by intermediaries. This is a critical development area because it will have a big impact on financial institutions and regulatory authorities. Blockchain processes payments in just a few minutes, while it takes several hours to make payments using third parties.

The fundamental feature of distributed ledger architecture is that it maintains an audit trail. It validates and authenticates the chain of value transfers in an open and transparent fashion so that each transaction is checked and validated by every participant in the network. Moreover, funds transfers can be recorded using private keys by both originator and beneficiary. Thus, it will be increasingly difficult to lose track of the source and destination.

R3 Consortium is a leading firm that handles complex financial transactions around the world using blockchain. As a distributed database technology company, it leads a consortium of more than 70 of the world's biggest financial institutions. This is the biggest banks' response to blockchain, though what it will result in is still unclear.

It created an open-source distributed ledger platform called "Corda." Corda provides a platform with common services to ensure that any services built on top are compatible.

Digital Medical Records

The next big thing to look out for in the healthcare industry is the disruptive impact of blockchain in the way patients' records are managed. Users can now take a look at health records from the comfort of their own homes. Blockchain technology makes it possible to access and store medical information about people in real time. This will also result in an opportunity for the health community to share ideas and, in turn, help generate more accurate answers to many questions about different illnesses.

However, customer records will remain secure because of features such as privacy and anonymity. Privacy ensures that only authorized parties may access the medical record while anonymity will ensure that identifiable information is omitted and only summary or partial data is shared.

Electronic Voting

Another application for blockchain is online voting. You can now cast a vote right from your digital device. This action will be recorded in the database as a transaction. The blockchain will keep track of the tallies of the votes. Since blockchain is an unchangeable, permanent record of transactions, everyone can agree on the final count of votes, and no recounts are needed.

In Australia, the *Australia Post* has floated this idea in a paper presented to a parliamentary Electoral Matters Committee. *Australia Post* believes that an e-voting system with the aid of blockchain will boost democracy.

They believe that blockchain would be used to store a cryptographic representation of ballots which would be verifiable by voters who value privacy.

Clearing and Settlement

The post-trade settlement is an important part of the trading process. This can be very slow, taking an average of two days; and expensive, requiring several intermediaries.[264] As of now, transactions pass through various intermediaries, and the records are stored in a centralized ledger. Entities that facilitate transactions are custodians, depositories, brokers, and clearing houses. Blockchain allows for irrevocable transactions and real-time activity, which in turn achieves high levels of accuracy and low levels of settlement risk.

Using blockchain technology, the centralized ledger, which is traditionally maintained by the clearing house, would now become a distributed ledger that would require authentication from each party. If any of the parties does not authenticate it, the transaction becomes invalid. The biggest hurdle in making this a reality, rather than technology, is reaching an agreement between different players in the industry. This doesn't mean that we will never see clearing and settlement through a distributed ledger. It just means that it will take significant time to achieve.

Smart Assets

Smart assets are those assets whose ownership is recorded on a blockchain. Since blockchain is a record of the history of transactions, the trading history of the asset is recorded, and the audit trail is kept so that facts about the asset can be verified before making a purchase. It is useful, at a personal level, to store a clear record of everything you buy for guarantees insurance and sales. It is also useful for businesses. For example, trade finance takes a lot of documentation. Documentation slows down processes, so by digitizing it, speed is gained. The blockchain can also record many kinds of relevant information, such as who is sending the asset, when it will expire, what taxes are due, and so forth. By having more information, the asset becomes more valuable, and further efficiencies can be gained.

Digital Identity

Traditionally, we are used to proving our identity using physical passports, driver's licenses and other government-issued IDs. Today, there are several companies using blockchain technology to provide digital identity. The idea of having our identities securely stored on the net is very appealing. The reliable and decentralized nature of information as well as the immutability of the network makes blockchain a key enabler. We look into this use case in detail in the "Identification, Cybersecurity, and RegTech" chapter.

The Future in a Flash

The areas where we can expect disruption by blockchain and distributed ledgers are:
- Identification, where identities will become stronger and well secured using cryptography
- Accounting, where transparency will make life easier for regulators to review financial reporting and audit firms
- Insurance, where actuarial risks will be easier to calculate for individuals and firms
- Moving value, where payments and purchases will be faster and cheaper
- Storing value, where checking and savings accounts could be revolutionized
- Lending, where the blockchain could be used for issuing, trading, and settling

Blockchain is currently in its infancy, but over the coming years, we will start to see growth based on the pilots and experiments that have been successful. New operating models will emerge and will be implemented globally, and some processes will become obsolete. We can expect the technology to be fully embedded by 2025.

Chapter 12
The Rise of InsurTech

The Rise of InsurTech in a Flash

The use of technology in the insurance industry is leading to innovation and is helping it meet the needs of the modern world. Industry disruptors can offer a state-of-the-art way to reduce costs and increase customer engagement. Changes in customer habits mean fintechs can offer customized products and services that may make incumbent insurers lose market share.

Blockchain and smart contracts are usable in insurance technology and are beneficial as they create immutable ledgers of valuable assets. InsurTech also benefits from the internet of things, as valuable information can be retrieved from devices attached to assets that have been insured. Insurers can use InsurTech to customize their products to make them adaptable to dynamic circumstances, and they can also harness the benefits of wearables to personalize their insurance products and upgrade the delivery of health care. Lastly, peer-to-peer networks can provide a more efficient end-to-end process, changing the standard insurance business model.

 ## How Insurance Works

The concept of insurance dates back to the time when sailing ships suffered damage or lost their cargo. Merchants realized that if they divided their goods between different ships, they could protect themselves from heavy losses. This meant that if one ship suffered damage, they would only lose a small portion of their cargo. In doing so, they insured themselves against total financial ruin.

Today, insurance takes many forms. A person can buy insurance and join other people who pay premiums to the insurer, who uses that money to pay claims made by people they have insured. A person receives a legal document called a policy when they buy insurance. This policy contains the insurance details, including the items covered, the premiums, and the payment frequency. It is important for the potential client to understand the insurance policy before they sign on the dotted line.

Insurance is protection against any accidental or unexpected events. There are different kinds of insurance. The main ones are:
- Agricultural insurance, for unexpected weather and crop production
- Health insurance, for covering medical fees
- Liability insurance, for paying off lawsuits and claims
- Life insurance, for covering loved ones in the case of a significant person's death

DOI 10.1515/9781547401055-012

- Mortgage insurance, for continuing mortgage payments in case of job loss
- Property insurance, for covering most risks related to property such as fire, theft, and weather damage
- Reinsurance, for insurance companies managing the risk that there might not be enough money to pay for claims

Insurance firms pool funds from individuals to pay for claims and pay expenses for the provision and selling of insurance protection. They also invest the money, and any earnings from their investments offset the insurance costs. For 2018, a growing number of insurers are taking an active role in investing. Many insurers have already set up their own investment arms, which enables them to be more aggressive in acquiring start-ups. Also, the fact that regulators are striving to understand InsurTech can only be beneficial to the sector as regulations will be mainly related to customer data protection and on possible ways to use this increased data for pricing purposes.

Unlike other products, rate setting for insurance is complex. Individuals pay premiums in advance, so insurers do not know the actual costs of a particular insurance policy. In essence, they compute premiums based on the cost of every claim and the frequency of claims.

Insurance fraud is always rampant after major catastrophes and during recessions. Individuals and even organized crime syndicates can perpetuate fraudulent insurance transactions like inflating actual claims and submitting claims for nonexistent damages, injuries, or medical bills.

Many countries regulate insurance companies to ensure that they follow the insurance laws that protect not only the insured individuals but the companies themselves. However, these statutes vary from country to country.

In 2017, InsurTech became a buzz word for customers seeking to plan strategies related to their health, wealth, and families. A range of InsurTech solutions have been developed to enhance the traditional touch points of the customer value chain, including quoting, purchasing policies, servicing policies, and claims. At the same time, the introduction of insurance wearables, sensors, and telematics opened up a host of ways to engage and personalize the customer experience.

For 2018, InsurTech trends are expected to be increasingly related to APIs and the insurance ecosystem. Insurance carriers with API-enabled policy administration systems can build off API-enabled value chain solutions to offer a higher quality product and capitalize on the generated benefits. This, in concert with an advanced insurance ecosystem that can bring the insurer, insured, and provider together in a seamless way will further enhance the ability of preventative care through the use of wearables, telematics, smart sensors, and the IoT.

 **Market Size**

In 2015, InsurTech received at least $3 billion in investment. This is not as impressive as it sounds, considering that car insurance firms spend at least $6 billion on marketing each year. However, large insurers are adapting to meet the demands of the digital world.[265] Venture capital firms are betting on start-ups that can bring life to the sector.

In 2015, venture funding for digital health care hit about $5.8 billion. Health care start-ups continue to grow in number. They collect personal data from customers to improve the insurer-customer relationship and hedge risks, reduce expenses, and provide excellent customer service. In Q3 2017, VC investment in InsurTech reached $1.5 billion across 179 deals, down by 16.7% from $1.8 billion across 203 deals in 2016.[266] Cumulatively, in the period 2012-2017, InsurTech start-ups gradually became a hot area for fintech investment with $2.2 billion in 2017, up 536.5% from $348 million in 2012.[267] In 2018 trends looked like investments started to concentrate, and more capital was channelled to proven entities in late-stage and follow up rounds.

According to Technavio, a company focused on technology research and advising, InsurTech will grow by at least 10% every year between 2016 and 2020. Technavio looked at investment in various InsurTech platforms in Europe, the Americas, Africa, Asia-Pacific, and the Middle East. In its Global InsurTech Market 2016-2020 report, it focused on the increased need for customer satisfaction, rationalization of transaction procedures, and for the growth of online business ecosystems.[268] Numerous insurers and financial institutions will enhance their products and services or collaborate with financial technology firms to offer innovative solutions to their clients, who are demanding improved online experiences.

Furthermore, transaction processes will become easier thanks to new technology. For example, insurance companies now use electronic payment systems. They will invest in adopting technology that will enhance the functionality of these payment systems. They will spend money on the prevention of cyberattacks by ensuring that they have systems in place to ascertain, control, enhance, and reduce risk.

With the emergence of the new generation and the aging of the baby boomers, InsurTech products can take advantage of these new opportunities by offering customized services and insurance security support. Different venture capitalists are investing in InsurTech innovators, which use software for portfolio management and insurance products. These InsurTech companies can disrupt the insurance industry by using powerful analytics tools and Big Data.

Drivers of Disruption

Insurers have been meeting customers' expectations by innovating little by little. Yet opportunities still abound for new business models and radical innovation. The main causes of disruption are increased customer expectations, an increased pace of innovation, and the appearance of new players.

As in other sectors, scaled cloud computing, open source frameworks, and on-demand development have broken down the barriers to entering this industry. New players can innovate to fill the gaps that present insurers cannot.

Although many people believe that the insurance industry will experience major disruption, only a few incumbents are relying on the use of InsurTech, even though 74% of insurance companies believe that innovations in financial technology pose a challenge to them.[269]

Despite emerging trends, traditional insurance providers are not innovating fast enough. 43% of these insurers believe that they already use financial technology as their corporate strategy, yet only 28% of them have explored collaboration with financial technology start-ups. Only 14% of these insurance companies participate in incubator programs and/or ventures.

Existing companies are focusing on playing catch-up with their competitors and failing to be proactive. They have no consistent strategy for dealing with disruption and are not thinking long term. Executives need to specify how they want their companies to benefit from InsurTech and embrace a strategy of innovation.

Consumer habits are changing, and they expect more personalized products and services that cater to their needs. InsurTech can act as a facilitator, but it must be a priority for companies because stand-alone competitors may eventually put them at risk of losing market share.

Although InsurTech is still in its infancy, new business models have already emerged, such as pay-as-you-go insurance and micro-insurance. Financial technology could make products and services more cost-friendly, personalized, and easy-to-use.

Peer-to-Peer Insurance

Several firms are betting on peer-to-peer insurance. In this model, some of the responsibilities and the risks of the insurance firms are passed onto the policyholders. Decisions can include defining risk pools, deciding where to use the proceeds of the pool, and having a say on who to adjudicate claims to.

The model differs depending on the country's legislation and the type of risks covered. Some firms support a model where there is an insurer that manages claims above a certain limit (broker model), and others don't depend on an insurer at all but take on reinsurance if the funds run out (carrier model). In both models, if there are funds left at the end of the year, these are credited to the policyholders to be used in the future.

Creating affinity networks is key for this model to work, as this deters people from inflating claims or raising fraudulent claims. They are also key to keeping acquisition costs down, as word of mouth is very effective.

The main players right now in the western world are US-based Lemonade and German-based Friendsurance.

Blockchain Insurance and Machine Learning

Financial technology is benefiting from blockchain innovation, and InsurTech is no exception. Reputational systems built on blockchain, through decentralized insurance markets, have the potential to enable insurers to calculate actuarial risk better for every customer, leading to better quotes for customers. Current distrust in the central databases has caused very high levels of underinsurance.

Blockchain can also help with fraud and risk prevention. By holding a decentralized digital repository, policies, transactions, and customers can be verified by considering a historical record. This would allow detection of duplicate transactions, and those done by suspicious parties.

Luther Systems is one of the companies working in this space. Based in the United Kingdom, it specializes in blockchain technology. In September 2016, Founders Factory and Aviva chose the company to participate in their accelerator program, a project that aims to help companies by providing them with mentoring and support.[270] Luther Systems is still relatively unknown but is working with Aviva to simplify smart contracts through templates that a customer can sign online. It also aims to improve efficiency and transparency in transaction management systems.[271]

A paper by Juniper Research forecasts that the use of InsurTech could cause product revenues to increase by combining machine learning and blockchain technology and creating more personalized products. Moreover, the paper claims that revenues could increase by up to 34% each year, from $175 billion in 2016 to $235 billion in 2021.[272]

Juniper also points out that blockchain investments will enable smart contracts to drive growth and allow for the creation of excellent mobile applications. The paper predicts that blockchain will help insurance companies to customize products to adapt to the changing circumstances of customers.

Wearables in Insurance

At present, buying health insurance has become easy. A person needs to fill in a form and provide a summary of their health condition. Later changes in their health can affect insurance risk, but insurers ignore them. Wearables may be able to change this practice. They may reform insurance by customizing risk and insurance and modifying health care delivery.

There are two ways that wearables could disrupt insurance. First, insurers will have a dynamic view of a person's health by taking advantage of wearables that can produce data signals. Insurance premiums could be reduced if a person becomes healthier. With wearables, insurers can get real-time data from an insured individual.

Second, things could change regarding health care delivery. Healthcare workers would be able to learn about patients through wearables so that they can deliver health care more cheaply, quickly, and effectively. Individuals with medical problems can use wearables to monitor heart rate, blood pressure, and pulse. Health care workers will be able to check the data from the wearables to make decisions.

Companies that self-insure their employees could use wearables because healthy employees are more productive, and their health care costs less. Venture capitalists invest in health insurance because there is a need for products and services.

Despite this, wearables still face many challenges. First, not everyone currently wants a wearable. Strategy Meets Action, a research firm in Boston, discovered that 22% of insurance companies were considering wearables as a strategy. Yet, in that same survey in 2014, the research company found out that only 3% of the insurers themselves wore a device.[273]

Second, wearables can detect a medical condition like diabetes. A person's insurance premiums could go up if they are wearing a device and their health deteriorates.

Third, countries regulate data privacy, yet regulations vary. In fact, in the United States, regulation can vary from state to state. Insurers must disclose that they will be using private data in their pricing to their clients. Insurance policyholders must be open to sharing their data with insurers and be aware of the potential for data hacking. As such, insurers must assuage the customers' fears by ensuring the security of their systems.

What Traditional Insurance Firms Can Do

Because InsurTech is booming, insurers are collaborating with financial technology innovators, who are willing to learn about the insurance industry. These financial technology start-ups may not always provide instantaneous solutions, but they are willing to adapt. Insurers must be able to communicate with start-ups and understand that these innovators may fail, while embracing innovation themselves.

Ingenious solutions can reduce losses and improve the customer claims experience. Insurance companies must employ individuals who can lead the search for innovative solutions. Finding the right partner to collaborate with may be difficult, and a financial technology company might form links with numerous global insurers.

Interesting InsurTech Ideas

Microinsurance

Microinsurance is about hand picking features that offer the right level of protection to a customer for the shortest amount of time. Several firms will start offering this type of coverage.

On August 4, 2016, Belgian multinational insurer Ageas launched Back Me Up,[274] an app-based insurance coverage that authorizes individuals to personalize their policies by specifying items that they wish to include in their coverage. Back Me Up is specifically for millennials, who are looking for better insurance products and services. There are no annual contract charges and penalty fees, and users can even upload photos of items they want their insurance to cover.

For £15 a month, an individual can protect three items from malicious and unforeseen destruction, loss, and theft. They can claim up to £3,000 per month. Aside from the three covered items, they can claim for a yearly mobile phone screen repair, are covered by UK and worldwide travel insurance for medical emergencies, cancellations, and lost items, and can claim a maximum of £1,500 for the replacement of house or car keys or locks.

Super Fast Car Insurance

Launched in October 2015, Cuvva is an iOS app for individuals who want car insurance coverage in less than 10 minutes.[275] A person needs to download the app and register. They also need to upload their picture, as well as an image of their driver's license, and have to input the car's details, like the estimated vehicle value and the registration number. Then they will receive numerous quotes for various durations of time.

Once they receive the quotes, the person can opt for the rate that suits their requirements. They upload a photo of their vehicle and authorize the payment. They can get coverage for as little as one hour. The next time they use the same insurance the process is quicker because they already have the customer's details.

Headquartered in Edinburgh, Cuvva aims to learn about risk and work with regulators and risk committees. According to Freddy Macnamara, Cuvva's CEO and Founder, for insurers, a car's time on the road is imperative. An underwriter decides the premium based on this time, the individual's driving history, location, and vehicle value.

Cuvva offers real value to the consumer when they want it most. The team behind it is flexible and responsive to the needs of its customers. It provides a customer experience that is straightforward, favorable, simple, and clean. Moreover, it has an excellent social element. Because of Cuvva, individuals can have insurance when they are behind the wheel even for a short time.

In January 2017, Cuvva launched pay-as-you-go car insurance through a mobile app to enable infrequent drivers to pay less expensive insurance for cars that are not frequently used.[276] It allows people to get insurance from one hour to 28 days.

Peer-to-Peer Car Insurance

Peer to peer insurance is another new business model idea, where an individual can opt to join a peer-to-peer pool if a family member or friend has invited them, or they could also be selected based on demographic features, geolocation, and risk profile using artificial intelligence. The result of being part of a small group would result in lower premiums for the mutual group by reducing the motivation to claim.

Germany-based Friendsurance operates in Germany and Australia, and use P2P to provide benefits to its users. It operates as an independent insurance broker with more than 70 domestic partners. It covers not only car insurance, but also home insurance, legal claims insurance, and private liability insurance.

UK-based Guevara has tried this model, introducing its initial version of its P2P car insurance platform in 2014. The app allowed its users to combine their premiums to reduce shared premiums, with excess funds being returned to them. Ninety percent of the app's users lowered their premiums since 2015.[277] However, Guevara had to close down in September 2017 as it could not find a fully capitalized underwriting vehicle.

Insurance Tailored for Digital Businesses

Digital Risks is a broker that uses media and technology to offer insurance to digital businesses. It collaborates with Aviva to ensure that its product meets the requirements of digitally focused and fast-growth SME businesses and start-ups. The product is available on a monthly subscription.[278]

Digital Risks is a UK-based firm that focuses on the digitization and legacy issues that had been plaguing the insurance industry for years. Utilizing the most recent technical frameworks, the systems provided by the company are scalable and responsive to changes. As an innovative InsurTech brand, Digital Risks offers its customers excellent products and services that meet their needs.

By working with Aviva, Digital Risks can expand its reach to fast-growth businesses. Its automated brokering infrastructure has enabled them to change the insurance buying process. Instead of offering the traditional price comparison feature, Digital Risks provides a platform that takes individual risks and location into consideration to provide the best-suited insurer.

Artificial Intelligence Led Insurance

The United Kingdom has its own AI insurance advisory app, named Brolly, which provides important insights through its mobile apps and website. Brolly empowers its customers to decide on their insurance. Through the app, clients learn if they are under- or over-insured. Furthermore, they receive information about insurers who provide cost-effective coverage that meets their needs.[279]

Brolly is an insurance company with a clean slate and a focus on the digital age. Its goal is to redesign the customer experience, based on its centralized approach and data analytics. Brolly aims to be the UK's insurance hub for policyholders and to distribute products directly to its users.

Established by experienced insurance executives, Spixii started its business distributing off-the-shelf products. It aims to be a brand that can connect customers with insurance products through Chatbot, an automated insurance agent. Clients feel that they are communicating with a real insurance agent online.

The ultimate goal of Spixii is to interact with its customers in a dynamic way to facilitate higher customization levels through automated underwriting functionalities, based on dynamic data. The insurer can assess risk based on exceptional information levels for a particular trip. This means that the insurance premium is more reflective of the needs of the customer.

In September 2017, Spixii announced its collaboration with Samsung for the 01/10/100 kick-off event for a six-month mentorship program intended to assist the innovative start-up to propel its business forward.[280]

Insurance as a Service

Instanda offers a customizable platform for the insurance industry. It is a self-service product, created by experts with hands-on experience, working together with software developers and insurers. Because of the challenges and demands of meeting market opportunities, the Instanda team provides a solution for insurers who deal with recurrent problems.[281]

Insurers can manage their businesses using Instanda's business toolkit without the need to hire developers. They can implement changes quickly and easily. Instanda's dynamic team of experienced practitioners and experts, with designers, developers, and senior consultants, provide large-scale projects for major insurers. Instanda is a member of the worldwide roster of alumni of Microsoft's Accelerator Program, an initiative that empowers entrepreneurs to be game changers.

Insly is a software-as-a-service platform designed for insurance brokers. Initially, it was only for the use of Estonian-based IIZI. The platform worked well, so IIZI sold it to other brokers. When the platform accumulated a client base of at least 30 brokers from Estonia, Finland, and Latvia, IIZI created the new spin-off Insly, to focus on capturing a larger market share.[282]

In 2014, Insly joined the Startupbootcamp Fintech Academy. Currently, it has a growing customer base in the UK, the US, and other countries. Customer support is only in English, although the platform runs in seven different languages.

As a cloud-based software-as-a-service platform, Insly does not involve license cost and software installation. An insurance broker pays for the subscription per month. They can also use professional services for standardizing reports or certain products.

UK-based RightIndem is a self-service platform for loss adjusters and insurers. As a software-as-a-service provider, RightIndem aims to improve customer service by transforming the claims for the entire insurance ecosystem.[283]

RightIndem promotes productivity, computes exact car valuations, and improves client retention. It has a model that enables the seamless transfer of multimedia, documents, and data between insurers and policyholders.

Key Players in InsurTech

oscar

Oscar Health's aim is to help develop the customer interface of health insurance by providing easy-to-understand health care products and tools like fitness monitors and smartwatches that save the customer time and discount insurance premiums. Founded in 2012, it uses technology that legacy insurers cannot offer.[284] It is very well funded, with more than $727 million invested in it and a valuation of more than $3 billion.

Oscar app users can communicate with a doctor and get prescriptions from the comfort of their home. The customer can also use geo-locational data and geofencing to select doctors within their neighborhood. They can monitor their medical history and earn discounts if they maintain an active lifestyle using the Misfit step tracker.

Oscar Health is available to families, couples, and individuals in Texas, California, New Jersey, and New York. It has at least 40,000 members in New Jersey and New York. Customers can pay lower premiums if they use fitness devices or trackers. The company expects $1 billion in revenues and 250,000 subscribers by the end of 2018, given a 150% increase in enrolments for Q1 2018 compared to Q1 2017.[285]

Clover

Clover Health is an up-and-coming health insurer that uses preventative care and data analysis to offer a cheaper alternative to Medicare private versions, as well as enhancing health care for the elderly. Backed by Alphabet, it uses technology that can recognize when patients need intervention and medical treatment to save money for both the insurer and the policyholder. Clover Health is for policyholders insured by Medicare Advantage—the Federal government has allowed Medicare to have private insurers such as Clover Health oversee the coverage. The Federal government finances the premium and pays for the claims. Its valuation in early 2018 was around $1.2 billion.

Clover Health has lower overhead costs because of its efficient operations. Its software and algorithms can determine if policyholders are at risk of expensive treatments or hospitalization. Furthermore, Clover Health can send nurse practitioners to check on patients and organize important tests. It monitors policyholders who have serious illness so that medical practitioners can counsel them to prevent costly treatments.

ZhongAn is a Chinese digital-first insurance provider founded in 2013 as a joint venture between Alibaba, Tencent, and Ping An Insurance. So far, it has written more than 3.6 billion policies, and in June 2015 raised $931 million from investors including Morgan Stanley, China International Capital Corp., and Keywise Capital Management. ZhongAn started selling return-delivery insurance, but it then moved on to most of the typical insurance categories such as auto insurance and health insurance.

ZhongAn is investing in blockchain and artificial intelligence, through an incubator that they recently created. In September 2017, ZhongAn held the world's first InsurTech IPO raising $1.5 billion, following the sale of 5.8 million policies to 460 million customers between 2013 and 2016.[286] ZhongAn competes with titans of insurance such as Ping An and China Life, and it is in a great position to take over millennials in a market that is highly underdeveloped.

Lemonade™

Insurance, in the past, used to excel at sharing risk by pooling funds from policyholders. Yet, at the turn of the 20th century, insurers became interested in profit, so they now compete with insured individuals for the same money. At present, both parties have misaligned priorities. Policyholders want support while the insurers want to meet their responsibilities to their shareholders. Due to high administrative and overhead sales costs, the insurer reduces the payout to claims, and claimants have to prove that their request is legitimate.

Launched in September 2016, Lemonade seeks to eliminate the conflict between the insurers and the policyholders through its platform. It does not profit from the non-payment of claims, yet enhances insurance engagement. It earns money through a flat fee users pay for using its platform.[287]

Lemonade is a peer-to-peer insurance platform that groups policyholders according to the good causes they wish to help. For instance, a group of users could be passionate about seeking a cure for cancer or helping local youth groups. Lemonade donates the group's unspent premiums to that good cause after every term. A policyholder who makes a fraudulent claim is aware that they are not only defrauding Lemonade but also their peers and a charitable cause.

Lemonade utilizes artificial intelligence to interact with its users. It provides an automated customer experience for everything, from sending out a quote to managing claims. Payout is easy as the claimant informs the company through the app. They create a brief video testimonial to explain the claim, and Lemonade will send the payment as soon as possible. Lemonade, using its claims bot "AI Jim," set a record by paying out an insurance claim in just three seconds in December 2016. Lemonade has set a benchmark for fast payouts in insurance.

During 2017, Lemonade obtained licenses in 25 states, and launched real estate and commerce websites and apps. In December 2017, SoftBank Group led a $120 million round of funding in Lemonade.[288] The company has partnered with Clarity Money and with WeWork to offer insurance to their customer bases.[289]

Based in San Francisco, Metromile is a vehicle insurance start-up that provides a driving app and pay-per-mile insurance. Founded in 2011 by Steve Pretre and David Friedberg, its usage-based insurance caters to low-mileage drivers. It does not consider driving behaviors or styles when deciding on discounts or rates.[290]

A policyholder needs the Metromile Pulse device to be attached to a port in his vehicle to relay mileage data to Metromile's servers. National General Insurance underwrites the insurance policies. Metromile insurance is available in several states in the United States. Uber drivers in some states can also avail themselves of this pay-per-mile insurance. Metromile is active across eight US states.

Moreover, Metromile's driving app provides insights to the driver, like a vehicle health monitor and alerts to notify the policyholder if they park their car in a street sweeping location. Users can recover their stolen cars through Metromile's car locator app feature.

Metromile raised $90 million in July 2018 which will be used toward improving its sensors and automation processes to better the claims experience.

 the **zebra**

The Zebra is an Austin-based start-up that makes online insurance shopping convenient and transparent to customers. It allows potential car insurance buyers to compare quotes from numerous insurers, and consumers are shown how insurers compute the insurance premiums.

Established in 2012, CEO and co-founder Adam Lyons worked in the vehicle insurance industry and understood brokerage and underwriting. He also realized that customers do not understand most insurance concepts. The Zebra aims to provide real-time quotes from car insurers when a consumer fills out a simplified form online.

However, The Zebra is not an insurer, so it has no interest in closing an insurance deal. It only offers quotes from at least 200 insurers in all US states.[291] Aside from receiving quotes, customers can also evaluate claims satisfaction, read customer reviews, and learn about the coverage offered by insurers. The purchasing process is also simplified through the website.

In September 2017, Zebra raised $40 million in a Series B round led by Accel Partners. The funds will be used toward the expansion of product offerings, including home policies.[292]

policy**genius**

Established in 2014, PolicyGenius serves customers wanting to receive customized quotes from different insurers around the US. PolicyGenius has built an insurance check-up interface so users can discover their coverage gaps and read about solutions for their exact needs. Founded by Francois de Lame and Jennifer Fitzgerald, former McKinsey consultants, it offers pet insurance, renters' insurance, long-term disability insurance, and life insurance.[293]

The founders of PolicyGenius aim to narrow the gap between the number of Americans that need life insurance and the actual number of citizens who have insurance. Currently, only 44% of American families can afford life insurance.

In May 2017, PolicyGenius raised $30 million in a Series C funding round with Norwest Venture Partners. To date, the company has raised $52 million in venture funding from Revolution Ventures, Karlin Ventures, and others.[294]

Gryphon Group Holdings Limited is an insurance start-up poised to launch an exciting new protection challenger under the 200-year-old Guardian brand name. The company's infrastructure will be based on digital and cloud-based technologies to generate higher consumer trust and an effortless adviser experience. In June 2017, Gryphon raised £180 million from investors.[295]

Bright Health is a Minneapolis-based VC-backed health insurance provider that offers health plans and health systems economic rewards for practicing efficient, high-quality healthcare. The company forms and maintains exclusive partnerships with a single health system in each market in order to be able to support the patient–provider interaction effectively. In June 2017, Bright Health raised $160 million in a Series B funding round led by Greenspring Associates and with the participation of Greycroft Partners, Redpoint Ventures and Cross Creek Advisors.[296]

Headquartered in Gurgaon and founded in 2008, Policybazaar.com is a leading online life insurance and general insurance aggregator in India backed by Softbank. The company performs comparative analysis of insurance products on the basis of price, quality, and key benefits through the collection of customer preferences and recent trends in the InsurTech industry. Policybazaar was valued at more than $1 billion in June 2018, and is considering a $1.5 billion IPO.[297]

The Future in a Flash

Purchasing insurance will become easier and faster as technology innovation advances, and a lot of information will be known about individuals and individual behavior using AI algorithms and risk profiles. This will open the door for offering additional products and reaching billions of uninsured customers who didn't even know they could benefit from these types of products.

Big Data analytics, together with wearables, the internet of things, blockchain and especially artificial intelligence will make the end-to-end process easier and cheaper. Calculating risks will be faster and more accurate as information gets stored and shared into distributed ledgers. Fraudulent cases will be significantly reduced. We can easily imagine a future that is preventive, with AI letting us know which is the safest route for us to travel on, sensors that can check damage produced to vehicles and alerting us to take pictures when we crash, and claims that are created automatically. We can also see usage-based insurance becoming the norm of pricing and annual renewals becoming obsolete. The role of agents will dramatically change to becoming an advisor on managing different risks rather than being an admin for one type of risk. Manual underwriting will become a thing of the past as automation will prevail for most cases. The claims department will become more focused on monitoring, preventing and mitigating. The number of those employed in claims will reduce significantly as IoT sensors and other data capture technologies will allow automation to save time and resources.

The winners will be the organizations that can implement AI technologies, create the right environment for technologies and talent to flourish, and create and implement a deep data strategy.

Chapter 13
Identification, Cybersecurity, and RegTech

Identification, Cybersecurity, and RegTech in a Flash

In this final chapter, we look at three topics that are hot in fintech and are supporting the growth of the industry.

Paper-based identification, where people hold passports and driver's licenses, is will become outdated. It is expensive to identify individuals, and it also leaves a proportion of the population unable to apply for financial services products. Technologies such as biometrics and blockchain can help make identification more inclusive and efficient.

Cybersecurity is a massive industry that has emerged alongside e-commerce. As more and more funds move digitally, cyber criminals have found easy ways to commit crimes and defraud people, without even needing to involve themselves in violent acts.

Regulation technology is the response from the technology industry to the efficiency problems generated by the large amount of regulatory requirements that financial institutions have. They aim to manage risks appropriately and keep firms compliant.

Traditional Ways of Using Identification

It is important to understand how identification processes work traditionally. In Western countries, citizens prove their identity using their social security card, passport, or driver's license. Yet, in many cases, people have trouble proving their identity. For instance, a homeless person in the US cannot provide a physical address, and without an address, they cannot apply for a job.

Furthermore, government-issued identification is important for opening a bank account. A person goes to a branch and provides identification to a bank officer to initiate security processes. Normally, an anti-money laundering group receives an automated notification to start the review process.

The initial phase of the anti-money laundering procedure is to identify the customer by collating and authenticating their information. Next, the bank performs customer due diligence to determine the anti-money laundering rating of the client. The client can only open a bank account after the whole process has been successfully completed.[298]

The use of digital identities is essential for a more efficient world. Annoying identification methods include creating and remembering passwords, as well as using technologies such as CAPTCHA. New solutions are necessary, especially with the

DOI 10.1515/9781547401055-013

proliferation of digital services. Millennials find it easier to entrust their identities to social media sites, while some people feel disturbed about sharing information on these sites.

Unique Identification System in India

A very innovative identification system is used in India. A project of the Indian government since January 2009, the Unique Identification Authority of India (UIDAI) aimed to assign a 12-digit unique identification to all Indian residents. The UIDAI was responsible for the plan and policies for the project's implementation, including the definition of processes and mechanisms interlinking it with other databases.

The UIDAI aimed to eliminate fake and duplicate identities by authenticating and verifying each resident's identity in a cost-effective and easy way at any time, anywhere around India. On December 16, 2010, the Indian government started accepting the UIDAI as an official document. UIDAI's Chairman Nandan Nilekani stressed that the 12-digit unique ID could provide residents with access to government, healthcare, and financial services.[299]

The UIDAI collects a resident's demographic and biometric data and then uses them to assign a 12-digit *Aadhaar*, an identity number, to every resident. At present, it is the largest project of its kind around the world. The Indian Parliament passed the *Aadhaar* (Targeted Delivery of Financial and other Subsidies, Benefits, and Services) Act of 2016 on March 11, 2016.[300]

According to a UIDAI report, as of July 2018, there are at least 1.22 billion residents enrolled. This represents 85% of India's population. Different forums opposed *Aadhaar* because of privacy issues. On September 2018, India's Supreme Court released a ruling that stated that *Aadhaar* must not be mandatory but voluntary and that the Indian government must provide services even if a resident does not have *Aadhaar*, and it is not mandatory for opening bank accounts, getting a mobile phone, or being admitted at school.

The Aadhar database has been compromised and over a billion records can be bought online. This was mostly due to app flaws and third party misuse, which allowed for the creation of duplicate cards, demographic data sale, and fraudulent payments.

Identification for the Unbanked

The number of people worldwide who state that they have an account at a financial institution or with a mobile money supplier has grown very fast in recent years. However, an estimated two billion adults lack access to an account. It is estimated that 38% of adults in the world are unbanked, 46% in developing countries.[301]

Even in the United States, many residents cannot use banks. In fact, some depositors take advantage of financial services provided by another entity for cashing checks and payday loans. For some people, it may not be practical to have access to a bank account since they cannot maintain it.

Unbanked is a term that refers to families that do not possess any accounts in any financial institution. In 2015, an estimated 7% of American families were unbanked, while about 19.9% of households were underbanked, meaning they have poor access to mainstream financial services. This means that at least 25 million families in the US were either unbanked or underbanked.[302]

An unbanked individual cannot receive a salary through direct deposit. They cannot build a credit history and may have trouble with savings and money transfers. Although there was a steady decline in the unbanked population of the US between 2013 and 2015, millions of residents still do not have a bank account.

In the 2015 National Survey of Unbanked and Underbanked Households by the Federal Deposit Insurance Corporation (FDIC), 57.4% of respondents claimed that they did not keep a bank account because they had no money to maintain one. Furthermore, they did not trust banks, wanted privacy, and did not want to pay excessive fees.

Unbanked residents also feel that the banks are unwilling to have them as clients. In the same FDIC survey, 55.8% of the respondents said that banks were uninterested in providing services to their households, so they, in turn, declared themselves uninterested in the services banks could provide.

Having a bank account provides several benefits. First, many governments insure deposits in the banking system against loss, and a bank account lets individuals take advantage of money managing services. What's more, the depositor receives an ATM card, which can also be used as a debit card, meaning they do not need to carry large amounts of cash. Other benefits include interest accrual and building up a credit history, which opens up opportunities for accessing affordable lending.

Using Biometrics as Identification

Biometrics uses electronic methodologies to recognize a customer through their biological traits and characteristics like voice recognition, iris pattern, finger vein patterns, and fingerprints. Every person has unique biometric characteristics, which are difficult to forge. As such, biometrics are beneficial not only in financial services, but also in forensic studies, law enforcement, and immigration control. Numerous financial institutions worldwide use biometrics to authenticate customers and employees.

Because of stricter employee and client identification protocols, and the digitization of financial services, biometric technology has become a strategic and important part of security platforms for countering identity fraud and theft. It also enhances brand reputation and customer trust, providing an excellent tool for secure online, branch, and ATM transactions. The need for biometrics became apparent because of the increased reliance on technology in financial services and the rise in cybercrime.

For financial institutions, biometrics can be a means for increasing their customer base, improving customer service, and reducing fraud. They help financial regulators crack down on money laundering and fraud.

There are several benefits of using biometrics as a method of identification, both generally and in the world of banking. These include having a unique identifier for each customer that is very hard to replicate. They also allow those without official documents to identify themselves without presenting any paperwork. In the short term, the construction of a centralized biometrics database that can be used by several institutions is likely, as it would reduce the cost of registering customers and generate a quick return on investment.

Using Biometrics in Bank Transactions

Financial institutions are replacing their old access methodologies like passwords, signature-based branch service, token-based electronic banking, and PIN-based ATMs and mobile banking with biometrics solutions to protect their customers and improve their services.

When a customer opens a bank account, a bank employee captures their biometric details, such as their fingerprints or facial picture. Then the bank's system checks for a match in its database to reduce the risk of fraud. Once an account is set up, bank personnel can verify a customer's biometrics before performing transactions. Bank branches like finger vein and fingerprint biometrics because they make identification faster and are easy-to-use, user-friendly, and reliable.

In ATMs, the use of biometrics is experiencing significant growth. A customer uses their biometrics together with their bank card or PIN. Banks frequently use fingerprints, face recognition, iris recognition, and finger vein patterns as these biometric methodologies are accurate, compact, and flexible. Japan has distributed at least 80,000 biometric ATMs around the country for its 15 million banking customers.[303]

In internet banking, biometric authentication is through voice, face, finger vein, and fingerprint recognition through scanners, microphones, and webcams. By requiring biometrics in addition to the conventional password for online transactions, banks can protect their customers against identity theft by cybercriminals.

By using a single biometric sign-in solution, banks can eradicate loopholes in the data security and vulnerability of passwords. Furthermore, they can protect their customers and themselves from data breaches and unauthorized access. They can also lessen regulatory fines and other security risks.

Latest mobile operating systems are prioritizing face recognition that is harder to breach than fingerprint recognition. Apple's Face ID has been very successful. It used infrared lighting and adds 3D readings from a separate sensor. Samsung has included iris scanning with its latest devices to authenticate people.

To provide great online identification, technology is required. The Fast Identity Online Alliance (FIDO) is an organization that focuses on developing specifications and certifying products that enable stronger and simpler online authentication. Launched in February 2013, it is a consortium of industry players founded by Lenovo, PayPal, and Nok Nok Labs, among others. As of September 2016, it had more than 260 members.[304]

The goal of FIDO is to reduce reliance on passwords while providing a better authentication experience. It uses a device-centric model and authentication is through the use of public-key cryptography. A user registers on their device by recording a unique public key in a server. They also unlock their device using biometrics.

It all started toward the end of 2009 when Validity Sensors' Ramesh Kesanupalli approached PayPal's Michael Barrett to discuss the possibility of PayPal using biometrics to identify online users. Barrett insisted that a biometrics solution should follow some sort of industry standard that supports numerous vendors. Kesanupalli approached other fingerprint sensor suppliers, industry experts, and device distributors to design a cryptographic key that could unlock a biometric device.[305]

In 2011, NXP, Yubico, and Google started working on a 2nd-factor, open standard device to facilitate web authentication, that no phishing scam could control. In April 2013, this group joined FIDO Alliance.

On December 9, 2014, FIDO published the completed Universal Authentication Framework and Universal 2nd Factor for device manufacturers to use. Recently introduced in 2018, FIDO2 is an open authentication standard that is the password-less evolution of the previous framework. It allows for strong security, privacy protection, a layered approach, and is cost efficient. Membership to FIDO continues to grow and includes top biometric suppliers, leading security hardware providers, and major software platform suppliers. Furthermore, FIDO aims to ensure that dominant software platforms include built-in FIDO technologies to ensure that the user experience becomes simple, intuitive, and secure.

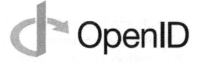

A perfect complement for FIDO is OpenID connect. OpenID is an authentication layer developed by the OpenID Foundation, which allows end users to authenticate themselves by using a different authentication provider and also retrieve information about themselves from the same server.

OpenID allows users to use their existing accounts to login to multiple websites, without needing to create new passwords for each of them. The user associates their information with their OpenID account and then shares this when visiting websites. The user is always in control regarding how much data they share. The OpenID account is the only one that holds the identification data, and that provider then confirms your identity to the websites you visit.

OpenID's main goal is to enable sharing identification on numerous sites. It delegates the authentication to other organizations such as FIDO, which makes these technologies complementary.[306]

Using Google, Twitter, LinkedIn, or Facebook, identifier portability is an approach that gives users the power to control the identity attributes that they want to use across numerous sites on the web. Furthermore, users control to whom they can prove their identity in a private and secure manner.

Although there is no authentication involved, OpenID Connect transmits authentication over the network. The users protect their identity through FIDO and use it across the World Wide Web through OpenID Connect. OpenID is quickly being adopted on the web, with over one billion OpenID enabled user accounts and over 50,000 websites accepting OpenID as a login mechanism.

Using a Distributed Ledger for Identification

Digital identification can be problematic because it involves legal, political, technical, and societal issues. Personally Identifiable Information (PII) defines a person's way of life. It is crucial because it ascertains a person's access to people they know, their past actions, their creditworthiness, their medical records, and so on.

Storing data in centralized data centers can be prone to hacking. In addition, data science technology can discover identities through PII data. For instance, it is possible to identify a person through their medical records or financial records, without the service provider knowing. Thus, it may be safer to store PII data in a blockchain.

Blockchain technology is decentralized, trustless, and inflexible. No institution or government can control the PII data. Furthermore, no entity can modify a record. It can only add amendments to a record.

Some banks see themselves as custodians of identity and believe they can be authenticators. Yet, various blockchain companies want to play an important part in the future of identity. Theoretically, blockchain technology promotes the independence of entities, as well as the reliance of these parties on an auditable, secure, and shared information source.[307] This is certainly a technology component that will enable the identification of the future.

The UN Identity Aspiration

By 2030, the United Nations wants every person on Earth to have biometric identities with a Geneva-based central database. Refugee populations are the first targets for this plan. Collaborating with Accenture, the United Nations plans to implement biometric identification to recognize and monitor refugees.[308]

The United Nations High Commissioner for Refugees (UNHCR) will adopt Accenture's BIMS (Biometric Identity Management System), which will collect fingerprints, iris patterns, and facial biometric data. Refugees will use this biometric identification card as their official documentation. BIMS and Accenture's Unique Identity Service Platform (UISP) will send the data to the Geneva-based central database system that UNHCR offices can use to track refugees.

A FindBiometrics report claims that nearly 1.8 billion adults worldwide have no official documentation. As such, they cannot avail themselves of important services and face difficulties with trans-border identification. The implementation of a biometric identification card for refugees will prove whether it is feasible to use the system on a larger scale. Thus, the United Nations is aiming toward the implementation of biometric identification worldwide through its Identification for Development initiative.

Cybercrime and Its History

Modern technology connects governments, financial institutions, businesses, and people. Digital technology offers the platform for this connectivity and provides numerous significant benefits. Yet, it also offers a way for unscrupulous individuals to perpetuate criminal activities, from vandalism to classified information theft.

Hacking can alter a procedure or product to either solve a problem or change the way it works. Coined in the 1960s, it describes the various activities performed by some MIT enthusiasts who altered model trains' operation. These people found ways to alter some functions without the need to re-engineer the whole device.[309]

The curiosity and resourcefulness of these individuals led them to learn the computer code of the early computer systems. Keith Thompson and Dennis Ritchie hacked the original system and developed the UNIX operating system. Most people know the term "hack" as an ingenious way to improve a function or fix a problem with a device or product.

In the 1970s, hacking became malicious. Phreakers or tech-savvy people found out the correct tones and codes of the early computerized phone systems that allowed free long distance calls. They imitated operators, performed different experiments, and went through Bell Telephone Company's rubbish to search for secret information. They hacked the software and hardware to take advantage of free long distance calls.

Law enforcement found it difficult to deal with hacking because there was no law for prosecuting hackers. Furthermore, the investigators had no technological skills. As communications and computer systems became more complex, cybercriminals also had more opportunities.

Lawrence Berkeley National Laboratory systems administrator Clifford Stoll noticed some accounting irregularities in 1986. He invented the first digital forensic techniques to detect if an unauthorized user was accessing his computer network. His honeypot tactic attracted hackers to return to the network until Stoll could gather enough data to find the source of the intrusion. Eventually, his strategy led to the arrest of Markus Hess and his associates, who sold stolen military data to the KGB.

In 1990, 150 FBI agents confiscated at least 20,000 floppy disks and 42 computers, that criminals had used for illegal telephone and credit card transactions. Yet, law enforcers could also make mistakes with their investigations. For instance, Steve Jackson Games publishing company was accused of having an illegally copied document in its possession. The Secret Service confiscated the company's computers. The seizure of computers forced the publishing company to miss deadlines and lay off employees. The Secret Service returned the computers but deleted computer data and accessed company emails. However, it did not press charges against the company.

In 1990, because of threats to civil liberties brought about by the mistakes and impulsive activities by law enforcement, lawyers, technologists, and other professionals formed the Electronic Frontier Foundation (EFF) to protect consumers from illegal prosecution.

Viruses like the ILOVEYOU and the Melissa infected millions of personal computers and caused the failure of email systems worldwide. They prompted the development of antivirus technology to recognize and prevent viruses. Furthermore, people became aware of the risks of opening emails and attachments from untrusted sources.[310]

In the late 2000s, credit cards became the focus of attacks. Albert Gonzalez headed a group of unscrupulous individuals who stole credit card information from customer transactions of the UK outlet TK Maxx and US retailer TJX. According to reports, the breach of security lost the company about $256 million.

In 2006, Sunshine Press in Iceland launched the website WikiLeaks, a non-profit organization that leaks secret news, information, and classified media from undisclosed sources. According to its website, the group had about 1.2 million documents it planned to publish. Julian Assange is touted as the group's founder, director, and editor-in-chief. Other publicly known associates of Assange include Sarah Harrison, Joseph Farrell, and Kristinn Hrafnsson.[311]

Many of the documents released by WikiLeaks became front-page news. Some released documents were about the wars in Iraq and Afghanistan, and, more recently, released documents were email leaks that damaged the US Democratic Party and Hillary Clinton.

The Cybersecurity Sector

Cybersecurity is one of the fastest growing sectors in the tech world. Worldwide, it had an estimated size of $152 billion in 2018. Its market size could grow to $250 billion by 2023.[312]

In the past 10 years, the US Federal government has spent close to $100 billion on cybersecurity alone. This is clearly important if we reflect on the fact that the 2016 US presidential election was certainly affected by cyber criminals. In 2016, the government allocated a budget of $14 billion. On average, cyberattacks cost businesses up to $500 billion per year, not including unreported cybercrimes.

In 2014, Heartbleed, a security bug that caused catastrophic damage to the corporate IT community, resulted in monetary damages costing billions of dollars. It is difficult to determine the possible cost-per-breach because a company has to compute the direct damage and the post-attack interruptions to business operations. Research companies and industry analysts, as well as suppliers, offer different formulas and estimates. As such, companies decide to calculate the damage on their own.

In the US, the cyber insurance market grew to $2.5 billion in 2015. This may grow significantly and may even expand worldwide in the next five years. Financial and banking services are also expanding into the cybersecurity market. The growth of the internet of things will also increase security spending.

In the global arena, Israel is the second largest cyber products exporter, behind the US. The Asia Pacific market is also developing cybersecurity plans due to denial-of-service attacks, and the adoption of mobile devices and cloud computing. In the Latin American region, cybersecurity and cybercrime spending are also growing. Yet, there is a labor shortage when it comes to global cybersecurity. In the US alone, there are at least 200,000 unfilled positions. By 2019, the shortage in cybersecurity workforce could reach 1.5 million.

Types of Cybercrime

There are different types of cybercrime. In this section, we provide a brief description of the main ones.

Backdoor

A backdoor is a secret way of circumventing security controls or normal authentication in an algorithm, a cryptosystem, or a computer system. It may occur due to poor configuration or original design. Authorized personnel may add a backdoor to provide others with unauthorized access. An unscrupulous person may add it for malicious intentions. Whatever the reason, a backdoor creates vulnerability.[313]

Distributed Denial of Service Attack (DDOS)

A denial-of-service attack can bring down a network or machine. It denies service to intended users by overloading the capabilities of a network or machine. It can also enter the wrong password deliberately to lock the victim's account. Adding a new firewall rule can block a network attack caused by an IP address. Yet it is difficult to defend a network from numerous Distributed Denial-of-Service attacks, which can come from a botnet and other techniques like amplification and reflection attacks. The cost of a DDOS attack averages half a million dollars.[314]

Phishing

Phishing instructs users to give out details to a fake site that is identical to the original site. It acquires user information like credit card details, passwords, and usernames. According to research undertaken by Ponemon Institute, the annual cost to a business in the event of a successful phishing attack is around $3.7 million.[315]

Clickjacking

Known as User Interface redress attack or UI redress attack, clickjacking allows an attacker to trick a user into clicking a link or button on a different web page. In other words, the attacker is hijacking the clicks of the user.

Spoofing

As a malicious or fraudulent activity, spoofing is when an attacker is disguised as a known source to the receiver and communicates with them. This is common to devices with low-level security.

Social Engineering

Social engineering is a type of fraud that convinces a user to disclose sensitive information. For instance, an attacker sends a fake CEO email to finance and accounting departments. According to the FBI, this scheme costs US enterprises at least $2 billion every two years.

Direct Access Attacks

An authorized user, who gains computer access, can copy data, modify the operating system, use wireless mice, or install covert listening devices, keyloggers, or software worms. Standard security measures may protect the system, but using a tool or booting another operating system can bypass such measures. It is possible to prevent direct access attacks through Trusted Platform Module and Disk encryption.

Eavesdropping

Eavesdropping is the unauthorized real-time interception of private communications. The programs NarusInsight and Carnivore, for example, eavesdrop on internet service providers' systems. It is also possible to eavesdrop on closed systems when there is a lack of encryption or when they are weak.

Cybersecurity Categories and Players

Cybersecurity is quite fragmented, and there is a profusion of start-ups. These fall under 11 categories. We can definitely expect consolidation in future.

Network and Endpoint Security

Network and endpoint security includes methods used to protect corporate networks from remote devices. Every remote device connecting to the corporate network can be a potential security threat. Thus, there is a need to secure both the corporate network and the endpoint.[316]

Red Canary is a leading start-up in this category. It specializes in protecting the computer networks of companies against vulnerabilities caused by remote connections of tablets, laptops, and other electronic devices of a companies' employees. Cylance, on the other hand, uses AI algorithms to identify and prevent malware and extreme threats in endpoints.

IoT/IIot Security

IoT security refers to the protection of connected networks and devices in the internet of things, which includes entities and objects that can initiate data transfer automatically and with unique identifiers. The main issue is that product design often does not include security. Most products in the internet of things have unpatched and old embedded software and operating systems. Thus, these devices are primary targets of security breaches.[317]

Securing the internet of things will become of paramount importance, as we have already seen the devastating consequences that hacking cars and other vehicles can have. Argus Cyber Security is a cybersecurity start-up that focuses on protecting connected vehicles. On the other hand, Indegy offers security for Industrial Control Systems in critical infrastructures like water utilities, manufacturing facilities, energy, petrochemical plants, and the like.

Threat Intelligence

Threat intelligence is refined, analyzed, and organized information about current or potential attacks against an organization. It aims to help corporations understand the risks of external threats. It provides in-depth information so that companies can protect themselves against damaging attacks.[318] A good threat intelligence provider is Flashpoint, which targets malicious activities on the web to expose and prevent threats and attacks.

Mobile Security

Mobile security involves securing business and personal information stored on mobile phones. Since smartphones compile sensitive information, it is necessary to protect the corporation's intellectual property and the smartphone user's privacy. Today, mobile phones have become preferred targets. As such, everyone must take part in securing information, from the developers to the end users.[319] Zimperium provides mobile threat protection for iOS and Android devices.

Behavioral Detection

Behavioral detection tracks the executable events of malicious software to prevent criminal actions from happening. Examples of prohibited operations include modifying system settings and deleting files.[320] Cloud security consists of control-based policies and technologies that protect infrastructure, data applications, and information related to the use of cloud computing. Furthermore, the policies and technologies comply with the rules of regulators.[321] Darktrace is a firm that identifies cyberattack threats and mitigates risks by detecting the organization's abnormal behavior.

Cloud Security

Cloud Security focuses on technologies and mechanisms that can secure data and applications that are held in the cloud. Tigera is a cybersecurity start-up focusing on securing the delivery of workload and application across private, public, and hybrid clouds.

Deception Security

Deception technology is a collection of techniques and tools to prevent an attacker within a network from damaging the system. It misdirects the attacker by using decoys. Furthermore, it prevents them from reaching their target and going deeper into the network. Its products mimic real IT assets and run either on emulated or real operating systems. These services dupe the attacker into thinking that they have already found their target. It does not take over the roles of the other security products but enhances them.[322] Illusive Networks can identify, deceive, and disrupt attackers before they can wreak any havoc to companies.

Continuous Network Visibility

Continuous network visibility allows the cloud to handle network security to detect enterprise threats, make them visible, and accelerate incident response. It uses the cloud to build a retention window with advanced visualization, automated retrospection, and full-fidelity forensics. With continuous network visibility, it becomes easier for security professionals to deal with threats in real time.[323] Protectwise visualizes and responds to network activity to thwart cyberattacks immediately.

Risk Remediation

Risk remediation is a technique that allows the application of countermeasures to lessen the susceptibility of cyber assets to various attack techniques, tactics, and procedures related to advanced persistent threats.[324] Web security can be public and internal. It is good if the network setup has tight permissions, the web applications and web server often receives updates and patches, and the website code is of high quality.[325]

AttackIQ focuses on identifying vulnerabilities in the processes, people, and technologies, and then offers solutions to solve the problem.

Website Security

Websites are unfortunately prone to many security risks, and so are any networks to which web servers are connected. Web servers and the sites hosted present the most serious sources of security risk for many companies, especially SMEs. This category consists of software installed on websites to prevent account takeover, content scraping, as well as other intrusions in websites. Shape Security and Distil Networks identify malicious website traffic.

Quantum Encryption

Quantum cryptography is the practice and study of techniques for secure communication in the presence of third parties called adversaries. Post-Quantum provides technology for the encryption of data and wireless communications using quantum mechanics.

Regulation Technology (RegTech)

Regulation technology, sometimes called RegTech, is the last topic we'll examine. It is defined as technology that is used to deal with regulatory challenges and helps deliver compliance requirements. RegTech is currently seen as being the next revolution to hit the financial services industry, used mostly to reduce the cost and complexity of complying with the profusion of regulations that have been instituted since the financial crisis of 2008.

Regulations and requirements have been tightened in several different industries, but especially in financial services. Regulators are issuing heavy fines for non-compliance, and new regulations around GDPR, PSD2, and MiFIDII/MIFIR are greatly challenging banks. This has led to a demand for technology that can help adapt quickly to changes in laws and regulations. Regulation projects can be very expensive, due to the amount of data that needs to be managed, the complexity of processes, as well as mandatory filings. In addition, regulators have tightened their grip through new legislation, thereby creating compliance gaps as the resources of firms are already strained. RegTech software digitizes compliance procedures and eliminates the backlog, enabling firms to streamline compliance workflows and reduce the margin for error.

Several industries need RegTech propositions, including financial services, government and legislation, environment, healthcare, vendor risk management—and even the cannabis industry.

A Sector Under Pressure

Financial institutions have seen how their compliance costs have surged, especially for global organizations operating in many jurisdictions. It is estimated that $270 billion are spent in annual compliance, 15% of all staff in banks work in risk management and compliance, and more than $321 billion has been spent on fines paid by banks since 2008.[326]

According to Thomson Reuters, a bank needs to interpret and implement a regulatory change every 12 minutes, based on the amount of annual changes required. This results in a lot of staff inside banks dedicated to compliance and heavy resources devoted to it. It is estimated that only 17% of firms have implemented RegTech solutions, which opens up an immense opportunity.

RegTech Evolution

In the beginning, compliance checking was done using Excel spreadsheets. The tool has been used very successfully for reporting, auditing, and this is the main tool that is still being used.

For organizations that require more, purpose built software started to be used, especially for automating workflows. This helped complete basic compliance activities and reduce risks involved with complying with reporting obligations. An example of the software used is MetricStream, founded in 1999. Other competitors include Workfusion and Ripcord.

Following that wave, a set of tools for monitoring transactions continuously was created. This allows bank to take a proactive stance regarding compliance, because as soon as an incident is detected it can be dealt with. An example of this type of software is Acadiasoft, which is used by most major banks, and OpenGamma, which is used for derivatives trading.

Finally, a set of providers started offering predictive software, which uses machine learning to provide new insights allowing them to have a strategic view of compliance risks and present solutions to deal with them. Companies create software that can be used for risk identification (Neurensic, Qumram), compliance intelligence (Ayasdi, Bigstream), identity management (BehaviosSec, Socure, Troo.ly) and background screening (ComplyAdvantage, Digital Reasoning, Onfido).

RegTech Funding

According to Fintech Global, VC-backed RegTech equity funding reached $6.1 billion across 529 deals since 2014. There are more than 60 European RegTechs in financial services, most of them based in the UK.[327] 2018 has been a great year for RegTech with more than $2.5 bn raised in the first half of the year. Some of the biggest deals include SignifyD for $100million, Checkr for $50 million, Symphony for $40million, Scality for $40 million, Auth0 for $39 million, Onapsis for $31 million, BigID for 30 million and Seal for $30 million.

RegTech Specialties

Within financial services, there are different RegTech firms that have different specialities.

KYC and AML

Know your Customer (KYC) and Anti-money laundering (AML) providers focus on technology that can help identify customers economically and ensure that they are not being used as vehicles for money laundering. Some example companies in this category are Trunomi, Contego, and ComplyAdvantage.

Operations and Portfolio Risk Management

Operations risk management providers manage day-to-day risks of financial services institutions, including issue identification, tracking and monitoring, data storage and reporting. Portfolio risk management firms analyze the risk inherent in investment portfolios to understand risks and ensure that banks are not overexposed. Enterprise risk management providers look at identifying other risks to the bank, including fraud risk and credit risk. Examples of companies in this space include Fenergo, Finomial, and Argos Risk.

Reporting

Reporting providers like Capital Confirmation and Certent aim to incorporate data analytics into reporting to make this process more efficient. It includes automation of regular and ad hoc reporting. Tax management providers offer software to make the collection of tax revenue easy, as well as keeping good records and making filing easy. Finally, trade-monitoring providers allow companies to monitor employees to ensure that they are not performing unauthorized transactions from a trade perspective.

Blockchain

These firms have been looking at increasing the security for distributed ledgers. Companies such as Skry and Elliptic look into transactions done on cryptocurrencies to ensure that they can build audit trails and other tools to provide comfort to organizations and individuals.

Tax Management

These firms will automate tax processes and the required government filings. These solutions are being built on the cloud, and can be consumed as software as a service. Companies in this segment include Exactor, Canopy Tax and Avalara.

Trade Monitoring

These firms will monitor employees and customers to ensure there is compliance to trade restrictions, as well as risk management boundaries. Companies in this segment include Opengamma, Droit, Ancoa and ComplySci.

Quantitative Analytics

These firms provide tools that help organizations manage liquidity, market and credit risks by using advanced analytics and quantitative risk models, which can include valuation and complex model solving. Companies in this segment include FINCAD and Ayasdi.

Looking forward, RegTech is expected to leverage advanced technology like cryptography, machine learning, robotics, artificial intelligence, natural language processing (NLP), biometrics, and blockchain to wholly automate and replace existing regulatory compliance policies and procedures. RegTech's short-term effect may be to help firms switch from passive to proactive regulatory interpretation and response. In the longer term, RegTech solutions are seen to lessen the need for human or centralized intervention for firms, and perhaps even for regulators themselves.

The Future in a Flash

We predict a global identification system, which might be one of the most rewarding changes that we get to experience in the next few decades. A global, inclusive system could not only make our lives easier but also increase the quality of life of millions of people in developing countries.

We can expect cybercrimes to continue growing and new strategies to be developed as technologies evolve. We can also expect cybersecurity firms to consolidate and huge security companies to evolve.

Regulation will continue changing as the world alters and faces new challenges. RegTech firms will mature over the next five years, and this will help financial institutions to be better protected when legislation and rules change.

Join our Newsletter

If you want to keep up to date with the latest financial technology news, please subscribe to our blog at www.fintechflash.co.uk. We send short summaries on the latest news, and provide our views on why we consider the news we select to be important to the industry.

Thank You!

Before you go, we'd like to say "thank you" for purchasing this guide.

We know that you could have picked from many different books on the topic, but you chose to buy this one.

So we'd like to say a big thanks for picking this book and reading all the way to the end. If you like what you've read, then we need your help.

Please take a moment to leave a review for this book on Amazon.

Feedback will help us continue to write more books that for you to enjoy. If you've loved it, please let us know at info@fintechflash.co.uk

DOI 10.1515/9781547401055-014

Endnotes

1 The Pulse of Fintech Q3 2017, Jonathan Lavender, Ian Pollari, Murraey Raisbeck, Brian Hughes, and Arik Speier, https://assets.kpmg.com/content/dam/kpmg/xx/pdf/2017/11/pulse-of-fintech-q3-17.pdf

2 UK fintech investment set for record-breaking year in 2017, Polina Ivanova and Jemima Kelly, https://www.reuters.com/article/us-britain-fintech-investment/uk-fintech-investment-set-for-record-breaking-year-in-2017-idUSKBN1CO026

3 CB Insights, Fintech Trends to Watch in 2018, https://www.cbinsights.com/reports/CB-Insights_Fintech-Trends-2018-Briefing.pdf?utm_campaign=fintech-trends_2018-01&utm_medium=email&_hsenc=p2ANqtz-98_rZXoHhViFaPI4PjIU3YJ8-aUyFxHIjrtVRLLfO2ecnIcJCJai6HjAPRR2af9NWygJh-0DGlrdVOjIiBVjIWkOdarRA&_hsmi=60234658&utm_content=60234658&utm_source=hs_automation&hsCtaTracking=bcd310ce-ae49-4230-b97f-23fae91ae767%7C0f816b71-bd5a-490f-8a81-18a3865bef74

4 The Pulse of Fintech Q3 2017, Jonathan Lavender, Ian Pollari, Murraey Raisbeck, Brian Hughes, and Arik Speier, https://assets.kpmg.com/content/dam/kpmg/xx/pdf/2017/11/pulse-of-fintech-q3-17.pdf

5 Credit Karma Takes On TurboTax, H&R Block With Free Tax Filings, Lauren Gensler, https://www.forbes.com/sites/laurengensler/2016/12/07/credit-karma-free-tax-filings/#497b62182c9d

6 Symphony, https://www.linkedin.com/company/2708824/

7 Alibaba's Ant Financial IPO Delayed Until 2018 at Earliest, Daniel Shane, https://www.barrons.com/articles/alibabas-ant-financial-ipo-delayed-until-2018-at-earliest-1494907150

8 Coupa up 87% in software IPO, Katie Roof, https://techcrunch.com/2016/10/06/coupa-up-87-in-software-ipo/

9 China Rapid Finance Announces Pricing of Initial Public Offering, https://www.prnewswire.com/news-releases/china-rapid-finance-announces-pricing-of-initial-public-offering-300447820.html

10 Financial service provider Markit's IPO raises $1.28 bln, https://www.cnbc.com/2014/06/19/financial-service-provider-markits-ipo-raises-128-bln.html

11 Chinese online insurer ZhongAn to seek $11 billion valuation in HK IPO: IFR, https://www.reuters.com/article/us-zhongan-online-ipo-shareissue/chinese-online-insurer-zhongan-to-seek-11-billion-valuation-in-hk-ipo-ifr-idUSKCN1BP0Z2

12 Is Qudian A Bargain Or A Falling Knife? Hongtao Li, https://seekingalpha.com/article/4133221-qudian-bargain-falling-knife

13 Chinese fintech Rong360 targets $200m US IPO for subsidiary Jianpu, Nguyen Thi Bich Ngoc, https://www.dealstreetasia.com/stories/china-fintech-company-rong360-targets-200m-us-ipo-wholly-owned-unit-84998/

14 Further, faster: Mastering digital reinvention in retail banking, Dirk Vater, Mike Baxter and Richard Fleming, http://www.bain.com/Images/BAIN_BRIEF_Mastering_digital_reinvention_in_retail_banking.pdf

15 The Second Payment Services Directive (PSD2): A briefing from Payments UK, http://www.paymentsuk.org.uk/sites/default/files/PSD2%20report%20June%202016.pdf

16 4 Banking Business Models For The Digital Age, Ben Robinson, http://fintechnews.ch/fintech/4-banking-business-models-for-the-digital-age/7566/

17 Application Programming Interface, David Orenstein, http://www.computerworld.com/article/2593623/app-development/application-programming-interface.html

18 Strong growth continues at Shawbrook in 2014, https://www.shawbrook.co.uk/newsroom/2014/09/strong-growth-continues-at-shawbrook-in-2014/

19 2014: Another Record Year, http://www.aldermore.co.uk/about-us/newsroom/2015/02/2014-another-record-year/

20 About Fidor Bank, https://www.fidorbank.uk/about-fidor/about-us

21 Revolution in Mobile Banking: Fidor Bank and Telefónica Germany to launch O2's first mobile

DOI 10.1515/9781547401055-015

bank account - O2 Banking, Ben Rose, https://www.fidor.de/documents/2016_05_12_Fidor_Bank_Telefonica_ENG.pdf

22 Rocketbank weathers Russia banking storms, https://www.ft.com/content/3ecb8bfa-d495-11e5-829b-8564e7528e54

23 Number26 is now a true bank as it now has a full banking license, Romain Dillet, https://techcrunch.com/2016/07/21/number26-is-now-a-true-bank-as-it-now-has-a-full-banking-license/

24 Number26 Now Uses TransferWise For International Transfers, Romain Dillet, https://techcrunch.com/2016/02/25/number26-now-uses-transferwise-for-international-transfers/

25 N26 announces plans to launch in the US by mid-2018, Romain Dillet, https://techcrunch.com/2017/10/23/n26-announces-plans-to-launch-in-the-us-by-mid-2018/

26 This guy turned 22 last week — but he's about to launch a startup RBS wants to partner with, Oscar Williams-Grut, http://uk.businessinsider.com/loot-bank-ceo-ollie-purdue-interview-2015-8

27 Digital banking startup Loot secures £2.2 million seed round, https://www.finextra.com/newsarticle/31467/digital-banking-startup-loot-secures-22-million-seed-round

28 Monzo, a UK digital-only challenger bank, granted full banking license, Steve O'Hear, https://techcrunch.com/2017/04/05/monzo-a-uk-digital-only-challenger-bank-granted-full-banking-license

29 Atom Bank raises $102M at $320M valuation for a mobile-only bank for millennials, Ingrid Lunden, https://techcrunch.com/2017/03/03/atom-bank-102-million/

30 Tandem Bank welcomes its first customers; Loot steps into the fray, https://www.finextra.com/newsarticle/29714/tandem-bank-welcomes-its-first-customers

31 Tandem's acquisition of Harrods Bank, the banking arm of UK department store, is approved by regulators, Steve O'Hear, https://techcrunch.com/2017/12/20/tandems-acquisition-of-harrods-bank-the-banking-arm-of-uk-department-store-is-approved-by-regulators/

32 Mobile-only bank Starling wins its licence, Tim Wallace, http://www.telegraph.co.uk/business/2016/07/14/mobile-only-bank-starling-wins-its-licence/

33 Monese, the UK banking app for immigrants and expats, finally lands on iOS, Steve O'Hear, https://techcrunch.com/2016/07/28/monese-ios/

34 Monese, the mobile current account banking app, expands to Europe, Steve O'Hear, https://techcrunch.com/2017/06/27/monese-adds-euro-support/

35 Remittances: Funds for the Folks Back Home, Dilip Ratha, http://www.imf.org/external/pubs/ft/fandd/basics/remitt.htm

36 Remittances to Recover Modestly After Two Years of Decline, Indira Chand and Huma Imtiaz, http://www.worldbank.org/en/news/press-release/2017/10/03/remittances-to-recover-modestly-after-two-years-of-decline

37 Trends in Migration and Remittances 2017, http://www.worldbank.org/en/news/infographic/2017/04/21/trends-in-migration-and-remittances-2017

38 Online-Remittances, *Life.SREDA VC, http://fintechranking.com/2016/03/26/online-remittances/*

39 Remittance prices worldwide, https://remittanceprices.worldbank.org/en

40 Peer to Peer Money Transfer Firms, http://moneytransfercomparison.com/peer-to-peer/

41 Digital Payments 2020, Alpesh Shah, Prateek Roongta, Chilman Jain, Vibha Kaushik, and Abhishek Awadhiya, http://image-src.bcg.com/BCG_COM/BCG-Google%20Digital%20Payments%202020-July%202016_tcm21-39245.pdf

42 Transferwise, https://en.wikipedia.org/wiki/TransferWise

43 Skype For Cash: How TransferWise Is Upending The Way Consumers Move $3 Trillion Around The Globe, Samantha Sharf, http://www.forbes.com/sites/samanthasharf/2016/05/26/skype-for-cash-how-transferwise-is-upending-the-way-consumers-move-3-trillion-around-the-globe/#77d-356784f3a

44 TransferWise raises $280M to Fund Global Expansion, Jeff John Roberts, http://fortune.com/2017/11/02/transferwise-latin-america-asia/

45 CB Insights, Fintech Trends to Watch in 2018,]f74

46 Venmo users sent $8 billion last quarter — twice as much as a year ago, Rani Molla, https://www.recode.net/2017/7/26/16044528/venmo-8-billion-transaction-volume-growth-rate-chart

47 Fintech CurrencyCloud tapped up investors months before Google raise, Oscar Williams-Grut, http://uk.businessinsider.com/currencycloud-2016-accounts-fintech-raised-from-investors-months-before-google-2017-7

48 How social media is reshaping global money transfer, See Kit Tang, http://www.cnbc.com/2015/11/12/start-up-fastacashs-xopo-app-lets-users-transfer-money-through-social-media.html

50 Should You Send Money to Friends Through Facebook Messenger?, Susan Johnston Taylor, http://money.usnews.com/money/personal-finance/articles/2015/04/07/should-you-send-money-to-friends-through-facebook-messenger

51 Facebook given licence to launch Messenger payments in Europe, Rian Boden, https://www.nfcworld.com/2016/12/09/348944/facebook-given-licence-launch-messenger-payments-europe/

52 WeChat, https://en.wikipedia.org/wiki/WeChat#WeChat_Payment

53 Western Union and Viber to provide cross-border money transfer capabilities, Jumat, http://www.antaranews.com/en/news/102976/western-union-and-viber-to-provide-cross-border-money-transfer-capabilities

54 How nanopayments finally came of age, Tom May, http://www.techradar.com/news/internet/how-nanopayments-finally-came-of-age-614212/2

55 Peer-to-peer lender Zopa moves towards bank launch after raising £32m, Lucy Burton,http://www.telegraph.co.uk/business/2017/06/01/peer-to-peer-lender-zopa-moves-towards-bank-launch-raising-32m/

56 Big News for Prosper: Marketplace Lender Signs Agreement for $5 Billion in Loan Purchases from Consortium of Investors, JD Alois, https://www.crowdfundinsider.com/2017/02/96722-big-news-prosper-marketplace-lender-signs-agreement-5-billion-loan-purchases-consortium-investors/

57 https://help.claritymoney.com/investments-loans-and-insurance/loans/prosper-loans

58 Peer-to-peer lending: everything you need to know about the leading websites, Tara Evans, http://www.telegraph.co.uk/personal-banking/savings/peer-to-peer-lending-everything-you-need-to-know-about-the-leadi/

59 CreditEase's Online Platform Yirendai Becomes the Third Major P2P Lender to IPO and China's First, Jason Jones, http://www.lendacademy.com/crediteases-online-platform-yirendai-becomes-third-major-p2p-lender-ipo-chinas-first/

60 Startup Spotlight: LendingRobot simplifies peer-to-peer lending for investors, Taylor Soper, http://www.geekwire.com/2014/lendingrobot/

61 Startup LendingRobot launches automated hedge fund investing in loans, Anna Irrera, https://www.reuters.com/article/us-lendingrobot-hedgefund/startup-lendingrobot-launches-automated-hedge-fund-investing-in-loans-idUSKBN15A28S

62 Digital Disruption, A UK Report, March 2015, BBA with Accenture, pp. 25-26,

63 Retail Banks Wake Up To Lending, Richard Fleming and John Fielding, http://www.bain.com/publications/articles/retail-banks-wake-up-to-digital-lending.aspx

64 Online Lending, http://fintechranking.com/2016/03/24/online-lending/

65 Affirm launches app to break purchases into monthly payments, Katie Roof, https://techcrunch.com/2017/10/23/affirm-launches-app-to-break-purchases-into-monthly-payments/

66 Max Levchin's Affirm raises $200 million at a nearly $2 billion valuation, Katie Roof, https://techcrunch.com/2017/12/11/max-levchins-affirm-raised-200-million-at-nearly-2-billion-valuation/

67 Kreditech raises €110M from Naspers' PayU in strategic financing partnership, Ingrid Lunden, https://techcrunch.com/2017/05/10/kreditech-payu/

68 ZestFinance Introduces Machine Learning Platform to Underwrite Millennials and Other Consumers with Limited Credit History, Sarah Arvizo, https://www.businesswire.com/news/home/20170214005357/en/ZestFinance-Introduces-Machine-Learning-Platform-Underwrite-Millennials

69 LendUp gets strategic investment from PayPal and adds to its executive team, Ryan Lower, https://techcrunch.com/2017/06/28/lendup-paypal/

70 http://www.independent.co.uk/student/student-life/finances/graduates-who-fail-to-make-student-loan-repayments-should-face-arrest-like-new-zealanders-education-a7158396.html

71 The Rise Of Peer To Peer Student Loans, Robert Farrington, http://www.forbes.com/sites/robert-farrington/2014/08/13/the-rise-of-peer-to-peer-student-loans/#55aed3bf5027

72 SoFi, https://en.wikipedia.org/wiki/SoFi

73 SoFi Tried To Sell Itself For $8B Earlier This Year https://www.pymnts.com/news/alternative-financial-services/2017/sofi-tried-to-sell-itself-for-8b-last-year/

74 How Commonbond Started, https://commonbond.co/about

75 Why CommonBond Will Make You Forget Everything You Thought You Knew About Student Loans, Murray Newlands, http://www.forbes.com/sites/mnewlands/2015/11/04/why-commonbond-will-make-you-forget-everything-you-thought-you-knew-about-student-loans/3/#49df3054360b

76 Lending Startup Earnest Jumps Into The Student Loan Refinancing Game, Laura Shin, http://www.forbes.com/sites/laurashin/2015/01/27/lending-startup-earnest-jumps-into-the-student-loan-refinancing-game/#3f886d0b36a9

77 Lending Startup Earnest Jumps Into The Student Loan Refinancing Game, Laura Shin, http://www.forbes.com/sites/laurashin/2015/01/27/lending-startup-earnest-jumps-into-the-student-loan-refinancing-game/#3f886d0b36a9

78 Earnest, An Online Student Lender, Bought By Navient For $155 Million, Lauren Gensler , https://www.forbes.com/sites/laurengensler/2017/10/04/earnest-acquired-by-navient-fintech-student-loans/#70aadbb17e19

79 With $63 Million Under Management, Student Loan Hero Joins The "Mint For Student Loans" Crowd, Sarah Perez, https://techcrunch.com/2013/02/19/with-63-million-under-management-student-loan-hero-joins-the-mint-for-student-loans-crowd/

80 LendEDU Is Making Student Loan Refinancing Easier, Jonathan Shieber, https://techcrunch.com/2016/02/09/lendedu-is-making-student-loan-refinancing-easier/

81 A Case of Regulatory Evolution: A Review of the UK Financial Conduct Authority's Approach to Crowdfunding, Robert Wardrop & Tania Ziegler, http://www.crowdfundinsider.com/2016/07/88046-case-regulatory-evolution-review-uk-financial-conduct-authorKs-approach-crowdfunding/

82 A Case of Regulatory Evolution: A Review of the UK Financial Conduct Authority's Approach to Crowdfunding, Robert Wardrop & Tania Ziegler, http://www.crowdfundinsider.com/2016/07/88046-case-regulatory-evolution-review-uk-financial-conduct-authorKs-approach-crowdfunding/

83 In Defence of Online Lending, Ryan Weeks, https://techcrunch.com/2016/06/02/in-defense-of-online-lending/

84 Factoring: What It Is and How to Choose a Service, Sara Angeles, http://www.businessnewsdaily.com/9336-choosing-factoring-service.html

85 Kabbage, https://en.wikipedia.org/wiki/Kabbage

86 The Six-Minute Loan: How Kabbage Is Upending Small Business Lending -- And Building A Very Big Business, Darren Dahl, http://www.forbes.com/sites/darrendahl/2015/05/06/the-six-minute-loan-how-kabbage-is-upending-small-business-lending-and-building-a-very-big-business/#421059a53a17

87 Billion-Dollar Unicorns: Kabbage Mulling An IPO, Sramana Mitra, https://seekingalpha.com/article/4130221-billion-dollar-unicorns-kabbage-mulling-ipo

88 PayPal Working Capital, https://www.paypal.com/workingcapital/

89 PayPal's "Bill Me Later" Service Becomes "PayPal Credit," As Company Expands Credit Products Globally, Sarah Perez, https://techcrunch.com/2014/07/30/paypals-bill-me-later-service-becomes-paypal-credit-as-company-expands-credit-products-globally/

90 Why PayPal Is Acquiring Swift Financial, Naomi Gray, http://marketrealist.com/2017/09/why-paypal-is-acquiring-swift-financial

91 Square Capital Starts Offering Loans More Broadly, Leena Rao, http://fortune.com/2016/08/10/square-capital-loans/

92 Square is expanding its lending business through partners to try to reach millions more small businesses, Jason Del Ray, https://www.recode.net/2017/10/24/16521474/square-capital-bigcommerce-partnership-loans-small-business

93 With New Funding In Tow, Lendio And Creditera Are Helping Small Businesses Secure Loans And Avoid Bad Credit, Rip Empson, https://techcrunch.com/2013/08/28/with-new-funding-in-tow-lendio-and-creditera-are-helping-small-businesses-secure-loans-and-avoid-bad-credit/

94 Lendio of South Jordan passes $500M mark in loans to small businesses nationwide, Tom Harvey, https://www.sltrib.com/news/business/2017/07/29/lendio-of-south-jordan-passes-500m-mark-in-loans-to-small-businesses-nationwide/

95 Habito, an app that helps you find the right mortgage, raises £18.5M Series B led by Atomico, Steve O'Hear, https://techcrunch.com/2017/09/03/habito-atomico/

96 Why SoFi Will Take Mortgage Market Share from Wells Fargo and JPMorgan Chase, Peter Cohan, http://www.forbes.com/sites/petercohan/2015/11/30/why-sofi-will-take-mortgage-market-share-from-wells-fargo-and-jpmorgan-chase/#46d4988c78ba

97 Online Mortgage Startup Lenda Expands, Aims To Shake Up Industry, Laura Shin, http://www.forbes.com/sites/laurashin/2015/02/25/online-mortgage-startup-lenda-expands-aims-to-shake-up-industry/#715ed2612227

98 loanDepot Rises to Become 5th Largest Mortgage Lender in US, JD Alois, http://www.crowdfundinsider.com/2016/11/91973-loandepot-rises-become-5th-largest-mortgage-lender-us/

99 Sindeo launches 5-minute digital mortgage, Brena Swanson, http://www.housingwire.com/articles/38273-sindeo-launches-5-minute-digital-mortgage

100 World Economic Forum, The Future of FinTech A Paradigm Shift in Small Business Finance, Michael Koenitzer, Giancarlo Bruno, Peer Stein, Arnaud Ventura & Peter Tufano, http://www3.weforum.org/docs/IP/2015/FS/GAC15_The_Future_of_FinTech_Paradigm_Shift_Small_Business_Finance_report_2015.pdf

101 Edinburgh Group, Growing the global economy through SMEs, Roberto D'Imperio, http://www.edinburgh-group.org/media/2776/edinburgh_group_research_-_growing_the_global_economy_through_smes.pdf

102 Federation of Small Businesses,http://www.fsb.org.uk/media-centre/small-business-statistics

103 Annual Report on European SMEs 2016/2017

104 BBVA, https://www.bba.org.uk/news/statistics/sme-statistics/bank-support-for-smes-4th-quarter-2015/#.Vv09BcvruM8

105 World Economic Forum, The Future of FinTech A Paradigm Shift in Small Business Finance, Michael Koenitzer, Giancarlo Bruno, Peer Stein, Arnaud Ventura & Peter Tufano, http://www3.weforum.org/docs/IP/2015/FS/GAC15_The_Future_of_FinTech_Paradigm_Shift_Small_Business_Finance_report_2015.pdf

106 BBVA, The 'fintech' revolution: A threat for banks or an opportunity?, http://www.centrodeinnovacionbbva.com/en/news/fintech-revolution-threat-banks-or-opportunity

107 WhiteCase, How fintech deals are reshaping financial services, Prof. Dr. Roger Kiem, Gavin Weir, Guy Potel, and Dr. Philip Trillmich, http://www.whitecase.com/publications/insight/how-fintech-deals-are-reshaping-financial-services

108 Fortune, Your Neighborhood Bank Is About to Have Its 'Uber Moment', Ian Mount, http://fortune.com/2016/03/31/citi-bank-staffing-uber-moment/

109 Why fintech won't kill banks, http://www.economist.com/blogs/economist-explains/2015/06/economist-explains-12

110 Harvard Business School, The State of Small Business Lending: Credit Access during the Recovery and How Technology May Change the Game, Karen Gordon Mills, and Brayden McCarthy, http://www.hbs.edu/faculty/Publication%20Files/15-004_09b1bf8b-eb2a-4e63-9c4e-0374f770856f.pdf

111 Citigroup, Digital Disruption - How FinTech is Forcing Banking to a Tipping Point, Kathleen Boyle, https://ir.citi.com/SEBhgbdvxes95HWZMmFbjGiU%2FydQ9kbvEbHIruHR%2Fle%2F2W-za4cRvOQUNX8GBWVsV

112 McKinsey, Engaging customers: The evolution of Asia–Pacific digital banking, Vinayak HV, Stuart Kamp, Sergey Khon, and Gillian Lee, http://www.mckinsey.com/industries/financial-services/our-insights/engaging-customers-the-evolution-of-asia-pacific-digital-banking?cid=other-eml-alt-mip-mck-oth-1701

113 Techcrunch, BBVA continues its fintech acquisition run, buys Holvi, an online-only business bank, Ingrid Lunden, https://techcrunch.com/2016/03/07/bbva-continues-its-fintech-acquisition-run-buys-holvi-an-online-only-business-bank/

114 Finance Magnets, Leumi, CIBC and NAB Form Strategic Alliance for Fintech Innovation, Avi Mizrahi, http://www.financemagnates.com/cryptocurrency/news/leumi-cibc-and-nab-form-strategic-alliance-for-fintech-innovation/

115 Reuters, Santander UK launches money management app with Kalixa Payments and Monitise, http://www.reuters.com/article/idUSFWN10105B20150722

116 Cogni, http://www.cogninow.com/

117 Holvi, https://about.holvi.com/

118 Revolut for Business, https://business.revolut.com/

119 Revolut launches business accounts in U.K. and Europe, Steve O'Hear, https://techcrunch.com/2017/06/13/revolut-launches-business-accounts/

120 CB Insights, Fintech Trends to Watch in 2018, https://www.cbinsights.com/reports/CB-Insights_Fintech-Trends-2018-Briefing.pdf?utm_campaign=fintech-trends_2018-01&utm_medium=email&_hsenc=p2ANqtz-98_rZXoHhViFaPI4PjIU3YJ8-aUyFxHIjrtVRLLf02ecnIc-JCJai6HjAPRR2af9NWygJh0DGlrdV0jIiBVjIWkOdarRA&_hsmi=60234658&utm_content=60234658&utm_source=hs_automation&hsCtaTracking=bcd310ce-ae49-4230-b97f-23fae91ae767%7C0f816b71-bd5a-490f-8a81-18a3865bef74

121 Tide, https://beta.tide.co/

122 Banking startup Tide raises $14 million to 'give small businesses back their time, Camilla Hodgson, http://uk.businessinsider.com/fintech-startup-tide-14-million-boost-from-spotify-backers-creandum-2017-7

123 Tochka, https://tochka.com/banking

124 Accenture, SME Banking 2020, https://www.accenture.com/t20160505T043700__w__/gb-en/_acnmedia/PDF-16/Accenture-Unlocking-Revenue-SME-Banking.PDF

125 NatWest selects FreeAgent for business banking platform, https://www.finextra.com/pressarticle/67700/natwest-selects-freeagent-for-business-banking-platform

126 Zenefits, https://www.zenefits.com/services/

127 Gusto, https://gusto.com/partners/accountants

128 Gusto Raises $50M At A $1B Valuation To Take On Zenefits, Matthew Lynley, https://techcrunch.com/2015/12/21/gusto-is-looking-for-another-50m-to-take-on-zenefits/

129 Hibob, https://www.hibob.com/

130 Hibob raises $7.5M to help SMEs manage their people, Steve O'Hear, https://techcrunch.com/2016/06/06/hibob/

131 HR and employee benefits platform Hibob raises $17.5M led by U.S.-based Battery Ventures, Steve O'Hear, https://techcrunch.com/2017/04/25/hr-and-employee-benefits-platform-hibob-raises-17-5m-led-by-u-s-based-battery-ventures/

132 Sprout, http://sproutsocial.com/

133 Most Innovative Social Media Platform: Sprout Social, Kin Davis, http://www.dmnews.com/marketing-strategy/most-innovative-social-media-platform-sprout-social/article/481846/

134 http://www.chicagobusiness.com/section/fast-50

135 Forbes, Most Innovative Growth Companies, http://www.forbes.com/companies/xero/

136 Rocketing through $300 million, Rod Drury, https://www.xero.com/blog/2016/11/rocketing-through-300m/

137 Mobile consumer behavior reshaping digital commerce, Lauren Horwitz, http://searchcrm.techtarget.com/feature/Mobile-consumer-behavior-reshaping-digital-commerce

138 How does a POS system work?, Ben Taylor, http://www.mobiletransaction.org/how-pos-system-work/

139 Two Unique Models for mPOS Success, http://blog.mondato.com/two-unique-models-for-mpos-success/

140 The Evolution of mPOS: The Payments Industry in Flux, http://www.mahindracomviva.com/wp-content/uploads/2015/08/The-Evolution-of-mPOS_White-Paper.pdf

141 Mobile is revolutionizing the way merchants accept payments and manage their businesses, John Heggestuen, http://www.businessinsider.com/mobile-is-revolutionizing-the-way-merchants-accept-payments-and-manage-their-business-2014-12?nr_email_referer=1&utm_source=Sailthru&utm_medium=email&utm_content=TechSelect

142 Square notes EMV pickup in first-quarter earnings, BI Intelligence, http://www.businessinsider.com/square-notes-emv-pickup-in-first-quarter-earnings-2016-5

143 This is Square's plan to maintain its growth after a successful first quarter, Andrew Meola, http://www.businessinsider.com/square-plans-to-grow-capital-instant-deposit-invoices-2016-3

144 About Us, https://www.klarna.com/us/about-us

145 Klarna, A Unicorn, Is Coming To The U.S. And Going After U.S. Credit Card Companies, Connie Loizos, https://techcrunch.com/2015/10/28/klarna-a-unicorn-is-coming-to-the-u-s-and-going-after-u-s-credit-card-companies/

146 Klarna Is Making The Jump To Real-World Commerce, http://www.pymnts.com/news/international/europe/2016/klarna-physical-commerce/

147 Klarna gets a full banking license, gears up to go beyond financing payments, Ingrid Lunden, https://techcrunch.com/2017/06/19/klarna-gets-a-full-banking-license-gears-up-to-go-beyond-financing-payments/

148 CB Insights, Fintech Trends to Watch in 2018, https://www.cbinsights.com/reports/CB-Insights_Fintech-Trends-2018-Briefing.pdf?utm_campaign=fintech-trends_2018-01&utm_medium=email&_hsenc=p2ANqtz-98_rZXoHhViFaPI4PjIU3YJ8-aUyFxHIjrtVRLLf02ecnIc-JCJai6HjAPRR2af9NWygJh0DGlrdV0jIiBVjIWkOdarRA&_hsmi=60234658&utm_content=60234658&utm_source=hs_automation&hsCtaTracking=bcd310ce-ae49-4230-b97f-23fae91ae767%7C0f816b71-bd5a-490f-8a81-18a3865bef74

149 LifePay Launched Internet Acquiring And Lending Services, http://fintechranking.com/2015/03/27/lifepay-launched-internet-acquiring-and-lending-services/

150 About SumUp, https://sumup.com/about

151 Allset, https://www.crunchbase.com/organization/allset#/entity

152 Allset raises $5M to help restaurants deliver a more efficient dining experience, Anthony Ha, https://techcrunch.com/2017/10/17/allset-series-a/

153 About One97, http://www.one97.com/about-one97

154 iPad Cash Registers: Coming To a Store Near You?, Jacqueline Emigh, http://www.tabletpcreview.com/feature/ipad-cash-registers-coming-to-a-store-near-you/

155 Toast, From Endeca Vets, Orders Up $30M For Restaurant Software, Jeff Engel, http://www.xconomy.com/boston/2016/01/05/toast-from-endeca-vets-orders-up-30m-for-restaurant-software/

156 Restaurant tech startup Toast raising more money as it hits 1,000 customers, Curt Woodward, http://www.betaboston.com/news/2015/08/07/restaurant-tech-startup-toast-raising-more-money-as-it-hits-1000-customers/

157 Toast Debuts an Inventory Management and Reporting Solution, http://hospitalitytechnology.

edgl.com/news/Toast-Debuts-an-Inventory-Management-and-Reporting-Solution107612

158 Shopify's iPad Point-of-Sale System Gets Its Own Apps, Sarah Perez, https://techcrunch.com/2015/07/21/shopifys-ipad-point-of-sale-system-gets-its-own-apps/

159 E La Carte Raises $35 Million to Expand Pay-at-the-Table Technology, Lora Kolodny, http://blogs.wsj.com/venturecapital/2014/09/24/e-la-carte-raises-35-million-to-expand-pay-at-the-table-technology/

160 Revel Systems, https://en.wikipedia.org/wiki/Revel_Systems

161 Internet Acquiring, http://www.okkocapital.com/en/out-services/internet-acquiring/

162 About Us, https://stripe.com/about

163 Here's your ultimate list of payment gateway providers and key industry players, Andrew Meola, http://www.businessinsider.com/list-payment-gateway-providers-2016-11

164 Stripe Ramps Up Payments Fraud Prevention, Leena Rao, http://fortune.com/2016/10/19/stripe-fraud-prevention/

165 Stripe launches Works With Stripe, a directory of apps that integrate with its payments, Ingrid Lunden, https://techcrunch.com/2016/11/07/stripe-launches-works-with-stripe-a-directory-of-apps-that-integrate-with-its-payments/

166 How to Sell Online, https://squareup.com/ecommerce

167 About Us, https://www.paypal.com/ph/webapps/mpp/about

168 About Braintree, https://www.braintreepayments.com/about-braintree

169 Two Years After Acquisition, Braintree's Authorized Payment Volume to Cross $50B this Year, Bill Ready, https://www.braintreepayments.com/blog/two-years-after-acquisition-braintrees-authorized-payment-volume-to-cross-50-billion-this-year/

170 Business, https://www.klarna.com/uk/business

171 Online acquiring: Stripe and Competitors, http://fintechranking.com/2016/03/20/online-acquiring-stripe-and-competitors/

172 Apple v. Google v. PayPal: Who Will Win The $4.5TN Mobile Wallets War? http://www.forbes.com/sites/groupthink/2016/05/16/apple-v-google-v-paypal-who-will-win-the-4-5tn-mobile-wallets-war/#1c36a7297cbe

173 Are we on the brink of a T-Commerce revolution?, *Ben Sutherland,* http://vizeum.co.uk/p/are-we-on-the-brink-of-a-t-commerce-revolution/

174 American Express Pushes E-Commerce to TV Commerce, Brian Steinberg, http://adage.com/article/media/american-express-pushes-e-commerce-tv-commerce/240048/

175 American Express Pushes E-Commerce to TV Commerce, Brian Steinberg, http://adage.com/article/media/american-express-pushes-e-commerce-tv-commerce/240048/

176 The venture capital funnel, https://www.cbinsights.com/blog/venture-capital-funnel/

177 CrowdExpert.com Investment Crowdfunding Industry Size Estimate, David Pricco, http://crowdexpert.com/crowdfunding-industry-statistics/

178 Kickstarter, https://en.wikipedia.org/wiki/Kickstarter

179 How Kickstarter Grew Fast--by Slowing Down, Zoe Henry, http://www.inc.com/zoe-henry/kickstarter-slowed-down-to-stay-in-control.html

180 AngelList, https://en.wikipedia.org/wiki/AngelList

181 A Pretty Insane Internal Rate of Return for AngelList Investors, JD Alois, http://www.crowdfundinsider.com/2016/10/91479-pretty-insane-internal-rate-return-angellist-investors/

182 Indiegogo, https://en.wikipedia.org/wiki/Indiegogo

183 Indiegogo, https://en.wikipedia.org/wiki/Indiegogo

184 6 Top Crowdfunding Websites: Which One Is Right For Your Project?, Kate Taylor, http://www.forbes.com/sites/katetaylor/2013/08/06/6-top-crowdfunding-websites-which-one-is-right-for-your-project/#b982db765f80

185 Crowdfunder, https://en.wikipedia.org/wiki/Crowdfunder

186 GoFundMe, https://en.wikipedia.org/wiki/GoFundMe

187 RocketHub, https://en.wikipedia.org/wiki/RocketHub

188 6 Top Crowdfunding Websites: Which One Is Right For Your Project?, Kate Taylor, http://www.forbes.com/sites/katetaylor/2013/08/06/6-top-crowdfunding-websites-which-one-is-right-for-your-project/#6e9bf8c265f8

189 How to Fundraise, https://gogetfunding.com/how-to-fundraise/

190 6 Top Crowdfunding Websites: Which One Is Right For Your Project?, Kate Taylor, http://www.forbes.com/sites/katetaylor/2013/08/06/6-top-crowdfunding-websites-which-one-is-right-for-your-project/#6e9bf8c265f8

191 About Us, https://startsomegood.com/about?view=what_we_do

192 What is Equity Funding?, https://www.syndicateroom.com/investors/what-is-equity-crowd-funding

193 CrowdCube, https://en.wikipedia.org/wiki/Crowdcube

194 SeedRs, https://en.wikipedia.org/wiki/Seedrs

195 Top 10 Equity Crowdfunding Sites for Investors & Entrepreneurs, Brian Martucci, http://www.moneycrashers.com/equity-crowdfunding-sites-investors-entrepreneurs/

196 CircleUp announced $125 million venture fund, Katie Roof, https://techcrunch.com/2017/10/31/circleup-announced-125-million-venture-fund/

197 Companisto, https://en.wikipedia.org/wiki/Companisto

198 10 Disruptive trends in wealth management, Gauthier Vincent, et al, https://www2.deloitte.com/content/dam/Deloitte/us/Documents/strategy/us-cons-disruptors-in-wealth-mgmt-final.pdf

199 How Wealth Managers Can Ride the Financial technology Wave, Rohit Mahna, http://www.wealthmanagement.com/technology/how-wealth-managers-can-ride-financial technology-wave

200 Robo-retirement, http://www.investopedia.com/terms/r/roboadvisor-roboadvisor.asp

201 10 Disruptive trends in wealth management, Gauthier Vincent, et al, https://www2.deloitte.com/content/dam/Deloitte/us/Documents/strategy/us-cons-disruptors-in-wealth-mgmt-final.pdf

202 The Rise of Robo-Advice: Changing the Concept of Wealth Management, Accenture, https://www.accenture.com/_acnmedia/PDF-2/Accenture-Wealth-Management-Rise-of-Robo-Advice.pdf

203 Robo Advisors to Run $2 Trillion by 2020 if This Model Is Right, Michael Regan, https://www.bloomberg.com/news/articles/2015-06-18/robo advisors-to-run-2-trillion-by-2020-if-this-model-is-right

204 THE ROBO-ADVISING REPORT: Market forecasts, key growth drivers, and how automated asset management will change the advisory industry, Sarah Kocianski, http://www.businessinsider.com/the-robo-advising-report-market-forecasts-key-growth-drivers-and-how-automated-asset-management-will-change-the-advisory-industry-2016-6

205 The US still has the robo-advisor lead, Intelligence, http://www.businessinsider.com/the-us-still-has-the-robo-advisor-lead-2017-4

206 10 Disruptive trends in wealth management, Gauthier Vincent, et al, https://www2.deloitte.com/content/dam/Deloitte/us/Documents/strategy/us-cons-disruptors-in-wealth-mgmt-final.pdf

207 Financial technology firms are taking on the 1%, but can they fix finance?, Nicole Kobie, http://www.wired.co.uk/article/future-of-investment-wired-money-2016

208 10 Disruptive trends in wealth management, Gauthier Vincent, et al, https://www2.deloitte.com/content/dam/Deloitte/us/Documents/strategy/us-cons-disruptors-in-wealth-mgmt-final.pdf

209 Number of social media user worldwide from 2010 to 2021, https://www.statista.com/statistics/278414/number-of-worldwide-social-network-users/

210 How Wealth Managers Can Ride the Financial technology Wave, Rohit Mahna, http://www.wealthmanagement.com/technology/how-wealth-managers-can-ride-financial technology-wave

211 eToro Review – Must Read Before Investing, Andrew Black, http://www.modestmoney.com/etoro-review-must-read-investing/35963

212 This App Makes Investing As Easy As Swiping Your Debit Card, Libby Kane, http://www.businessinsider.com/acorns-investing-app-2014-10

213 Acorns Acquires Vault to Expand Product Offerings and Tap into Portland's Fintech Talent https://www.prnewswire.com/news-releases/acorns-acquires-vault-to-expand-product-offerings-and-tap-into-portlands-fintech-talent-300551281.html

214 This new app is like fantasy sports for the stock market — and it's offering cash prizes, Nathan McAlone, http://www.businessinsider.com/vestly-is-like-fantasy-sports-for-the-stock-market-2016-4

215 Ellevest: What to Know about This Robo advisor, Barbara Friedberg, http://www.investopedia.com/articles/investing/061516/ellevest-what-know-about-roboadvisor.asp

216 Wealthfront, https://en.wikipedia.org/wiki/Wealthfront

217 How Robinhood Makes Money (AAPL, EFTC), Steven Richmond, http://www.investopedia.com/articles/active-trading/020515/how-robinhood-makes-money.asp

218 Nutmeg, https://en.wikipedia.org/wiki/Nutmeg_(investment_company)

219 7 Top Non-U.S. Robo advisors, Zina Kumok, http://www.investopedia.com/articles/financial-advisors/032216/7-top-nonus-roboadvisors.asp

220 9 Top Robo advisors for Financial Advisors, Barbara A. Friedberg, http://www.investopedia.com/articles/financial-advisor/062316/9-top-roboadvisors-financial-advisors.asp

221 7 Robo Advisors That Make Investing Effortless, Rob Berger, http://www.forbes.com/sites/robertberger/2015/02/05/7-robo advisors-that-make-investing-effortless/4/#6941778e4420

222 This former JPMorgan trader built a free app that sends custom financial signals to your smartphone, Nathan McAlone, http://www.businessinsider.com/trigger-app-sends-you-custom-financial-signals-2016-6

223 Riskalyze draws $20 million in capital for robo platform and other advisor products, Liz Skinner, http://www.investmentnews.com/article/20161031/FREE/161029901/riskalyze-draws-20-million-in-capital-for-robo-platform-and-other

224 Addepar's strategy: Focus on HNW, arm advisors with digital tools, Suleman Din, http://www.financial-planning.com/news/addepars-strategy-focus-on-hnw-arm-advisors-with-digital-tools

225 Wealth management data startup Addepar raises $140 million, Anna Irrera, https://www.reuters.com/article/us-addepar-investment/wealth-management-data-startup-addepar-raises-140-million-idUSKBN18Z1IO

226 SumZero, https://en.wikipedia.org/wiki/SumZero

227 Hedge Fund Manager Puts Profile on Social Media, Lures $20 Million, Selina Wang, https://www.bloomberg.com/news/articles/2016-02-16/hedge-fund-manager-puts-profile-on-social-media-lures-20-million

228 PFM isn't dead: it's just that nobody has got it right yet, Chris Ward, http://www.maparesearch.com/pfm-isnt-dead-its-just-that-nobody-has-got-it-right-yet/

229 The Hollerith Machine, https://www.census.gov/history/www/innovations/technology/the_hollerith_tabulator.html

230 How Much Information? Peter Lyman and Hal R. Varian, http://www2.sims.berkeley.edu/research/projects/how-much-info/

231 Big data: The next frontier for innovation, competition, and productivity, McKinsey Global Institute, http://www.mckinsey.com/business-functions/digital-mckinsey/our-insights/big-data-the-next-frontier-for-innovation

232 Using big data to make better pricing decisions, Walter Baker, Dieter Kiewell, and Georg Winkler, http://www.mckinsey.com/business-functions/marketing-and-sales/our-insights/using-big-data-to-make-better-pricing-decisions

233 Big Data: A Competitive Weapon for the Enterprise, https://blogs.adobe.com/digitalmarketing/wp-content/uploads/2015/10/laxalt-fig1.jpg

234 Big Data Executive Survey 2016, Randy Bean, http://newvantage.com/wp-content/uploads/2016/01/Big-Data-Executive-Survey-2016-Findings-FINAL.pdf

235 Avant, Rates & Terms, https://www.avant.com/rates_terms

236 WeLab raises US$160M in Series B financing from Khazanah and ING Bank, http://www.welab.

co/series_b_release?locale=en

237 Financial tech startup WeLab raises $220M from investors including Alibaba, the IFC and Credit Suisse, Catherine Shu, https://techcrunch.com/2017/11/09/financial-tech-startup-welab-raises-220m-from-investors-including-alibaba-the-ifc-and-credit-suisse/

238 Qualtrics, https://www.qualtrics.com/

239 This is Watson, IBM Journal of Research and Development, http://ieeexplore.ieee.org/xpl/tocresult.jsp?reload=true&isnumber=6177717&cm_mc_uid=98990303915214833709656&cm_mc_sid_50200000=1483373577

240 Alteryx, http://www.alteryx.com/

241 Gooddata, https://www.gooddata.com/

242 Gartner Says 6.4 Billion Connected "Things" Will Be in Use in 2016, Up 30 Percent From 2015, Rob van der Meulen, http://www.gartner.com/newsroom/id/3165317

244 Here are IoT trends that will change the way businesses, governments, and consumers interact with the world, John Greenough and Jonathan Camhi, http://www.businessinsider.com/top-internet-of-things-trends-2016-1?IR=T

245 Institute of Southeast Asian Studies, Urbanisation in Southeast Asian Countries, https://www.iseas.edu.sg/images/centres/asc/pdf/UrbanSEAsia-prelimasof13Jul10.pdf

246 Demographia World Urban Areas, Built Up Urban Areas or World Agglomerations, 12th Annual Edition, April 2016, http://www.demographia.com/db-worldua.pdf

247 New Geography, Largest 1,000 cities on earth: World urban areas: 2015 Edition, http://www.newgeography.com/content/004841-largest-1000-cities-earth-world-urban-areas-2015-edition

248 Statista, Number of smartphone users worldwide from 2014 to 2020 (in billions), https://www.statista.com/statistics/3360695/number-of-smartphone-users-worldwide/

249 The Hub, Smartphone Penetration By Country - Top 10, Phillip Kissonergis, http://thehub.smsglobal.com/smartphone-penetration-by-country-top-10/

250 TechSci Research, Global Internet of Things (IoT) Services Market By Type, By Application, By Region, Competition Forecast & Opportunities, 2011 – 2021

251 eMarketer, https://www.emarketer.com/Article/Slowing-Growth-Ahead-Worldwide-Internet-Audience/1014045?SOC1001

252 RFID Forecasts, Players and Opportunities 2016-2026, Raghu Das and Peter Harrop, http://www.idtechex.com/research/reports/rfid-forecasts-players-and-opportunities-2016-2026-000451.asp

253 Forbes, Roundup Of Cloud Computing Forecasts And Market Estimates, Louis Columbus, http://www.forbes.com/sites/louiscolumbus/2016/03/13/roundup-of-cloud-computing-forecasts-and-market-estimates-2016/#4e0886cf74b0

254 Statista, Quarterly revenue of Amazon Web Services from 1st quarter 2014 to 3rd quarter 2016 (in million U.S. dollars), ehttps://www.statista.com/statistics/250520/forecast-of-amazon-web-services-revenue/

255 Forbes, Microsoft tops Amazon, https://www.forbes.com/sites/bobevans1/2018/04/27/microsoft-tops-amazon-in-q1-cloud-revenue-6-0-billion-to-5-44-billion-ibm-third-at-4-2-billion/#4498281f5d4b

256 McKinsey Are today's CFOs ready for tomorrow's demands on finance?, Survey, http://www.mckinsey.com/business-functions/strategy-and-corporate-finance/our-insights/are-todays-cfos-ready-for-tomorrows-demands-on-finance?cid=other-alt-mip-mck-oth-1612

257 Deloitte University Press, The derivative effect: How financial services can make IoT technology pay off, The Internet of Things in the financial services industry, Jim Eckenrode, https://dupress.deloitte.com/dup-us-en/focus/internet-of-things/iot-in-financial-services-industry.html

258 Reuters, Fintech growth accelerates in Asia with record $4.5 billion investments, Elzio Barreto, http://www.reuters.com/article/us-asia-fintech-idUSKCN0WD0O0

259 eMarketer, Understanding China's O2O Commerce Marketplace, https://www.emarketer.com/Article/Understanding-Chinas-O2O-Commerce-Marketplace/1014374

260 Can cryptocurrencies fulfill the function of money? http://capitalism.columbia.edu/files/ccs/workingpage/2016/ammous_cryptocurrencies_and_the_functions_of_money.pdf

261 Easiest way to track Cryptocurrencies https://www.coingecko.com/en

262 Bitcoin: is it a bubble waiting to burst or a good investment? https://www.theguardian.com/business/2017/dec/02/bitcoin-is-it-a-bubble-waiting-to-burst-or-a-good-investment

263 The Future of Financial Infrastructure http://www3.weforum.org/docs/WEF_The_future_of_financial_infrastructure.pdf

264 Rebooting financial services: http://santanderinnoventures.com/wp-content/uploads/2015/06/The-Fintech-2-0-Paper.pdf

265 How InsurTech Is Rapidly Changing Insurance And Health Tech Industries, Vladislav Solodkiy, http://www.forbes.com/sites/vladislavsolodkiy/2016/10/20/how-InsurTech-is-rapidly-changing-insurance-and-health-tech-industries/#3e1d16084ba9

266 The Pulse of Fintexh Q3 2017, Jonathan Lavender, Ian Pollari, Murraey Raisbeck, Brian Hughes, and Arik Speier, https://assets.kpmg.com/content/dam/kpmg/xx/pdf/2017/11/pulse-of-fintech-q3-17.pdf

267 CB Insights, Fintech Trends to Watch in 2018, https://www.cbinsights.com/reports/CB-Insights_Fintech-Trends-2018-Briefing.pdf?utm_campaign=fintech-trends_2018-01&utm_medium=email&_hsenc=p2ANqtz-98_rZXoHhViFaPI4PjIU3YJ8-aUyFxHIjrtVRLLf02ecnIc-JCJai6HjAPRR2af9NWygJh0DGlrdV0jIiBVjIWkOdarRA&_hsmi=60234658&utm_content=60234658&utm_source=hs_automation&hsCtaTracking=bcd310ce-ae49-4230-b97f-23fae91ae767%7C0f816b71-bd5a-490f-8a81-18a3865bef74

268 Global InsurTech market forecast to grow at compound annual growth rate of more than 10% between 2016 and 2020, new report suggests, Canadian Underwriter, http://www.canadianunderwriter.ca/insurance/global-InsurTech-market-forecast-grow-compound-annual-growth-rate-10-2016-2020-new-report-suggests-1004104479/

269 Opportunities await: How InsurTech is reshaping insurance, PwC, https://www.pwc.com/ca/en/insurance/publications/pwc-how-InsurTech-is-reshaping-insurance-2016-07-en.pdf

270 Aviva and Founders Factory searching for "the next big thing", Paul Lucas, http://www.insurancebusinessmag.com/uk/news/breaking-news/aviva-and-founders-factory-searching-for-the-next-big-thing-37828.aspx

271 11 UK InsurTech startups to watch: from peer-to-peer and by-the-hour insurance, to back office tools for insurers, Scott Carey, http://www.techworld.com/picture-gallery/startups/11-uk-InsurTech-startups-watch-3645315/

272 Blockchain to Help InsurTech Soar to $235 Billion Industry, Justin OConnell, https://www.cryptocoinsnews.com/InsurTech-blockchain-industry/

273 Wearables could help to heal Health & Life insurance, https://dailyfintech.com/2016/10/06/wearables-may-heal-health-life-insurance/

274 Insurance app Back Me Up launches, https://www.finextra.com/pressarticle/65594/insurance-app-back-me-up-launches

275 Cuvva launches an InsurTech app for short term, instant car insurance, Rick Huckstep, https://dailyfintech.com/2015/12/17/cuvva-launches-an-InsurTech-app-for-short-term-instant-car-insurance/

276 Cuvva launching pay-as-you-go car insurance aimed at infrequent drivers, Steve O'Hear, https://techcrunch.com/2017/01/24/cuvva-localglobe/

277 Guevara, http://www.the-digital-insurer.com/dia/guevara-peer-to-peer-car-insurance/

278 InsurTech Futures: Digital Risks partners with Aviva, Sian Barton, http://www.insuranceage.co.uk/insurance-age/news/2462195/InsurTech-futures-digital-risks-partners-with-aviva

279 Brolly – An AI driven Insurance Advisory Application, http://www.the-digital-insurer.com/dia/brolly-ai-driven-insurance-advisory-application/

280 SPIXII is changing the world of insurance with the aid of Samsung's mentorship, Vaughn Highfield, http://www.alphr.com/startups/1006993/spixii-is-changing-the-world-of-insurance-with-the-aid-of-samsung-s-mentorship

281 About Us, http://instanda.com/insurance-software-providers/#about-us-intro

282 Insly – a global Software as a Service insurance platform, Rick Huckstep, https://dailyfintech.com/2015/05/07/insly-a-global-software-as-a-service-insurance-platform/

283 RightIndem – SaaS platform that speeds up the claims process, http://www.the-digital-insurer.com/dia/rightindem-saas-platform-speeds-claims-process/

284 Oscar Health – The Health Insurance Startup That Wants To Revolutionise Healthcare, http://www.the-digital-insurer.com/dia/oscar-health-health-insurance-startup-wants-revolutionise-health-care/

285 Oscar Health expects to generate $1 billion in revenue and sign up 250,000 members in 2018, Sarah Buhr, https://techcrunch.com/2017/12/21/oscar-health-expects-to-generate-1-billion-in-revenue-and-sign-up-250000-members-in-2018/

286 Chinese online insurer ZhongAn raises $1.5bn in IPO, Don Weinland and Oliver Ralph, https://www.ft.com/content/424e7b36-9f5d-11e7-9a86-4d5a475ba4c5

287 Lemonade are Live. Insurance will never be the same again!, Rick Huckstep, http://www.the-digital-insurer.com/blog/InsurTech-lemonade-are-here-and-insurance-will-never-be-the-same-again/

288 SoftBank Leads $120 Million Funding in Fintech Startup Lemonade, Julie Verhage, https://www.bloomberg.com/news/articles/2017-12-19/softbank-leads-120-million-funding-in-fintech-start-up-lemonade

289 https://help.claritymoney.com/investments-loans-and-insurance/insurance/lemonade-insurance

290 Metromile, https://en.wikipedia.org/wiki/Metromile

291 The Zebra, A "Kayak For Auto Insurance," Grabs $17 Million To Better Educate Drivers About Rates & Coverage, Sarah Perez, https://techcrunch.com/2016/01/27/the-zebra-a-kayak-for-auto-insurance-grabs-17-million-to-better-educate-drivers-about-rates-coverage/

292 Fintech Startup Zebra Raises $40M, Seremedi, Alice & More Texas News, Angela Shah, https://www.xconomy.com/texas/2017/09/19/fintech-startup-zebra-raises-40m-seremedi-alice-more-texas-news/

293 PolicyGenius, https://en.wikipedia.org/wiki/PolicyGenius

294 PolicyGenius raises $30 million from Norwest Venture Partners, Ryan Lawler, https://techcrunch.com/2017/05/24/policygenius-30m-norwest/

295 Start-up insurer Gryphon scoops £180 million, Paul Lucas, https://www.insurancebusinessmag.com/uk/news/breaking-news/startup-insurer-gryphon-scoops-180-million-70346.aspx

296 Bright Health Raises $160 Million in Series B Funding Round, https://www.businesswire.com/news/home/20170601005540/en/Bright-Health-Raises-160-Million-Series-Funding

297 PolicyBazaar eyes $1.5 billion value in IPO, Samidha Sharma, https://timesofindia.indiatimes.com/business/policybazaar-eyes-1-5bn-value-in-ipo/articleshow/61973103.cms

298 The AML KYC Onboarding Lifecycle Process Flow, http://www.advisoryhq.com/articles/the-aml-kyc-onboarding-lifecycle-process-flow/

299 How India's Unique ID System is Changing Lives, Lauren Clyne Medley, http://blogs.worldbank.org/voices/how-indias-unique-id-system-changing-lives

300 Aadhaar, https://en.wikipedia.org/wiki/Aadhaar#Aadhaar-enabled_biometric_attendance_systems

301 Greater financial inclusion for the unbanked is possible, http://www.gallup.com/businessjournal/182945/greater-financial-inclusion-unbanked-possible.aspx

302 The Problems of Being Unbanked, ValuePenguin, http://www.nasdaq.com/article/the-problems-of-being-unbanked-cm716881

303 The Power of Biometrics: Banking the Unbanked, Elaine Bliss, http://www.cartes-america.com/files/the_power_of_biometricsbanking_the_unbanked__elaine_bliss.pdf

304 FIDO, https://en.wikipedia.org/wiki/FIDO_Alliance

305 History of FIDO Alliance, https://fidoalliance.org/about/history/

306 Introducing Digital Identity Week on Daily Fintech, https://dailyfintech.com/2016/12/12/intro-ducing-digital-identity-week-on-daily-fintech/,

307 How Blockchain Fits into the Future of Digital Identity, Bryan Yurcan, http://www.amer-icanbanker.com/news/bank-technology/how-blockchain-fits-into-the-future-of-digital-identi-ty-1080345-1.html

308 The UN Plans To Implement Universal Biometric Identification For All Of Humanity By 2030, Michael Snyder, http://www.infowars.com/the-un-plans-to-implement-universal-biometric-identifi-cation-for-all-of-humanity-by-2030/

309 A Brief History of Cyber Crime, https://www.floridatechonline.com/blog/information-technolo-gy/a-brief-history-of-cyber-crime/

310 Defining Moments in the History of Cyber-Security and the Rise of Incident Response, Ted Julian, http://www.infosecurity-magazine.com/opinions/the-history-of-cybersecurity/

311 WikiLeaks, https://en.wikipedia.org/wiki/WikiLeaks

312 Cybersecurity Market Global Forecast, https://www.prnewswire.com/news-releases/cyberse-curity-market---global-forecast-to-2023-innovation-spotlight-on-splunk-cyberbit-carbon-black--bal-bix-300720906.html

313 Computer security, https://en.wikipedia.org/wiki/Computer_security

314 What DDOS really cost businesses, https://lp.incapsula.com/rs/incapsulainc/images/eBook%20-%20DDoS%20Impact%20Survey.pdf

315 The cost of phishing & value of employee training, https://info.wombatsecurity.com/hubfs/Ponemon_Institute_Cost_of_Phishing.pdf

316 Endpoint Security, Vangie Beal, http://www.webopedia.com/TERM/E/endpoint_security.html

317 IoT security (Internet of Things security), Margaret Rouse, http://internetofthingsagenda.techtarget.com/definition/IoT-security-Internet-of-Things-security

318 Threat Intelligence, Margaret Rouse, http://whatis.techtarget.com/definition/threat-intelli-gence-cyber-threat-intelligence

319 Mobile Security, https://en.wikipedia.org/wiki/Mobile_security

320 Behavior Detection, http://www.pcmag.com/encyclopedia/term/67445/behavior-detection

321 Cloud computing security, Margaret Rouse, http://searchcompliance.techtarget.com/definition/cloud-computing-security

322 Deception technology, Margaret Rouse, http://whatis.techtarget.com/definition/deception-tech-nology

323 About Us, https://www.protectwise.com/about.html

324 Cyber Risk Remediation Analysis, https://www.mitre.org/publications/systems-engineer-ing-guide/enterprise-engineering/systems-engineering-for-mission-assurance/cyber-risk-remedia-tion-analysis

325 Web Security Basics, http://www.beyondsecurity.com/web-security-and-web-scanning.html

326 There's a revolution coming - https://home.kpmg.com/content/dam/kpmg/uk/pdf/2018/09/regtech-revolution-coming.pdf

327 CB Insights, Fintech Trends to Watch in 2018, https://www.cbinsights.com/reports/CB-Insights_Fintech-Trends-2018-Briefing.pdf?utm_campaign=fintech-trends_2018-01&utm_medium=email&_hsenc=p2ANqtz-98_rZXoHhViFaPI4PjIU3YJ8-aUyFxHIjrtVRLLf02ecnIc-JCJai6HjAPRR2af9NWygJhODGlrdVOjliBVjIWkOdarRA&_hsmi=60234658&utm_con-tent=60234658&utm_source=hs_automation&hsCtaTracking=bcd310ce-ae49-4230-b97f-23fae91ae767%7C0f816b71-bd5a-490f-8a81-18a3865bef74

Index

DOI 10.1515/9781547401055-016

CPSIA information can be obtained
at www.ICGtesting.com
Printed in the USA
LVHW101003180820
663505LV00007B/719

9 781547 417162